TWENTIETH CENTURY VIEWS

The aim of this series is to present the best in contemporary critical opinion on major authors, providing a twentieth century perspective on their changing status in an era of profound revaluation.

Maynard Mack, *Series Editor*
Yale University

MATTHEW
ARNOLD

A COLLECTION OF CRITICAL ESSAYS

Edited by

David J. DeLaura

Prentice-Hall, Inc. *Englewood Cliffs, N.J.*

A SPECTRUM BOOK

Library of Congress Cataloging in Publication Data

DeLaura, David J.   comp.
    Matthew Arnold: a collection of critical essays.

    (Twentieth century views) (A Spectrum Book)
    CONTENTS: Eliot, T. S. Arnold and Pater.—Eliot,
T. S. Matthew Arnold.—Miller, J. H. Matthew Arnold. [etc.]
    1. Arnold, Matthew, 1822–1888.   I. Title.
PR4024.D4   821'.8   73–316
ISBN 0–13–046425–2
ISBN 0–13–046417–1 (pbk)

10 9 8 7 6 5 4 3 2 1

PRENTICE-HALL INTERNATIONAL, INC. (*London*)
PRENTICE-HALL OF AUSTRALIA PTY. LTD. (*Sydney*)
PRENTICE-HALL OF CANADA LTD. (*Toronto*)
PRENTICE-HALL OF INDIA PRIVATE LIMITED (*New Delhi*)
PRENTICE-HALL OF JAPAN, INC. (*Tokyo*)

Contents

Matthew Arnold: Poetry as Religion

Matthew Arnold: Conservative Revolutionary

Introduction

by David J. DeLaura

It is not entirely easy to explain why it is important to continue reading Matthew Arnold, why in fact he is an essential poet and critic even in our time. Despite the large volume and high quality of Arnold studies in the past twenty years, his reputation continues to need defending. One critic flatly declares Arnold to be a "bad" poet, and another finds most of his elegies "pretty bad poems" and questions whether Arnold "can maintain his position among the Big Three of Victorian poetry." [1] Jonathan Middlebrook, cheerfully celebrating contemporary popular poets who "take the sun as the real light of the world" and sing of "knowledge and joy," has no doubts. For him, Arnold's moonlit landscapes and nostalgia are part of the discarded past, his ideal of "rational calm" a delusion, and his emotions "debilitating." [2] Within recent years Arnold has even been denied the title of literary critic, and his theory of literature is dismissed by some as feeble and self-contradictory.

And yet, though Arnold requires explanations, he hardly needs a defense. He is not unpopular or underrated in the way that his friend Arthur Hugh Clough continues to be. His name appears in countless discussions of the claims of "culture" as against the "anarchy" that has threatened to take over so many of our institutions in recent years. The scope and effect of his poetry, though explicated through dozens of articles and a goodly shelf of books, stand more in need of defining. Geoffrey Tillotson explained that Arnold is "one of the really powerful emotional forces" in English poetry, whose subjects are "aching hearts, longing, frustration, the depths of blankness and isolation," and a man "marvellously gifted in the expres-

[1] *The Genius of John Ruskin* (Boston: Houghton Mifflin Company, 1963), p. 11; *JEGP*, 66 (July 1967), 473.
[2] "Sunshine Supermen," *College English*, 30 (March 1969), 418–23.

sion of sorts and shades of emotion." [3] Lionel Stevenson provides another clue when he describes Arnold as everywhere expressing "the dilemma of the modern intellectual, who can find satisfaction neither as a recluse in a cloister nor as a participant and policy-maker in public affairs." [4]

That last quotation will open Arnold to the easy charge of being an "academic" poet (or at least an academic's poet). But Walter Houghton has shown that a figure like Arnold's Empedocles ex-hibited, long before Hardy or Yeats or Eliot, many of the elements of a widespread "modern" consciousness: "the skepticism of any ulti-mate truths, the search for some constructive outlook that can give 'the courage to be,' the distate for a society that seems devoid of moral values, the acute self-consciousness, the sense of isolation and loneliness, the suspicion of a 'pure' intellectualism, the desire for a wholeness in which the total personality may be alive and active, above all, perhaps, the nostalgia—though firmly repressed today and rarely mentioned—for a lost world of youth and peace." [5] In-deed, since Houghton wrote in 1958, an important and quite explicit force in world politics is the search for new modes of community and the abatement of strident modern individualism and unfettered competitiveness.

A unifying element in both Arnold's poetry and prose is a large gallery of complex, morally sensitive men and women who cannot simply abandon the highly "interiorized" values of the waning tradi-tional culture, and who find the "pride of life" of modern activism deeply repugnant. One by one they come before us—Obermann, Empedocles, Balder, the Scholar-Gipsy, Lucretius, Marcus Aurelius, Joubert, the Guérins, Falkland. They are often very like Matthew Arnold; they embody important aspects of ourselves. But Arnold is never, even in the relatively conservative politics of his later career, merely a reactionary, the last noble Roman at the gates as the bar-barian hordes sweep in. As much as any revolutionary, he knew the immensity of the change overtaking institutions and human con-sciousness in the nineteenth century. He remains of permanent value because, perhaps more than any other single figure of his period in

[3] *Times Literary Supplement* (London), April 2, 1954; reprinted in *Mid-Vic-torian Studies* (London: Athlone Press, 1965), pp. 152–56.

[4] "Matthew Arnold's Poetry: A Modern Appraisal," *Tennessee Studies in Lit-erature,* 4 (1959), 39.

[5] "Arnold's 'Empedocles on Etna,' " *Victorian Studies,* 1 (June 1958), 336.

England, he tried to spell out those elements of traditional culture —religious, social, imaginative—that must be carried over into the new world if a manipulative technology and a value-free search for fact were not to have the future entirely to themselves. And Arnold persistently tried, with increasing success and hopefulness, to imagine himself ahead, to sketch out the essential elements of a "transformed" human society. Scorned by traditionalists and radicals alike, he has survived them handily. His politics was the liberalism of the future; his church was the religion of the future.

The divided Arnold that criticism has made so much of is thus partly the honest Arnold who gave substance to a permanently available vision of painful modern dislocation. He has a Romantic sensibility, but intellectually he cannot make the residual Romantic assertion about the benevolence of Nature and the shadowy Spirit interpenetrating it. His classicism is in one aspect a demand for "form" and "architectonicè" in a literary climate worshipful of freaks of "expression" and isolated "beauties"; but in another sense, it is a very "romantic" search for an innocent wholeness of nature imagined to exist before modern fragmentation set in. (Long before T. S. Eliot, Arnold had mapped out the causes and consequences of the modern "dissociation of sensibility.") His criticism is divided between an insistence on "form" and subject matter that acts as a check to mere subjectivity and a "touchstone" method that acknowledges the "magical" power of words that the Symbolists were later to push to an extreme.

To say that Arnold is divided is also to say that he is at the "center" of modern culture in a number of ways. He is everywhere the "mediator": between past and present (and future), between inward and outward, between the claims of a "dissolving" modern intellect and the claims of man's permanent emotional needs and values. He for the most part resists the more "prophetic" and rousing stances possible in his time. He does not, like Newman or Kierkegaard, fiercely and exclusively affirm the claims of transcendence; and yet his deep concern for man's essential religious nature explains much that is neglected but central in his later humanism. Temperamentally and intellectually he was too mindful of human continuity to welcome the overthrow of all institutions imagined by a Carlyle or by the radicals of the left; nevertheless, his critique of the complacencies and shortsightedness of liberal ideology remains, as Trilling and others have noted, one of the keenest ever made, and an almost millennial sense of a transformed society ministering to human "expansion" informs his later social, religious, and educational writing.

In all periods, Arnold comes before his readers in the guise of a teacher and a judge. Even in Arnold's most troubled early poetry, in which he admits his own impotence and alienation—in "Empedocles," "Tristram and Iseult," "Obermann," the Marguerite poems, "The Grande Chartreuse"—he is in effect defending his own painful withdrawal and perplexity as more honest and more integral than the prideful and self-satisfied activism of the mid-nineteenth century. This is even more explicit, of course, in the more positive social writings of the 1860s and later. He is saying that his kind of complex consciousness—valuing *being* as much as *doing,* inwardness as much as action, reverence as much as control of nature—is the better model for the society of the future. The mere worldling, "doing as he likes," is easily condemned. But for Arnold, even the secular moralist and the social revolutionary are building without foundations by neglecting the historical and inward basis of ethics. The religionist, on the other hand, is too willing to hand over the secular order to anarchy and brutishness in the expectation of a transcendent and post-terrestrial recovery of order. The aesthete, a new source of danger, will accept the "inward" values of high percipience inherited from the older culture, but he will neatly sever them from Arnold's demand for a "general" expansion of society in which the ideal of individual development is shared by the community at large.

There are obvious limitations in Arnold's vision. He managed to irritate almost every segment of contemporary opinion by suggesting its narrowness; his effectiveness in his own time, in the various areas of his activity, is in question, though his long-term influence is undoubtedly very pervasive. Worse, his cool assumption in the prose of superior clarity and even of virtue is no doubt accompanied by a kind of snobbishness and elitism that does not sit well with his later readers. More dangerously, perhaps, in insisting that a proper ordering of the "distinterested" mind was prerequisite to defensible action, he too often hints that once our minds have been informed by "right" reason, changes in the practical order will somehow come about of themselves. Despite his pose of reasonableness and moderation, there is a strong "mystical" streak in his nature that leads him to flirt with an apocalypse he could not welcome while underplaying the hard and gradual work of social amelioration.

Arnold remains "modern," however, in an important and permanently valuable way. He prophetically discriminates shades of feeling—a limited range, no doubt, centering in isolation, unsatisfied longing, a sense of a disintegrating culture context and of being left unfit for participation in the work of the modern world—that were to become integral to the experience of large numbers of sensitive individuals later in the century. This range of easily abused emotions is constantly, and increasingly as he enters mid-career, offset by a hardening of the features as he insists upon maintaining his moral and emotional equipoise amid the (alternately) numbing or agitating pressures of contemporary life. A couple of generations of later English and American poets responded to the alienation and impotence Arnold had been the first to work out for English poetry, but in general those less strenuous generations chose—to use Trilling's terms—the self-pity and forgot about the self-control.

A. Dwight Culler has brilliantly established that the metaphorical unity of much of Arnold's poetry lies in a series of landscapes that recapitulate the characteristically "modern" experience.[6] Adapting a pattern used earlier by Wordsworth and by Carlyle in *Sartor Resartus,* Arnold's various personae move from the innocence of the Forest Glade through a "fall" or crisis down onto the Burning Plain of contemporary alienation. Increasingly, in the poetry written after 1855, Arnold asserts the possibility of a satisfactory reintegration of society and of the human soul, in either the naturalistic Wide-glimmering Sea or the more Christian City of God. A flaw in this implicitly "progressive" scheme is the fact that almost all readers find the more hopeful assertions of the major later poems—"Rugby Chapel," "Thyrsis," and "Obermann Once More"—less convincingly embodied than the alienated states of the best earlier poems. Only in the religious writings of the 1870s, when his own poetry had virtually ceased to be written, did Arnold work out with authority the conditions of "the joy whose grounds are true" and of what Carlyle had called "the new firm lands of Faith" beyond contemporary doubt and disintegration.

Arnold decided in 1852–53, for a complex of reasons spelled out in the essay by Kenneth Allott included here, not to write more poems of the sort best represented by "Empedocles on Etna." Most recent readers regard the Preface to the *Poems* of 1853 as the asser-

---

[6] *Imaginative Reason* (New Haven and London: Yale University Press, 1966).

tion of a pseudoclassical ideal that repudiated his own richest vein of poetry. As Frank Kermode puts it, "the answer to his dilemma, in the terms in which he undoubtedly understood it, lay in the cruel effort and continued self-expenditure of a series of Empedoclean victories, not in the carefully qualified betrayal, the compromise of art and life, action and inaction, which his Mask as Critic represents." [7] Arnold reconstructed himself, and in the criticism of the 1860s and after sought to create the climate in which an adequate poetry might be written, and in which the lives of individual men and women might be reintegrated. But unquestionably, after, say, "The Scholar-Gipsy" (1853), Arnold's creativity worked in a diminished mode.

The other lingering doubt concerns the poetic—and verbal—authority and authenticity of Arnold's poetry. The poetry does to some extent fall under the blanket indictments of nineteenth-century poetry developed by Eliot in the 1920s, and by F. W. Bateson and F. R. Leavis from the 1930s on. At the level of poetic artistry, Arnold failed to develop a language and a symbolic mode equal to the subtlety of his emotional perceptions about the cost and conditions of "modernity." Even his best performances borrow too heavily from a sort of Romantic thesaurus of language and image: adjectives like sweet, dear, and fair soften the texture; stage properties like night, dark, gloom, forlorn, cold, grave and graves, moon and moonlight are wheeled on and off by the score; "tears" (used sixty-eight times) flow too freely; poems are awash in images of the river and sea of life. Thematically, Leavis's charges of "evasion" and "escapism" in nineteenth-century poetry have this much relevance to Arnold: "The Scholar-Gipsy" is simply the most impressive example of his continuing failure to develop a model of life combining integrity and interiority with a capacity for action in the modern world. Despite one or two recent defenders, the hopefulness and the calls for action in the poems of the 1860s seem strained and are couched in a cruder language and a less sensitive rhythm than are found in the best of the early poetry.

Still, after all the deductions have been made, Arnold's verbal and technical achievements are not inconsiderable. Though the elegiac tone suffuses many of the poems and is one source of the unity of Arnold's effort, the range of mode and texture is surprisingly wide.

---

[7] *Romantic Image* (New York: Vintage Books, 1964), pp. 18–19.

The irregular cadences of "Dover Beach" are highly effective but hard to analyze; it is, so far as I know, the first free-verse poem in the language. "The Buried Life" combines irregular rhyme with variously stressed lines, the effect being one of "murmurous" elasticity and continuity. Arnold frequently favored the "unpoetic" short line of three or four stresses, as in a "conversation" poem like "Epilogue to Lessing's Laocoön." But in "Resignation" Arnold achieved with a four-stress line and a deliberate austerity of diction an impressive and even mysterious elevation of tone not unlike the finest incantatory passages in Wordsworth.

> Before him he sees life unroll,
> A placid and continuous whole—
> That general life, which does not cease,
> Whose secret is not joy, but peace;
> That life, whose dumb wish is not miss'd
> If birth proceeds, if things subsist;
> The life of plants, and stones, and rain,
> The life he craves—if not in vain
> Fate gave, what chance shall not control,
> His sad lucidity of soul.
>
> (11. 189–98)

The blank-verse songs of Callicles in "Empedocles on Etna" easily rank with the best examples of the line in the nineteenth century. The flower-laden sensuousness of "The Scholar-Gipsy" and "Thyrsis," indebted to Keats in form, theme, and diction, testifies to Arnold's lingering affinity for the verbalism and local elaborateness consciously repudiated in the letters to Clough and in the Preface of 1853.

The variety of Arnold's forms and effects is thus wider than is often recognized. What he lacks is wit, meaning both humor and unexpected "metaphysical" juxtapositions in order to reveal fresh aspects of reality. Of his contemporaries, Clough is closest to seventeenth-century boldness and concision and to the Augustan snap of antithesis, especially for satirical effects. (The tradition was best kept alive for the nineteenth century by Byron.) Arnold's own frequent complaints are closer to Tennysonian and "spasmodic" railings against the insensitivity and materialism of the age. Still, in his most austere mood there are detectable elements of neoclassical neatness and precision, as in Empedocles' "sermon" in Act I.

The understanding of Arnold's artistry in prose has advanced rapidly in recent years, especially in the studies by Holloway and Tillotson partially included here. Arnold was a part-time journalist and polemicist through much of his career, and some of his most important essays were written in sooty trains and drafty hotels after numbing days of school inspecting. Much of his prose is densely topical and allusive, and even the primary meaning of his words, let alone the intended effect, is often hard to recover without an annotated modern edition like R. H. Super's. His own theory of prose style was parallel to the theory of poetic diction outlined in the Preface of 1853: he advocated a more flexible variant of the eighteenth-century "middle" style, the emphasis being on simplicity, clarity, and urbanity. The insistence on restraint in both poetry and prose is part of Arnold's broadly conceived "moral" theory of the function of style in literature. His theory fits his practice in both the rather severe style of his education reports and the more colloquial tone of his best uncontroversial essays. But there are other modes too, notably the stinging and sometimes wounding satire he directed against a very wide range of contemporary brands of opinion, as well as the more "polyphonic" set pieces on Oxford, on George Sand, and on Cardinal Newman. Tillotson notes that Arnold set about both to persuade and to make his own literary personality "striking." It would be a nice exercise to determine whether the qualities that lead us to continue reading Arnold with relish are lacking in the equally spirited controversial prose of Macaulay or Leslie Stephen or Huxley.

Arnold's effort to change the tone and direction of English and American culture—in literary criticism, as well as in his religious and educational writings—was so generally successful as to make his widespread influence hard to trace. His theory of disinterestedness in criticism, his call for a cosmopolitan culture, his keen historical sense of the great shift in values through which his own society was dangerously passing, have permanently elevated the level of literary and "cultural" thinking in the English-speaking world. This might be called the "conscious" level of his influence: to a Goethean comprehensiveness he added a very English moralism. Later "general" critics as diverse as T. S. Eliot, Edmund Wilson, F. R. Leavis, and Lionel Trilling are distinctly Arnoldian in their historical sense, in the range of their interests, and in their passion for integrity. The best of the early poetry also still speaks to us, but differently, at a level below the "surface stream," at an almost preconscious depth of awareness of life's "central stream." Arnold was the first poet in English to express the universal loss of primal innocence, the fact that

> Too fast we live, too much are tried,
> Too harass'd, to attain
> Wordsworth's sweet calm, or Goethe's wide
> And luminous view to gain.
> ("Stanzas in Memory of the Author of
> 'Obermann,' " ll. 77–80)

And yet he held out, even in a post-Wordsworthian world, the possibility of "tracking out our true, original course," of recovering an innocence of perception that only former generations possessed as a birthright:

> Yet still, from time to time, vague and forlorn,
> From the soul's subterranean depth upborne
> As from an infinitely distant land,
> Come airs, and floating echoes, and convey
> A melancholy into all our day.
> . . . .
> The eye sinks inward, and the heart lies plain,
> And what we mean, we say, and what we would, we know.
> A man becomes aware of his life's flow,
> And hears its winding murmur; and he sees
> The meadows where it glides, the sun, the breeze.
> ("The Buried Life," ll. 72–76, 86–90)

Arnold was uniquely equipped to record these elusive signals from the now almost silent heart of being. He remains indispensable.

Arnold and Pater

by T. S. Eliot

The purpose of the present paper is to indicate a direction from Arnold, through Pater, to the 'nineties, with, of course, the solitary figure of Newman in the background.

It is necessary first of all to estimate the aesthetic and religious views of Arnold: in each of which, to borrow his own phrase against him, there is an element of *literature* and an element of *dogma*. As Mr. J. M. Robertson has well pointed out in his *Modern Humanists Reconsidered,* Arnold had little gift for consistency or for definition. Nor had he the power of connected reasoning at any length: his flights are either short flights or circular flights. Nothing in his prose work, therefore, will stand very close analysis, and we may well feel that the positive content of many words is very small. Culture and Conduct are the first things, we are told; but what Culture and Conduct are, I feel that I know less well on every reading. Yet Arnold does still hold us, at least with *Culture and Anarchy* and *Friendship's Garland.* To my generation, I am sure, he was a more sympathetic prose writer than Carlyle or Ruskin; yet he holds his position and achieves his effects exactly on the same plane, by the power of his rhetoric and by representing a point of view which is particular though it cannot be wholly defined.

But the revival of interest in Arnold in our time—and I believe he is admired and read not only more than Carlyle and Ruskin, but than Pater—is a very different thing from the influence he exerted in his own time. We go to him for refreshment and for the companionship of a kindred point of view to our own, but not as disciples. And therefore it is the two books I have mentioned that are most readable. Even the *Essays in Criticism* cannot be read very often; *Literature and Dogma, God and the Bible,* and *Last Essays on Church and Religion,* have served their turn and can hardly be read through. In these books he attempts something which must be austerely impersonal; in them reasoning power matters, and it fails him; furthermore, we have now our modern solvers of the same problem Arnold there set himself, and they, or some of them, are more accomplished and ingenious in this sort of rationalizing than Arnold was. Accordingly, and this is my first point, his Culture survives better than his Conduct, because it can better survive vagueness of definition. But both Culture and Conduct were important for his own time.

Culture has three aspects, according as we look at it in *Culture and Anarchy,* in *Essays in Criticism,* or in the abstract. It is in the first of these two books that Culture shows to best advantage. And the reason is clear: Culture there stands out against a background to which it is contrasted, a background of definite items of ignorance, vulgarity and prejudice. As an invective against the crudities of the industrialism of his time, the book is perfect of its kind. Compared with Carlyle, it looks like clear thinking, and is certainly clearer expression; and compared with Arnold, Ruskin often appears long-winded and peevish. Arnold taught English expository and critical prose a restraint and urbanity it needed. And hardly, in this book, do we question the meaning of Culture; for the good reason that we do not need to. Even when we read that Culture "is a study of perfection," we do not at that point raise an eyebrow to admire how much Culture appears to have arrogated from Religion. For we have shortly before been hearing something about "the will of God," or of a joint firm called "reason and the will of God"; and soon after we are presented with Mr. Bright and Mr. Frederic Harrison as foils to Culture; and appearing in this way between the will of God and Mr. Bright, Culture is here sufficiently outlined to be recognizable. *Culture and Anarchy* is on the same side as *Past and Present* or *Unto this Last.* Its ideas are really no clearer;—one reason why Arnold, Carlyle and Ruskin were so influential, for precision and completeness of thought do not always make for influence. (Arnold, it is true, gave something else: he produced a kind of illusion of precision and clarity; that is, maintained these qualities as ideals of style.)

Certainly, the prophets of the period just before that of which I

am supposed to be writing excelled in denunciation (each in his
own way) rather than in construction; and each in his own fashion
lays himself open to the charge of tedious querulousness. And an
idea, such as that of Culture, is apt to lead to consequences which
its author cannot foresee and probably will not like. Already, in the
Essays, Culture begins to seem a little more priggish—I do not say
"begins" in a chronological sense—and a little more anaemic. Where
Sir Charles Adderley and Mr. Roebuck appear, there is more life
than in the more literary criticism. Arnold is in the end, I believe,
at his best in satire and in apologetics for literature, in his defence
and enunciation of a needed attitude.

To us, as I have said, Arnold is rather a friend than a leader. He
was a champion of "ideas" most of whose ideas we no longer take
seriously. His Culture is powerless to aid or to harm. But he is at
least a forerunner of what is now called Humanism, of which I
must here say something, if only to contrast it and compare it with
the Aestheticism of Pater. How far Arnold is responsible for the
birth of Humanism would be difficult to say; we can at least say that
it issues very naturally from his doctrine, that Charles Eliot Norton
is largely responsible for its American form, and that therefore Arnold is another likely ancestor. But the resemblances are too patent
to be ignored. The difference is that Arnold could father something
apparently quite different—the view of life of Walter Pater. The
resemblance is that literature, or Culture, tended with Arnold to
usurp the place of Religion. From one point of view, Arnold's theory
of Art and his theory of Religion are quite harmonious, and Humanism is merely the more coherent structure. Arnold's prose writings
fall into two parts; those on Culture and those on Religion; and the
books about Christianity seem only to say again and again—merely
that the Christian faith is of course impossible to the man of culture.
They are tediously negative. But they are negative in a peculiar
fashion: their aim is to affirm that the emotions of Christianity can
and must be preserved without the belief. From this proposition two
different types of man can extract two different types of conclusion:
(1) that Religion is Morals, (2) that Religion is Art. The effect of
Arnold's religious campaign is to divorce Religion from thought.

In Arnold himself there was a powerful element of Puritan morality, as in most of his contemporaries, however diverse. And the
strength of his moral feeling—we might add its blindness also—
prevented him from seeing how very odd might look the fragments

of the fabric which he knocked about so recklessly. "The power of Christianity has been in the immense emotion which it has excited," he says; not realizing at all that this is a counsel to get all the emotional kick out of Christianity one can, without the bother of believing it; without reading the future to foresee *Marius the Epicurean,* and finally *De Profundis.* Furthermore, in his books dealing with Christianity he seems bent upon illustrating in himself the provincialisms which he rebuked in others. "M. de Lavelaye," he says in the preface to *God and the Bible,* with as deferential a manner as if he were citing M. Renan himself, "is struck, as any judicious Catholic may well be struck, with the superior freedom, order, stability, and religious earnestness, of the Protestant Nations as compared with the Catholic." He goes on complacently, "Their religion has made them what they are." I am not here concerned with the genuine differences between Catholic and Protestant; only with the tone which Arnold adopts in this preface and throughout this book; and which is in no wise more liberal than that of Sir Charles Adderley or Mr. Roebuck or "Mr. Tennyson's great broad-shouldered Englishman." He girds at (apparently) Herbert Spencer for substituting *Unknowable* for *God;* quite unaware that his own Eternal not ourselves comes to exactly the same thing as the Unknowable. And when we read Arnold's discourses on Religion, we return to scrutinize his Culture with some suspicion.

For Arnold's Culture, at first sight so enlightened, moderate and reasonable, walks so decorously in the company of the will of God, that we may overlook the fact that it tends to develop its own stringent rules and restrictions.

> Certainly, culture will never make us think it an essential of religion whether we have in our Church discipline "a popular authority of elders," as Hooker calls it, or whether we have Episcopal jurisdiction.

Certainly, "culture" in itself can never make us think so, any more than it can make us think that the quantum theory is an essential of physical science: but such people as are interested in this question at all, however cultured they be, hold one or the other opinion pretty strongly; and Arnold is really affirming that to Culture all theological and ecclesiastical differences are indifferent. But this is a rather positive dogma for Culture to hold. When we take *Culture and Anarchy* in one hand, and *Literature and Dogma* in the other, our minds are gradually darkened by the suspicion that Arnold's objection to Dissenters is partly that they do hold strongly to that which they believe, and partly that they are not Masters of Arts of Oxford. Arnold, as Master of Arts, should have had some scruple about the use of words. But in the very preface to the second edition of *Literature and Dogma* he says:

> The *Guardian* proclaims "the miracle of the incarnation" to be the "fundamental truth" for Christians. How strange that on me should devolve the office of instructing the *Guardian* that the fundamental thing for Christians is not the Incarnation but the imitation of Christ!

While wondering whether Arnold's own "imitation" is even a good piece of mimicry, we notice that he employs *truth* and *thing* as interchangeable: and a very slight knowledge of the field in which he was skirmishing should have told him that a "fundamental truth" in theology and a "fundamental thing" in his own loose jargon have nothing comparable about them. The total effect of Arnold's philosophy is to set up Culture in the place of Religion, and to leave Religion to be laid waste by the anarchy of feeling. And Culture is a term which each man not only may interpret as he pleases, but must indeed interpret as he can. So the gospel of Pater follows naturally upon the prophecy of Arnold.

Matthew Arnold

by T. S. Eliot

March 3rd, 1933

"The rise of the democracy to power in America and Europe is not, as has been hoped, to be a safeguard of peace and civilisation. It is the rise of the uncivilised, whom no school education can suffice to provide with intelligence and reason. It looks as if the world were entering upon a new stage of experience, unlike anything heretofore, in which there must be a new discipline of suffering to fit men for the new conditions."

I have quoted the foregoing words, partly because they are by Norton[1] and partly because they are not by Arnold. The first two sentences might well be Arnold's. But the third—"a new stage of experience, unlike anything heretofore, in which there must be a new discipline of suffering": these words are not only not Arnold's, but we know at once that they could not have been written by him. Arnold hardly looks ahead to the new stage of experience; and though he speaks to us of discipline, it is the discipline of culture, not the discipline of suffering. Arnold represents a period of stasis; of relative and precarious stability, it is true, a brief halt in the endless march of humanity in some, or in any direction. Arnold is neither a reactionary nor a revolutionary; he marks a period of time, as do Dryden and Johnson before him.

Even if the delight we get from Arnold's writings, prose and verse, be moderate, yet he is in some respects the most satisfactory man of letters of his age. You remember the famous judgement which he pronounced upon the poets of the epoch which I have just been

[1] Letter to Leslie Stephen, January 8th, 1896.

considering; a judgement which, at its time, must have appeared startlingly independent. "The English poetry of the first quarter of this century," he says in his essay on *The Function of Criticism,* "with plenty of energy, plenty of creative force, did not know enough." We should be right too, I think, if we added that Carlyle, Ruskin, Tennyson, Browning, with plenty of energy, plenty of creative force, had not enough wisdom. Their culture was not always well-rounded; their knowledge of the human soul was often partial and often shallow. Arnold was not a man of vast or exact scholarship, and he had neither walked in hell nor been rapt to heaven; but what he did know, of books and men, was in its way well-balanced and well-marshalled. After the prophetic frenzies of the end of the eighteenth and the beginning of the nineteenth century, he seems to come to us saying: "This poetry is very fine, it is opulent and careless, it is sometimes profound, it is highly original; but you will never establish and maintain a tradition if you go on in this haphazard way. There are minor virtues which have flourished better at other times and in other countries: these you must give heed to, these you must apply, in your poetry, in your prose, in your conversation and your way of living; else you condemn yourselves to enjoy only fitful and transient bursts of literary brilliance, and you will never, as a people, a nation, a race, have a fully formed tradition and personality." However well-nourished we may be on previous literature and previous culture, we cannot afford to neglect Arnold.

I have elsewhere tried to point out some of Arnold's weaknesses when he ventured into departments of thought for which his mind was unsuited and ill-equipped. In philosophy and theology he was an undergraduate; in religion a Philistine. It is a pleasanter task to define a man's limitations within the field in which he is qualified; for there, the definition of limitation may be at the same time a precision of the writer's excellences. Arnold's poetry has little technical interest. It is academic poetry in the best sense; the best fruit which can issue from the promise shown by the prize-poem. When he is not simply being himself, he is most at ease in a master's gown: *Empedocles on Etna* is one of the finest academic poems ever written. He tried other robes which became him less well; I cannot but think of *Tristram and Iseult* and *The Forsaken Merman* as charades. *Sohrab and Rustum* is a fine piece, but less fine than *Gebir;* and in the classical line Landor, with a finer ear, can beat Arnold every time. But Arnold is a poet to whom one readily returns. It is a pleasure, certainly, after associating with the riff-raff of the early part of the century, to be in the company of a man *qui sait se conduire;* but Arnold is something more than an agreeable Professor of Poetry. With all his fastidiousness and superciliousness and officiality, Arnold is more intimate with us than Browning, more intimate than Tennyson ever is except at moments, as in the passionate flights in *In Memoriam.* He is the poet and critic of a period of false stability. All his writing in the kind of *Literature and Dogma* seems to me a valiant attempt to dodge the issue, to mediate between Newman and Huxley; but his poetry, the best of it, is too honest to employ any but his genuine feelings of unrest, loneliness and dissatisfaction. Some of his limitations are manifest enough. In his essay on *The Study of Poetry* he has several paragraphs on Burns, and for an Englishman and an Englishman of his time, Arnold understands Burns very well. Perhaps I have a partiality for small oppressive nationalities like the Scots that makes Arnold's patronising manner irritate me; and certainly I suspect Arnold of helping to fix the wholly mistaken notion of Burns as a singular untutored English dialect poet, instead of as a decadent representative of a great alien tradition. But he says (taking occasion to rebuke the country in which Burns lived) that "no one can deny that it is of advantage to a poet to deal with a beautiful world"; and this remark strikes me as betraying a limitation. It is an advantage to mankind in general to live in a beautiful world; that no one can doubt. But for the poet is it so important? We mean all sorts of things, I know, by Beauty. But the essential advantage for a poet is not to have a beautiful world with which to deal: it is to be able to see beneath both beauty and ugliness; to see the boredom, and the horror, and the glory.

The vision of the horror and the glory was denied to Arnold, but he knew something of the boredom. He speaks much of the "consolatory" power of Wordsworth's poetry, and it is in connexion with Wordsworth that he makes many of his wisest observations about poetry.

> But when will Europe's latter hour
> Again find Wordsworth's healing power?
> Others will teach us how to dare,
> And against fear our breast to steel:
> Others will strengthen us to bear—
> But who, ah who, will make us feel?

The cloud of mortal destiny,
Others will front it fearlessly—
But who, like him, will put it by? [2]

His tone is always of regret, of loss of faith, instability, nostalgia:

And love, if love, of happier men.
Of happier men, for they, at least,
Have *dreamed* two human hearts might blend
In one, and were through faith released
From isolation without end
Prolonged, nor knew, although no less
Alone than thou, their loneliness.

This is a familiar enough sentiment; and perhaps a more robust comment on the situation is, that if you don't like it, you can get on with it; and the verse itself is not highly distinguished. Marguerite, at best, is a shadowy figure, neither very passionately desired nor very closely observed, a mere pretext for lamentation. His personal emotion is indeed most convincing when he deals with an impersonal subject. And when we know his poetry, we are not surprised that in his criticism he tells us little or nothing about his experience of writing it, and that he is so little concerned with poetry from the maker's point of view. One feels that the writing of poetry brought him little of that excitement, that joyful loss of self in the workmanship of art, that intense and transitory relief which comes at the moment of completion and is the chief reward of creative work. As we can forget, in reading his criticism, that he is a poet himself, so it is all the more necessary to remind ourselves that his creative and his critical writing are essentially the work of the same man. The same weakness, the same necessity for something to depend upon, which make him an academic poet make him an academic critic. . . .

It was desirable after the surprising, varied and abundant contribution of the Romantic Period that this task of criticism should be undertaken again. Nothing that was done in this period was of the nature of what Arnold was able to do, because that was not the time in which it could be done. Coleridge, Lamb, Hazlitt, De Quincey, did work of great importance upon Shakespeare and the

---

[2] I do not quote these lines as good verse. They are very carelessly written. The fourth line is particularly clumsy, the sixth has a bathetic repetition. To "put by" the cloud of human destiny is not a felicitous expression. The dashes at the end of two lines are a symptom of weakness, like Arnold's irritating use of italicised words.

Elizabethan dramatists, and discovered new treasure which they left for others to calculate. The instruments of Arnold's time appear now, of course, very antiquated: his was the epoch of Ward's *English Poets,* and of *The Golden Treasury,* birthday albums and calendars with a poetical quotation for each day. Arnold was not Dryden or Johnson; he was an Inspector of Schools and he became Professor of Poetry. He was an educator. The valuation of the Romantic poets, in academic circles, is still very largely that which Arnold made. It was right, it was just, it was necessary for its time; and of course it had its defects. It is tinged by his own uncertainty, his own apprehensions, his own view of what it was best that his own time should believe; and it is very much influenced by his religious attitude. His taste is not comprehensive. He seems to have chosen, when he could—for much of his work is occasional—those subjects in connexion with which he could best express his views about morals and society: Wordsworth—perhaps not quite as Wordsworth would have recognised himself, Heine, Amiel, Guérin. He was capable of learning from France and from Germany. But the *use* to which he put poetry was limited; he wrote about poets when they provided a pretext for his sermon to the British public; and he was apt to think of the greatness of poetry rather than of its genuineness.

There is no poetry which Arnold experienced more deeply than that of Wordsworth; the lines which I quoted above are not so much a criticism of Wordsworth as a testimonial of what Wordsworth had done for *him.* We may expect to find in the essay on Wordsworth, if anywhere, a statement of what poetry meant to Arnold. It is in his essay on Wordsworth that occurs his famous definition: "Poetry is at bottom a criticism of life." At bottom: that is a great way down; the bottom is the bottom. At the bottom of the abyss is what few ever see, and what those cannot bear to look at for long; and it is not a "criticism of life." If we mean life as a whole—not that Arnold ever saw life as a whole—from top to bottom, can anything that we can say of it ultimately, of that awful mystery, be called criticism? We bring back very little from our rare descents, and that is not criticism. Arnold might just as well have said that Christian worship is at bottom a criticism of the Trinity. We see better what Arnold's words amount to when we recognise that his own poetry is decidedly critical poetry. A poem like *Heine's Grave* is criticism, and very fine criticism too; and a kind of criticism which is justified because it could not be made in prose. Sometimes Arnold's criticism is on a lower level:

> One morn, as through Hyde Park we walked,
> My friend and I, by chance we talked,
> Of Lessing's famed Laocoon.[3]

The poem about Heine is good poetry for the same reason that it is good criticism: because Heine is one of the *personae*, the masks, behind which Arnold is able to go through his performance. The reason why some criticism is good (I do not care to generalise here about all criticism) is that the critic assumes, in a way, the personality of the author whom he criticises, and through this personality is able to speak with his own voice. Arnold's Wordsworth is as much like Arnold as he is like Wordsworth. Sometimes a critic may choose an author to criticise, a rôle to assume, as far as possible the antithesis to himself, a personality which has actualised all that has been suppressed in himself; we can sometimes arrive at a very satisfactory intimacy with our anti-masks.

"The greatness of a poet," Arnold goes on to say, "lies in his powerful and beautiful application of ideas to life." Not a happy way of putting it, as if ideas were a lotion for the inflamed skin of suffering humanity. But it seems to be what Arnold thought he was doing. He presently qualifies this assertion by pointing out that "morals" must not be interpreted too narrowly:

> Morals are often treated in a narrow and false fashion; they are bound up with systems of thought and belief which have had their day; they are fallen into the hands of pedants and professional dealers; they grow tiresome to some of us.

Alas! for morals as Arnold conceived them; they are grown still more tiresome. He then remarks significantly in speaking of the "Wordsworthians":

> The Wordsworthians are apt to praise him for the wrong things, and to lay far too much stress upon what they call his philosophy. His poetry is the reality, his philosophy—so far, at least, as it may put on the form and habit of a "scientific system of thought," and the more that it puts them on—is the illusion.

[3] It may be said of Arnold's inferior work, as was said of that of an inferior poet, that he faggotted his verses as they fell. And if they rhymed and rattled, all was well. Of course we do not judge Arnold as a poet by such effusions as this, but we cannot be blamed for forming a lower opinion of his capacity for self-criticism. He need not have printed them.

Perhaps we shall one day learn to make this proposition general, and to say: Poetry is the reality, philosophy the illusion.

This seems to me a striking, dangerous and subversive assertion. Poetry is at bottom a criticism of life; yet philosophy is illusion; the reality is the criticism of life. Arnold might have read Lessing's famed Laocoon with a view to disentangling his own confusions.

We must remember that for Arnold, as for everyone else, "poetry" meant a particular selection and order of poets. It meant, as for everyone else, the poetry that he liked, that he re-read; when we come to the point of making a statement about poetry, it is the poetry that sticks in our minds that weights that statement. And at the same time we notice that Arnold has come to an opinion about poetry different from that of any of his predecessors. For Wordsworth and for Shelley poetry was a vehicle for one kind of philosophy or another, but the philosophy was something believed in. For Arnold the best poetry supersedes both religion and philosophy. I have tried to indicate the results of this conjuring trick elsewhere.[4] The most generalised form of my own view is simply this: that nothing in this world or the next is a substitute for anything else; and if you find that you must do without something, such as religious faith or philosophic belief, then you must just do without it. I can persuade myself, I find, that some of the things that I can hope to get are better worth having than some of the things I cannot get; or I may hope to alter myself so as to want different things; but I cannot persuade myself that it is the same desires that are satisfied, or that I have in effect the same thing under a different name.

A French friend said of the late York Powell of Oxford: *"il était aussi tranquille dans son manque de foi que le mystique dans sa croyance."* You could not say that of Arnold; his charm and his interest are largely due to the painful position that he occupied between faith and disbelief. Like many people the vanishing of whose religious faith has left behind only habits, he placed an exaggerated emphasis upon morals. Such people often confuse morals with their own good habits, the result of a sensible upbringing, prudence, and the absence of any very powerful temptation; but I do not speak of Arnold or of any particular person, for only God knows. Morals for the saint are only a preliminary matter; for the poet a secondary matter. How Arnold finds morals in poetry is not clear. He tells us that:

[4] "Arnold and Pater," in *Selected Essays*. [It is the essay preceding this in the present volume.—Ed.]

A poetry of revolt against moral ideas is a poetry of revolt against *life*; a poetry of indifference towards moral ideas is a poetry of indifference towards *life,*

but the statement left in suspension, and without Arnold's illustrating it by examples of poetic revolt and poetic indifference, seems to have little value. A little later he tells us why Wordsworth is great:

Wordsworth's poetry is great because of the extraordinary power with which Wordsworth feels the joy offered to us in nature, the joy offered to us in the simple primary affections and duties; and because of the extraordinary power with which, in case after case, he shows us this joy, and renders it so as to make us share it.

It is not clear whether "the simple primary affections and duties" (whatever they are, and however distinguished from the secondary and the complex) is meant to be an expansion of "nature," or another joy superadded: I rather think the latter, and take "nature" to mean the Lake District. I am not, furthermore, sure of the meaning of the conjunction of two quite different reasons for Wordsworth's greatness: one being the power with which Wordsworth *feels* the joy of nature, the other the power by which he makes us *share* it. In any case, it is definitely a communication theory, as any theory of the poet as teacher, leader, or priest is bound to be. One way of testing it is to ask why other poets are great. Can we say that Shakespeare's poetry is great because of the extraordinary power with which Shakespeare feels estimable feelings, and because of the extraordinary power with which he makes us share them? I enjoy Shakespeare's poetry to the full extent of my capacity for enjoying poetry; but I have not the slightest approach to certainty that I share Shakespeare's feelings; nor am I very much concerned to know whether I do or not. In short, Arnold's account seems to me to err in putting the emphasis upon the poet's feelings, instead of upon the poetry. We can say that in poetry there is communication from writer to reader, but should not proceed from this to think of the poetry as being primarily the vehicle of communication. Communication may take place, but will explain nothing. Or Arnold's statement may be criticised in another way, by asking whether Wordsworth would be a less great poet, if he felt with extraordinary power the horror offered to us in nature, and the boredom and sense of restriction in the simple primary affections and duties? Arnold seems to think that because, as he says, Wordsworth "deals with more of *life"* than Burns, Keats and Heine, he is dealing with more of moral ideas. A poetry which is concerned with moral ideas, it would appear, is concerned with life; and a poetry concerned with life is concerned with moral ideas. . . .

I do not mean to suggest that Arnold's conception of the use of poetry, an educator's view, vitiates his criticism. To ask of poetry that it give religious and philosophic satisfaction, while deprecating philosophy and dogmatic religion, is of course to embrace the shadow of a shade. But Arnold had real taste. His preoccupations, as I have said, make him too exclusively concerned with *great* poetry, and with the greatness of it. His view of Milton is for this reason unsatisfying. But you cannot read his essay on *The Study of Poetry* without being convinced by the felicity of his quotations: to be able to quote as Arnold could is the best evidence of taste. The essay is a classic in English criticism: so much is said in so little space, with such economy and with such authority. Yet he was so conscious of what, for him, poetry was *for*, that he could not altogether see it for what it is. And I am not sure that he was highly sensitive to the musical qualities of verse. His own occasional bad lapses arouse the suspicion; and so far as I can recollect he never emphasises this virtue of poetic style, this fundamental, in his criticism. What I call the "auditory imagination" is the feeling for syllable and rhythm, penetrating far below the conscious levels of thought and feeling, invigorating every word; sinking to the most primitive and forgotten, returning to the origin and bringing something back, seeking the beginning and the end. It works through meanings, certainly, or not without meanings in the ordinary sense, and fuses the old and obliterated and the trite, the current, and the new and surprising, the most ancient and the most civilised mentality. Arnold's notion of "life," in his account of poetry, does not perhaps go deep enough.

I feel, rather than observe, an inner uncertainty and lack of confidence and conviction in Matthew Arnold: the conservatism which springs from lack of faith, and the zeal for reform which springs from dislike of change. Perhaps, looking inward and finding how little he had to support him, looking outward on the state of society and its tendencies, he was somewhat disturbed. He had no real serenity, only an impeccable demeanour. Perhaps he cared too much for civilisation, forgetting that Heaven and Earth shall pass away, and Mr. Arnold with them, and there is only one stay. He is a representative figure. A man's theory of the place of poetry is not independent of his view of life in general.

Matthew Arnold

by J. Hillis Miller

Man is not only a creature of time and space, like a stone or a tree. He is also a social being, and can form relations to his fellows. Perhaps he can find in society or in the love of another person what he cannot find in time or space. In the lost epoch of harmony, love was still possible, and society was divinely ordered. This lost harmony would be regained if we could re-establish love or discover a valid society.

Only a still genuine society could be depended on to mediate between man and God. Present society does not appear to be so when seen from the point of view of isolated, self-conscious man, though this may be an illusion. The only way to make certain would be to accept the role society would have us play. There is in Arnold's writings a recurrent suspicion that the fault is not with the times, but with himself. His coldness and detachment may be preventing him from discovering whether any of the ways of living offered to him are valid ones.

Arnold is attracted by his own version of the strategy of role-playing. At present he is "an aimless unallay'd Desire" (481). If he could act for a while as if one of the given ways of being were proper, he might find that the costume would become habitual dress. Arnold's copying in his notebooks of quotations of a courageous and morally stiffening sort was in one of its aspects an

"Matthew Arnold." From J. Hillis Miller, *The Disappearance of God: Five Nineteenth-Century Writers* (Cambridge: Harvard University Press, The Belknap Press, 1963), pp. 241–48, 250–54, 257–66, and 267–69. Copyright 1963 by the President and Fellows of Harvard College. Reprinted by permission of the publisher.

Author's abbreviations: Numbers in parentheses refer to pages in C. B. Tinker and H. F. Lowry, eds., *The Poetical Works of Matthew Arnold* (London: Oxford University Press, 1957). *The Works of Matthew Arnold in Fifteen Volumes* (London, 1903, 1904) are cited by volume and page number alone.

CL.: Howard Foster Lowry, ed., *The Letters of Matthew Arnold to Arthur Hugh Clough* (London: Oxford University Press, 1957).

attempt to carry into practice this theory of role-playing. If he could go often enough through the act of writing down a solemn and constructive quotation from some wise man of the past, Bishop Wilson or Isaiah or Epictetus, he might come to believe in the quotation and be made over in its image. Then "the best that has been thought and said in the world" (VII, xxx) would be made current in Arnold's own life.

This method of role-playing never really works for Arnold, in spite of the bulk of his notebooks. He is never able to conquer his coldness. Arnold makes a bad actor, and his own anxious face is always present behind the mask of Bishop Wilson, Sophocles, or Spinoza. Arnold is never able to leap beyond the basic paradox of such a strategy. There is no way to be certain that a given course of imitative action will lead to its goal. But how, unless we are sure, can we give ourselves wholeheartedly to any path? There is an element of guesswork in any choice of a predetermined way toward an end. If we were certain the path would lead to the goal, we should already in some sense possess the goal, and should not need to go through any process to reach it. It is just this unpredictability which Arnold is unwilling to accept. He has to see the goal clearly before he takes the plunge. My "one natural craving," he says, is "a distinct seeing of my way as far as my own nature is concerned" (CL, 110). This is impossible. The goal stays hidden until it is reached. So Arnold remains permanently in his detachment, unable to accept any externally given code as the law of his being. At the crucial moment faith fails him, he throws down in disgust the mask of "duty self-denial etc.," and relaxes back into his usual inner slackness and anarchy: "What I must tell you," he writes to Clough, "is that I have never yet succeeded in any one great occasion in consciously mastering myself. I can go thro: the imaginary process of mastering myself and see the whole affair as it would then stand, but at the critical point I am too apt to hoist up the mainsail to the wind and let her drive. However as I get more awake to this it will I hope mend for I find that with me a clear almost palpable intuition (damn the logical senses of the word) is necessary before I get into prayer: unlike many people who set to work at their duty self-denial etc. like furies in the dark hoping to be gradually illuminated as they persist in this course" (CL, 110).

The key word here is "intuition," and the strain Arnold is put-

ting on the word is revealed in his exclamation about it. He
recognizes that he wants the word to express a contradiction: the
possession of the goal before one has gone through the process
necessary to reach it. The "intuition" of the goal which Arnold
requires before he starts praying must not be a vague supposition.
It must be "clear" and "almost palpable," or else he cannot be
sure enough that the goal is there to get under way at all. The
peculiarity of prayer, from the human point of view, is that it
creates in its own act the goal which is sought. Prayer brings us
into the realm where prayer is answered. The other acts which
Arnold is considering here are of the same nature. The strategy
of escaping inner emptiness by the playing of a role must accept
the initial obscurity and uncertainty of the method, but Arnold
is unwilling to work like a fury in the dark hoping for a gradual
illumination. So he remains withdrawn from life, the disinterested critic of the institutions, the literature, the society, the religion of his time. These present themselves to him never as
something he has experienced from the inside, but as a spectacle
to be regarded from a distance with a settled suspicion that the
truth is not in them. As a critic of society he seeks rather to understand than to sympathize. He wants to control society and to
keep it at arm's length by a discovery of its laws. His attitude
toward society is fundamentally defensive. The "demand for an
intellectual deliverance," he writes, "arises, because the present
age exhibits to the individual man who contemplates it the spectacle of a vast multitude of facts awaiting and inviting his comprehension. The deliverance consists in man's comprehension of
this present and past. It begins when our mind begins to enter
into possession of the general ideas which are the law of this vast
multitude of facts. It is perfect when we have acquired that harmonious acquiescence of mind which we feel in contemplating
a grand spectacle that is intelligible to us . . ."[1]

Arnold strives to understand the spectacle of life by looking at
it with the scientist's cold, detached eye, by "see[ing] the object
as in itself it really is" (III, 1). Another name for this disinterestedness is irony, the stylistic pose which separates itself from
what it describes, and, holding it at a distance, hollows it out with
subtle mockery. Arnold is a skillful ironist, but his irony is not,
as with the greatest ironists, turned on himself. Irony, like the

---

[1] *Essays by Matthew Arnold* (London: Oxford Univ. Press, 1914), pp. 455, 456.

stance of disinterestedness, is for Arnold a way of not being swallowed up by the world. He fears more than anything else the possibility that he might plunge into the "immense, moving, confused spectacle" of life (*Essays*, 456), and be lost in its inauthenticity. Society is a dangerous whirlpool. "The rush and roar of practical life will always have a dizzying and attracting effect upon the most collected spectator, and tend to draw him into its vortex" (III, 27), and therefore man "must begin with an Idea of the world in order not to be prevailed over by the world's multitudinousness" (CL, 97).

Arnold always keeps himself erect and aloof, like a man fording a rapid, muddy river, holding his head high and walking on tiptoe. He never has the courage to try that mode of understanding which seeks to comprehend the rationale of an alien way of life by seeing how it would feel to accept it as one's own. Arnold recognizes that this mode of understanding is an important one, and even that it is the way of knowing most proper to the poet. The poet, in order to recreate in words the spectacle of life around him, must "become what [he] sing[s]" (193), but, whereas the Gods can with pleasure see and participate in the vast panorama of life, the poet must pay the price of great pain for his knowledge. Though the Gods cannot share human sorrows, the poet must enter fully into the sufferings as well as the joys of the heroes of his poem: "—such a price/The Gods exact for song" (193). Being a poet seems to Arnold a matter of great suffering, the pain caused by breaking down the safe barriers of cold solitude, going outside oneself, and entering into the warmth and feeling of those who are engaged in life. Keats welcomes the chance to be "with Achilles shouting in the trenches." The more powerful the sensation the better. "Negative capability," sympathetic identification even with painful or melancholy things, is for Keats the very source of joy, of truth, and of beauty. Arnold fears such a loss of his self-possession, and goes out of himself with great reluctance. He wants to make poetry as much as possible a matter of assimilation and control rather than of diffusion and sympathy, though the process of taking the world into oneself rather than going outward into the world also seems to him a cause of suffering and effort: "For me you may often hear my sinews cracking under the effort to unite matter . . ." (CL, 65). Arnold fears that even this painful control over the world may be impossible. The world may slip away, rise up against the soul, and once more engulf it.

Arnold's fullest analysis of the danger of understanding through sympathy is in a famous letter to Clough. As is so often the case he projects into Clough as a *fait accompli* what he fears as a possibility for himself. Role-playing, he says, leads to a dispersal of the self, its absorption by the chaotic multiplicity of all the ways of living which society offers. "You ask me," he tells Clough, "in what I think or have thought you going wrong: in this: that you would never take your assiette as something determined final and unchangeable for you and proceed to work away on the basis of that: but were always poking and patching and cobbling at the assiette itself—could never finally, as it seemed—'resolve to be thyself'—but were looking for this and that experience, and doubting whether you ought not to adopt this or that mode of being of persons qui ne vous valaient pas because it might possibly be nearer the truth than your own: you had no reason for thinking it *was,* but it *might* be—and so you would try to adapt yourself to it. You have I am convinced lost infinite time in this way: it is what I call your morbid conscientiousness . . ." (CL, 130). Clough's conscientiousness is the tormenting awareness of the possibility that the other fellow has found the secret of inner certainty. Arnold's conscientiousness is that of the man who never takes the plunge into life because he fears all given ways of living are imposture, and will contaminate him. He is not sure that they are all false, but neither is he sure that any one of them is true, and so he loses infinite time, just as Clough, in Arnold's analysis of him, loses infinite time through being unable to take one mode of life as permanently his. No man in these damned times has a solid inner law and support for his being. In the absence of this man can neither accept society nor do without it, but must fluctuate between isolation and the halfhearted acceptance of a social role whose falseness he suspects from the start:

> Where shall [a man] fly then? back to men?—
> But they will gladly welcome him once more,
> And help him to unbend his too tense thought,
> And rid him of the presence of himself,
> And keep their friendly chatter at his ear,
> And haunt him, till the absence from himself,
> That other torment, grow unbearable;

> And he will fly to solitude again,
> And he will find its air too keen for him,
> And so change back; and many thousand times
> Be miserably bandied to and fro
> Like a sea-wave . . . (435, 436)

Arnold never really tries to reach the lost time of joy through society. The basis of his attitude toward society is an inability to believe that any social form embodies divine law, and his analysis of society, in his poetry and in his prose, is an attempt to persuade us of the truth of this presupposition. At one time society was in God's hand, but an originally good society has drifted further and further away from its holy beginning until mere empty husks are left. In terms of these husks, shells from which the spiritual vitality has departed, man in these days is forced to carry on his collective life. Social forms no longer draw strength from God, and, on the other hand, they are no longer appropriate to the life man leads. An awareness of the artificiality, the hollowness, the conventionality of present-day social forms characterizes the modern spirit: "Modern times find themselves with an immense system of institutions, established facts, accredited dogmas, customs, rules, which have come to them from times not modern. In this system their life has to be carried forward; yet they have a sense that this system is not of their own creation, that it by no means corresponds exactly with the wants of their actual life, that, for them, it is customary, not rational. The awakening of this sense is the awakening of the modern spirit" (III, 174).

The forms of society are laws, institutions, religion, the arts, language. Most of Arnold's prose is "criticism" in the sense that it is dedicated to showing the emptiness of one or another of these social forms. *Culture and Anarchy* is based on the assumption that all classes of contemporary society, barbarians, philistines, and populace alike, are wrong in their claims to be divinely justified. England possesses "an aristocracy materialised and null, a middle-class purblind and hideous, a lower class crude and brutal" (IV, 148, 149). Rather than being "culture" in the sense of a viable human embodiment of divine truth, the three classes are, in one way or another, baseless anarchy, the anarchy, for example, of "doing as one likes," without any extrahuman justification. In the same way, at the heart of Arnold's several books on religion is the assumption that language cannot incarnate God's truth.

St. Paul and Protestantism is an attempt to demolish the Puritan
claim to speak "scientifically" about God in the language of the
"covenant of redemption," "the covenant of works," "original sin,"
"free election," "effectual calling." The trouble with this kind
of language is that it is "talking about God just as if he were
a man in the next street" (IX, 8). We can never talk about God
in this way. St. Paul had the secret of righteousness and lived
in harmony with God's law, but Protestantism has reduced St.
Paul to empty formulas, and lives outside the divine kingdom.
In the chapter in *God and the Bible* called "The God of Metaphysics" Arnold attempts to demonstrate that the central words
of metaphysics, "is," "being," "essence," "existence," "substance,"
and so on, are derived from words for physical nature. Since they
all come from terms for earthly experience, they can tell us nothing whatever about God. "*Être*," says Arnold, "really means to
breathe" (VIII, 90), and to say "God is," is simply to say "God
operates, . . . the Eternal which makes for righteousness has operation" (VIII, 92, 93). Arnold assumes here that the origin of a
word permanently limits its meaning. Abstract words are metaphorical extensions of concrete terms. Therefore they can never be
anything but figurative. As abstractions they refer to nothing at all.
All we can honestly say about God and his heaven is: "We know
nothing about the matter, it is altogether beyond us" (VIII, 97).

This idea about the nature of language contains a theological
implication. It assumes that God transcends our speech. He can
only be defined negatively, as "not ourselves," that is, as unthinkable, and therefore unspeakable. We cannot even speak of God
as "He," for that is to anthropomorphize God, to think of It after
the model of a "magnified and non-natural man" (IX, 19). "It,"
the "not ourselves," can only be known through Its operation,
as what "makes for righteousness," whatever *that* may mean.
Arnold wishes to show that all our language, even the most abstract and seemingly worthy of the transcendent character of the
deity, is a "throwing out" of figurative language toward something which it cannot name and has no hope of reaching. He
believes in God, but he does not believe that God can be spoken
about as we speak of the things of this world. . . .

Man as a social being is condemned to remain an outlaw, but
once he could form an extrasocial relation to his fellows, the re-

lation of love. In the epoch of harmony lovers could be transparent to one another, and see truly into one another's souls. This communion of lovers was the microcosm of the universal harmony in which it participated. Perhaps if true love could be re-established the cosmic background of love would also be recovered. Arnold in his own life seeks this way out of the sterility and "aridity"[2] of his existence. The record of this attempt is the Marguerite poems.

These poems are dominated by nostalgia for an epoch when each person was not yet "enisled" (182) in the sea of life. Marguerite, on her Alpine heights, still belongs to the pastoral age, and if Arnold can love and be loved by her, he can return, through her, to the primal origin of things, for she is "a messenger from radiant climes" (208).

The poems express Arnold's discovery that love cannot be used in this way. Only someone who already participates in the divine life of nature would be a fit mate for Marguerite. Such a man would be himself an incarnation of the universal joy:

> His eyes be like the starry lights—
> His voice like sounds of summer nights—
> In all his lovely mien let pierce
> The magic of the universe! (202)

Unless Arnold already shares in the "magic of the universe," Marguerite will be opaque to him. Instead of permitting him access to her inner self, she will turn on him her "pure, unwavering, deep disdain" (202), the disdain of someone who has "look'd, and smiled, and [seen him] through" (202). Arnold is a hollow man, and because he needs from love the vitality which makes it possible to love, he is unable to love in Marguerite's way, the way of those who "bring more than they receive" (203). Marguerite is able to love because she contains her own springs of life and joy. She rejects disdainfully the modern sort of love, in which two people, as in "Dover Beach," need one another to fill up the void in their hearts. Such modern lovers plight their troth in the face of an awareness that there is no universal Love to guarantee particular acts of love. Aloneness is now man's real condition,

---

[2] Compare CL, 131: "God keep us . . . from aridity! *Arid*—that is what the times are."

and love is founded on its own despair. This is a modern "existentialist" kind of love, which says: "Since there is no 'Love,' in the sense of a power transcending man, let us create love out of nothing, in spite of the insecurity and even absurdity of such love." Marguerite has no need of this kind of love, and expects the same independence from her lover. She is one of those who "ask no love, [and] plight no faith,/For they are happy as they are" (203).

Just as Arnold must have a poet's nature first in order to write poetry, so he must participate in the universal harmony in order to create its miniature image in the intimacy of lovers. But Arnold is outside the timeless current of God's life, an island upon time's barren, stormy flow, and therefore love is impossible for him. He abandons Marguerite because he recognizes an essential lack in himself. He is "too strange, too restless, too untamed" (178), and she is right to reject him. He is right to leave her too, for rather than being a way to his true goal, the "establishment of God's kingdom on earth," love in these bad days leads man astray and diverts him from other possible ways out of the wilderness. Love tends to present itself to Arnold under the guise of passion, as a dangerous relaxation of moral stiffness, a "hoisting up of the mainsail and letting her drive." In "A Summer Night" the alternative to giving one's life to "some unmeaning taskwork" is the mad liberty of the "freed prisoner" who sails aimlessly across the tempestuous sea of life, "With anguish'd face and flying hair/Grasping the rudder hard,/Still bent to make some port he knows not where, /Still standing for some false impossible shore" (244). Against Clough's tendency to "welter to the parching wind," to *"fluctuate,"* Arnold feels it necessary to "stiffen [himself]—and hold fast [his] rudder" (CL, 146).

Along with this conviction that the only way to get through these bad times is aloofness and stiffness, the chin held high above the swirling waters, goes another attitude toward strong feeling. Arnold often feels guilty about his inability to abandon himself to passion: "I have had that desire of fulness without respect of the means, which may become almost maniacal: but nature had placed a bar thereto not only in the conscience (as with all men) but in a great numbness in that direction" (CL, 97); "I doubt whether I shall ever have heat and radiance enough to pierce the clouds that are massed round me" (CL, 126). It may be that his "coldness" and "invincible languor of spirit" (CL, 129) are not really good qualities at all. Though passion clouds intellectual clarity, this clarity may be the thing which is cutting him off from the divine vitality. If he could drown his lucidity in a current of powerful feeling he would find himself back in a realm where things blend in mutual interpenetration. While intellect coldly sets things against one another, and puts a void between them, feeling is a warm flow in which things lose their sharp edges, and the mind its separateness. Though speech belongs to surface life and is never authentic, the "nameless feelings that course through our breast" (246) come from the deep buried life and share its truth. In those rare moments when the buried life is liberated and "our eyes can in another's eyes read clear" (247) the vehicle of this possession of ourselves and of another person is not speech or intellect. It is the recovery of "a lost pulse of feeling" (247).

Religion, in Arnold's famous definition, is "morality touched with emotion." By itself morality is not strong enough to lead man to the good. Emotion comes, though distantly and obscurely, from God, and when morality is irradiated with this gracious element of feeling it is strong enough to guide man's steps toward heaven. Creeds and dogmas are not so important as the unspeakable feeling they express, and this feeling is the same whatever the creed. The fact that man is forced to use speech and concepts is merely proof of his separation from the fusing joy. In his religious books, as in his doctrine of poetry, Arnold wants to return to a time before abstract thought was necessary, a time when man lived his religion directly, in powerful feeling, without needing to think about it.

Arnold's theories of religion and love are strikingly similar, and he returns, in a religious context, to his notion that the loved one can serve as a mediator between man and God. In *St. Paul and Protestantism* he rejects the idea that Jesus is the Mediator either in the metaphysical sense of the divine Logos, or in the Old Testament sense of the Messiah. Science, he says, can neither prove nor disprove these ideas. They are something we can know nothing about. Arnold proposes as truly St. Paul's an analysis of the power of Jesus based on his own earlier theory of love between the sexes. Though there is a moral law which we should obey, by himself man is unable to know and follow this law. Jesus, alone of all men, was without sin, and He "lived to God" (IX, 59). Ordinary men are not strong enough to reach the kingdom of God by a cold performance of duty, but if they love Jesus, then the current of emotion and sympathy binding them to Him will allow them to reach God through Jesus. Only in this sense is Jesus the Mediator: "Every one knows how being in love changes for the time a man's spiritual atmosphere, and makes animation and buoyancy where before there was flatness and dulness. . . . [Being in love] also sensibly and powerfully increases our faculties of action." When Paul loved Jesus, "appropriated" the power of Jesus, "the struggling stream of duty, which had not volume enough to bear him to his goal, was suddenly reinforced by the immense tidal wave of sympathy and emotion" (IX, 56, 65). What was possible for St. Paul, reaching God through his love for Jesus, is by no means necessarily possible for Arnold. Even for St. Paul this loving attachment to Jesus was faith, the "power of holding on to the unseen" (IX, 65). For the deity is an "unseen God" (IX, 67). In religion as in love the ideas of separation, of unavailability, are essential for Arnold. He uses here his basic metaphor of human life, the stream. Religious life, like life in general, is a moving toward a goal which transcends man, as the ocean transcends any point on the river which flows toward it. . . .

Though Arnold tries all the ways to fly from himself, his attempts to escape lead him inevitably back to his original state of ennui. His unsuccessful flights from himself are the very causes of that state.

The failure of every effort to reach peace leads Arnold to discover the essential nature of his situation. When man dwelt in the divine kingdom he could reconcile opposites, for all qualities existed together in harmonious tension. When the world exploded into multiplicity the opposites were divided from one another. Man hungers for unity, for totality. His exploration of the world leads to the discovery that this need must be frustrated. He can have any half of each of the pairs of opposites, never both at once. Fire, ice; height, depth; isolation, society; feeling, thought; clearness, force; aridity, fluidity; too much air or too little; freedom, law; self-possession, possession of the All—man can have only one member of each of these pairs. To have one quality without its opposite is loss of selfhood, not its recovery. The antinomies can never be reconciled, and man is condemned to the either/or of the exploded world. Arnold's thought, both in its imagery and in its conceptual axes, is dominated by the theme of irreconcilable opposites, and the constant appearance of this theme is evidence of his inability to experience the world as other than broken and disintegrated. He is either too hot or too cold, either oppressed by the stuffy air of great cities or suffocating in the thin air on the mountaintop, either tormented by solitude or poisoned by the "unavoidable contact with millions of small [natures]," either alienated from himself by submission to a false law, or driven mad by an empty freedom. He hurries everywhere, like a rat in a maze, trying to find some way of life which will bring together the opposites and allow him to have the plentitude of an undivided life. Everywhere he finds one extreme or the other, never the central harmony from which all opposites flow. Arnold's search for some power or mode of existence which will mediate between himself and God has failed in every direction. It has turned out to be impossible to remain poised in a calm equilibrium. In spite of himself he falls back into one or another of the opposites and begins again the miserable process of wavering. It seems as if "only death /Can cut his oscillations short, and so/Bring him to poise. There is no other way" (436).

One last strategy remains, self-dependence: "Resolve to be thyself; and know that he,/Who finds himself, loses his misery!" (240). Man must cut himself off from everything outside, and seek to reach the "only true, deep-buried [self],/Being one with which we are one with the whole world" (440). It may be that in his own vital depths man still encompasses the divine current. If he could withdraw from all superficial engagements in life he might find himself back in the streets of the celestial city. "Sink . . . in thy soul!" Arnold cries; "Rally the good in the depths of thyself!" (235).

This movement of withdrawal means, in one direction, a total rejection of the social world as it is. Arnold hopes that this self-purification will destroy the inauthentic, and permit the authentic to be revealed. By repudiating the false selves which have engulfed him in the rush and hurry of urban life, Arnold will allow to rise up and fill his inner emptiness the deep buried self which is his real identity. At the same time this will be a possession of the "general life," the soul of the world, the All. To possess the All is at the same moment to reach God. The "spark from heaven" will fall, and man will be the source of true and fresh ideas from

God, a "bringer of heavenly light" (447). This light will illuminate human society. When man recovers his deep buried self he will himself become the mediator he has sought in vain.

The buried life is characterized by its individuality, and by the fact that to possess it coincides with possession of the totality of the world, therefore with possession of God. It is undifferentiated, like God himself, and yet it is *my* self, special to me alone. It is the self I recover when I escape from the successions of time and the divisions of space. The buried life dwells in the place where origin and ending are simultaneous. It comes from the depths of the soul in the form of floating, evanescent emotions which resist embodiment in words. It is truly a self—personal, and yet universal. To reach it would be to gain everything I lack.

In attempting to reach the buried life by cutting himself off from every contaminating influence Arnold makes his most frightening discovery, the discovery recorded in "Empedocles on Etna." At this moment the thin strand connecting the soul to the self and the self to God's joy is being cut, and the soul is being transformed into sheer emptiness. Whether by going down toward the deep buried self and finding it "infinitely distant" in the "unlit gulph of himself" (231), or by going up on the mountaintops toward the "unseen God," Arnold finds that by separation from everything external he gets not possession of himself, but the final loss of life and joy. Though he gets clearer and clearer, higher and higher above the turmoil of ordinary life, he does not get one inch closer to the buried self or to the divine spark. No revelation, no intuition, no presence of God is possible. What happens is a progressive evacuation of the soul, a progressive appearance of the true emptiness of consciousness. This emptiness is defined by its infinite distance from the buried self and from the divine transcendence. So Arnold writes, in "Stagirius," of the tragic situation,

> When the soul, growing clearer,
>   Sees God no nearer;
> When the soul, mounting higher,
>   To God comes no nigher . . . (38)

These lines, in their very banality of rhythm and expression, are of great importance to an understanding of Arnold. No other lines express so succinctly the pathos of his spiritual experience. The prosodic slackness of the verses, and the singsong of their feminine rhymes match the terrible spiritual slackness and despondency which is their meaning. In these lines is enacted that drama of the disappearance of God which makes the nineteenth century a turning point in the spiritual history of man. When every external way back to God has failed, the soul turns within, and hopes to reach the unseen self and the unseen God through rejection, simplification, clarification, the climb to the pure heights of the soul's solitude. Surely in its most secret places the soul is still bound to God. But clarity becomes vacuity, and the soul confronts at last the horror of its own nothingness. Though Arnold should climb forever he would not move a cubit closer to God, for no progress is possible along an infinite course, and he remains, however far he goes, an empty desire.[3]

In "Empedocles on Etna" the Greek philosopher-poet recognizes that there is still a thin strand connecting him to the universal life, a narrow channel through which he participates in the "immortal vigour" of earth, air, fire, and water. This "held-in joy" (438) of nature shares in God's life. Empedocles possesses God through nature, but at this very moment the fragile link to God is being broken. In a final attempt to save himself from isolation while there is yet time, Empedocles plunges into the crater. He sacrifices his separate existence for the sake of a total participation in the "All," the universal life which is diffused throughout nature (441).

Empedocles makes the extreme choice of suicide, and saves his soul, but Arnold only imagines this possibility. His rejection of suicide and his remorse for having considered it are clear enough in his repudiation of "Empedocles on Etna" in the "Preface" of 1853. Arnold chooses to remain behind as a survivor into those black times which Empedocles foresees. Empedocles kills himself at the moment he is about to become "Nothing but a devouring flame of thought—/But a naked, eternally restless mind!" (438). He knows that once a man is transformed into intelligence, he is doomed. His body will, after his death, find a home among the several elements from which it came, but mind can find no resting

---

[3] "Stagirius" is also called, in some printings, "Desire." Stagirius, as Arnold explained in a note of 1877, was a young monk to whom St. John Chrysostom addressed "three books" (487). (See Migne, *P.G.*, 47:423–494, for Chrysostom's Πρὸς Σταγείριον.) It is appropriate that Arnold should in the title of this poem make a cryptic allusion to the fourth-century Church Father who inherited the tradition of negative theology and preached so eloquently on the transcendence and "incomprehensibility" of God. A manuscript variant of the crucial lines in Arnold's poem reads: "When the soul rising higher, to God comes no nigher—/ When the mind waxing clearer sees God no nearer—" (38).

place in the universe. There is nothing it can blend with or find itself reflected in. The man who is all mind is condemned to wandering and solitude. He is irrevocably trapped in the prison of himself, and will remain one of "the strangers of the world" (439). The last consequence of man's transformation into mind is the worst of all. A man who is wholly mind is unable to die. He is doomed, as in a passage from Eastern philosophy which Arnold recorded in his notebooks,[4] to the horror of the eternal return. His endless life will be a constant repetition of the same failure to escape from himself. He will be born again and again, and in each new reincarnation will seek frantically to be absorbed back into the general life. The elements will reject him as always, for mind is allied to none of them. He will be thrust back into life, again to seek unsuccessfully for death and its obliteration of self-hood. He will endure a perpetual transmigration, and move endlessly across the surface of existence, his "ineffable longing for the life of life/Baffled for ever" (439). As in Kafka's terrifying story of "The Hunter Gracchus," the worst suffering is that man should seek death, and yet be unable to find it. The discovery that man may be condemned to "be astray for ever" (440) is the climax not only of "Empedocles on Etna," but of all Arnold's experience.

The breaking of the unity of man, nature, and God which Empedocles experienced in his time, and which Arnold experiences in ours, is not an isolated event. The moment of Empedocles' death is a true turning point or pivot of history. It is the instant when God withdraws from the world. Only at such a time does man experience himself as complete emptiness. All Arnold's frustrated attempts to escape back to the epoch when man could participate in the divine life have led him inexorably to the discovery of the truth about man's present condition: vacuity and distance are what man, in these bad times, really is. And this vacuity and distance, "the void which in our breasts we bear" (424), can in no way be escaped.

[4] See *The Note-Books of Matthew Arnold*, ed. H. F. Lowry, K. Young, and W. H. Dunn (London: Oxford University Press, 1952), p. 10: "Let him reflect on the transmigrations of men caused by their sinful deeds, on their downfall into a region of darkness, and their torments in the mansion of Yama; . . . on their agonizing departure from this corporeal frame, their formation again in the womb, and the glidings of this vital spirit through ten thousand millions of passages . . ." (from the *Mānava Dharma Śāstra; or The Institutes of Menu*, tr. Sir William Jones, II [London, 1825], 180, 181).

Though Arnold's explorations of the world seem to have led to an altogether negative revelation, the discovery that man is about to become a devouring flame of thought turns out to be an unexpected victory over wavering and vacillation. Arnold finds at last an assiette and a positive course to pursue.

This reversal is the strange denouement of Arnold's spiritual adventure. He discovers that true piety consists in accepting the withdrawal of God. The responsibility of man in a time when God is absent is to keep the void open for God's return. "I am nothing," said Arnold in a passage which goes to the heart of his sense of himself and of his time—"I am nothing and very probably never shall be anything—but there are characters which are truest to themselves by never being anything, when circumstances do not suit" (CL, 135).

After trying all the ways in which he might be something, Arnold resigns himself to being nothing. His work thereby becomes one of the most important testimonies to the spiritual situation of the nineteenth century. Arnold's constant desire for rest, for peace, is an attempt to refuse the situation in which he finds himself. He is condemned to be inwardly a void, to be always in motion, always an unsatisfied desire. He hates to be so "mobile, inconstant" (III, 96), and tries to believe that it is not a meaningful situation, but a shameful failing, a directionless eddying from one attitude or allegiance to another. His mobility is an endless rejection of whatever has been reached for the sake of something which has not yet been reached, a situation imposed by the disappearance of God and the consequent degradation of all human values. Arnold's last and most characteristic posture is that of the man who waits passively and in tranquil hope for the spark from heaven to fall, "the leaven to work, the let to end" (449). He is the man "Wandering between two worlds, one dead,/The other powerless to be born . . ." (302), the man of the no longer and not yet, a survivor who has persisted unwillingly into a time when all he cares for is dead. Arnold is fascinated by those who, like Obermann or the Scholar-Gipsy, withdraw from life and wait out the interim, isolating themselves to keep their emptiness pure. He sees in such figures an image of what he should be, of what he *is,* in spite of all his superficial engagements in life.

The proper literary form for such a situation is the elegy, the form of expression fitting for a man who sits by the body of a

loved one whose death is the death of a world. In his essay on
Emerson, Arnold quotes, with covert self-application, the Youths'
dirge over Mignon from Carlyle's translation of *Wilhelm Meister*.
In this passage Arnold's own situation is given in brief: "Well is
our treasure now laid up, the fair image of the past. Here sleeps
it in the marble, undecaying; in your hearts, also, it lives, it works.
Travel, travel, back into life! Take along with you this holy earnestness, for earnestness alone makes life eternity" (IV, 352). Like
Goethe's youth, Arnold is an elegist who mourns more than the
death of the loved one in his dirge. There are a great many elegies
among Arnold's poems. For him the truly poetic situation is the
death of a great man or of someone deeply loved. In poem after
poem, in "Thyrsis," "Rugby Chapel," "Balder Dead," "The Church
of Brou," "Memorial Verses," "Haworth Churchyard," "Heine's
Grave," and even in the several elegies for dead pets, Arnold
dramatizes in the death of one individual the whole situation of
his time. Though the past is dead, it is preserved undecaying in the
tomb, and we must fare forth in a present life which draws its
meaning from its relation to a treasure which lies in the tomb of
the past. The earnestness of a reverent memory that the past joy
once existed is all that connects the present to eternity. The mind
preserves its relation to this joy by accepting nothing in the
whirling quotidian world as a substitute for it. Man's inner emptiness holds the two realms, the authentic and the inauthentic,
rigidly apart. In keeping the two realms separate Arnold obeys the
divine decision, and participates, through suffering, in the mysterious withdrawal of God from the world. He becomes the void
where that withdrawal is completed and maintained.

Arnold's notebooks and his social, literary, and religious criticism are like the elegies in that they too reject the present and
embalm a dead wisdom. For "the best that has been thought and
said in the world" is no longer current in society. It is kept alive,
in these bad times, only by the effort of the critic to "learn and
propagate" it, as a corpse might be kept alive by mesmerism.
Though the tone of Arnold's prose is so different from that of his
poetry, this difference testifies not to Arnold's escape from his
earlier situation, but to the resigned acquiescence which he ultimately reaches. Arnold the critic can only say: "God exists, and
I know it, but I do not know it directly, and I know too that He
would be the only support of a civilization built on eternal values.

Unfortunately, at this particular moment I cannot tell you, and
no man can tell you, what those values are. Believe no man now
but the one who says, like the prophet crying in the wilderness
before the coming of Christ, that the truth is, but not here, not
yet." There is only one honest way for the man between two
worlds to testify to a God who is no longer immanent. He must
testify negatively: by denying truth to whatever is, and by formulas which are so general that though they assert the existence
of the absolute do not pretend to contain it in words.

Certain modes of language keep their authenticity in a time
when God is transcendent. All of these indicate somewhat vaguely
a direction rather than claiming to participate in the reality they
name. They are signposts which say: "God is somewhere over that
way," rather than labels on a captured truth. In his essay on Spinoza, Arnold makes it clear that for him the value of Spinoza's
philosophy lies not in what is expressed in rational language, but
only in what that language is "driving at" (III, 364), in what its
"tendencies" are. The value of a philosophical system lies not in
what is contained in the system, for the trans-human truth can be
contained in no system, but in the unspoken orientation of the
system. Philosophy is the pursuit of an unattainable object: "A
philosopher's real power over mankind resides not in his metaphysical formulas, but in the spirit and tendencies which have led
him to adopt those formulas" (III, 363, 364). In the same way
Arnold is extremely reluctant to limit the "sweet reasonableness
of Jesus" to any dogmatic interpretation. The divine truth cannot
be contained in concepts, nor in any maxims which can be ex-
tracted from Jesus' own words. The power of Jesus, his "secret,"
is something which is suggested by his sayings. It is transmitted
indirectly and mysteriously, and to each man differently, as a pure
inexhaustible well supplies fresh water to all who drink of it. "The
very *secret* of Jesus," says Arnold, " 'He that loveth his life shall
lose it, he that will lose his life shall save it,' does not give us a
command to be taken and followed in the letter, but an idea to
work in our mind and soul, and of inexhaustible value there. . . .
Christianity cannot be packed into any set of commandments.
. . . Christianity is a *source;* no one supply of water and refreshment that comes from it can be called the sum of Christianity.
It is a mistake, and may lead to much error, to exhibit any series
of maxims, even those of the Sermon on the Mount, as the ulti-

mate sum and formula into which Christianity may be run up"
(IV, 218, 216, 217).

In a similar fashion Arnold's expressions of the truths which
are the center of his own system are left deliberately vague. They
are scrupulously empty phrases. Their repetition empties them
further of meaning, and testifies to the fact that though there is
something to which the words refer, this something is not named
by the words: "make reason and the will of God prevail" (VI, 8);
"the best that has been thought and said in the world"; "high
seriousness"; "the laws of poetic truth and poetic beauty" (IV, 36);
the "Eternal, not ourselves, that makes for righteousness" (VIII,
26); the "stream of tendency by which all things strive to fulfil the
law of their being"; "the absolute beauty and fitness of things"
(III, 23). "Reason," "the will of God," "the best," "righteousness,"
"beauty," "fitness," "seriousness"—none of these terms is really
given any definition by Arnold. They are the blank places in his
discourse which testify to the fact that "we know nothing about
the matter, it is altogether beyond us." The empty phrases repeated so often in Arnold's essays are a way of keeping the void
open after the disappearance of God. Even when these phrases
have a meaning, that meaning is negative. The definition of God
as a "stream of tendency," besides using covertly Arnold's basic
poetic landscape, is a perfect definition of a God who remains
transcendent. Though God is the final end which pulls all things
toward him, he is only what things "tend" toward, not what they
possess already. Man tends to fulfill the law of his being in the
same way as iron filings tend to orient themselves in a magnetic
field—if the field is strong enough.

For Arnold the "Eternal not ourselves" at once is and is not the
guarantee of human values. It is impossible to say exactly what
human values are guaranteed. No one of them can at this time be
put into words. Whenever Arnold asserts that he is naming the
specific values which a given poet, philosopher, or religious thinker
expresses, the reader is aware once again that the Eternal and
man have not really been brought together through the words.
Instead, their relation has been asserted in such a way as to preserve their separation.

In spite of his penchant for elegy, Arnold faces toward the future
as well as toward the lost past. The fact that such men as Words-

worth, Heine, Arthur Stanley, and Thomas Arnold once lived is
proof that the joy which they possessed or believed in still exists.
The signal-tree which Thyrsis longed to reach is still there as a
goal toward which his monodist can direct his life. Thyrsis by
dying leaped ahead to his goal, and his death is proof that "the
light [they] sought is shining still" (269). In the same way the key
phrases in Arnold's essays are witnesses to a truth which may someday return. In these empty linguistic shells a vacant place is kept
intact, waiting to be filled, as the Scholar-Gipsy keeps himself un-
committed, waiting for the spark from heaven to strike him into
life. In his essay on Falkland, Arnold praises those who "by their
heroic and hopeless stand against the inadequate ideals dominant
in their time, kept open their communications with the future,
lived with the future" (X, 222). Like the Scholar-Gipsy, and like
Falkland and his friends, Arnold the critic waits in a purity and
emptiness which are carefully preserved by the rejection of false-
hood. He waits for the return of God, the descent of the "fugitive
and gracious light . . . ,/Shy to illumine" (268). Someday, he believes, "the harmony from which man swerved" will be "made his
life's rule once more" (314).

Arnold does not see history as a gradual exhaustion of the original vitality of creation. History is cyclical, the alternation of
periods of expansion and periods of concentration, periods of poetry and periods of criticism, times when God is within the world,
and times when he inexplicably disappears. The river of time is
a circle which returns on itself, so that the same moment of beginning is constantly repeated, as well as the same process of degradation and drying up. Or, rather, as in passages from Wordsworth and Goethe which Arnold knew,[5] time is a spiral. By a
"progress en ligne spirale" (CL, 80) history returns at different
levels to the same place, so that, though the same ideas, cultures,
and epochs of history are repeated, perhaps time will eventually
be fulfilled, and the promised land reached at last. . . .

To live in the present in terms of the future will be the best
title to esteem with posterity because only through our faith in
the future can we find strength to do the proper work of the
present, a work of rejection, demolition, dissolution. Man "must
be born again" (CL, 109), and in order to be reborn he must first

---

[5] See CL, 80. Lowry has identified the passages to which Arnold apparently
refers (CL, 82).

die to the old man and the old world. Balder, in "Balder Dead," sees destruction of the old as necessary to the creation of the new. Only when "o'er this present earth and Heavens/The tempest of the latter days hath swept,/And they from sight have disappear'd, and sunk," shall we "see emerge/From the bright Ocean at our feet an earth/More fresh, more verdant than the last . . ." (128). As in the Yeatsian picture of history, the stages of civilization are, first, creation, then gradual decay, and finally dissolution, followed by a new creation. Only on the ruins of the old can the new be built. Arnold ends "A Comment on Christmas" with a prophetic vision of our time as, like the time of Jesus, " 'the end of *the age*,' 'the close of *the period*,' " and he urges his readers to accept destruction as the price of renovation. "Sometimes," he says, "we may almost be inclined to augur that from some such 'end of the age' we ourselves are not far distant now; that through dissolution,—dissolution peaceful if we have virtue enough, violent if we are vicious, but still dissolution,—we and our own age have to pass, according to the eternal law which makes dissolution the condition of renovation" (XI, 329).

After the failure of every attempt to escape from himself Arnold is left with only one thing to do. He must hover in the void, in one direction waiting for the lightning to strike, the dawn to come, and in the other direction sternly and implacably criticizing all present cultural forms as false. Through his strategy of withdrawal from practical involvement, he attains at last what he has sought from the beginning. Arnold's final platform is the absence of God.

"The Scholar-Gipsy" best expresses this stance. Arnold's gypsy lives in the rhythm of the perpetual round of the seasons. The ebb and flow of nature is his milieu. His constant alignment toward the spark which has not yet fallen gives him stability in the midst of movement, continuity in the midst of succession. Like the Scholar-Gipsy, Arnold postpones indefinitely the attempt to repossess the buried life, but he recognizes that an escape from fluctuation can be obtained by the rejection of every life less than the buried life, and by a permanent orientation toward the infinite distance where it lies.

In the end Arnold no longer faces toward the lost past, but toward the future return of the divine spirit, a return which he can almost see, as he waits in passive tension, renouncing everything here and now for the sake of something which never quite, while he lives, is actual and present. In "Obermann Once More" the ghost of the Swiss solitary tells Arnold that the dawn of the new world is about to come, and the poet, in what is perhaps the most hopeful passage in all his work, imagines that he sees the morning break—but over there, at a distance, high in the mountains where all things begin. The glimpse of this distant dawn, a dawn which still remains just in the future, is the final prize of Arnold's patient repudiation of everything else:

> And glorious there, without a sound,
> Across the glimmering lake,
> High in the Valais-depth profound,
> I saw the morning break. (324)

Dover Revisited:
The Wordsworthian Matrix
in the Poetry of
Matthew Arnold

by U. C. Knoepflmacher

Much has been written on Matthew Arnold's qualification of Romanticism, on his fluctuating estimates of the English Romantic poets in general and of William Wordsworth in particular. Such studies are generally limited to Arnold's critical opinions.[1] Only occasionally, and then very succinctly, have students of Arnold's poetry dwelled on his creation of what a recent and perceptive critic has called "ironic echoes of Wordsworth": "a version of Wordsworth which is also a criticism and a rejection of Wordsworth's view."[2]

Arnold's poetry is, to a large extent, derivative. It draws on the classics for much of its mythic substance and the stateliness of its rhythm; on Goethe for intellectual content; on sources as remote as the *Bhagavad Gita* for that "wider application" which Arnold felt was "the one thing wanting to make Wordsworth an even greater poet than he is." But the core of Arnold's emotional power is Words-

"Dover Revisited: The Wordsworthian Matrix in the Poetry of Matthew Arnold" by U. C. Knoepflmacher. From *Victorian Poetry*, 1 (January 1963), 17–21, 24–26. Copyright 1963 by West Virginia University. Reprinted by permission of the publisher.

[1] Among the more recent studies see D. G. James, *Matthew Arnold and the Decline of English Romanticism* (Oxford 1961), and William A. Jamison, *Arnold and the Romantics* (Copenhagen, 1958).

[2] W. Stacy Johnson, *The Voices of Matthew Arnold: An Essay in Criticism* (New Haven, 1961), pp. 48, 47. See also Paull F. Baum, *Ten Studies in the Poetry of Matthew Arnold* (Durham, 1958), p. 25ff.: Lionel Trilling, *Matthew Arnold* (New York, 1955), pp. 75ff.; and E. D. H. Johnson, *The Alien Vision of Victorian Poetry* (Princeton, 1952), pp. 152–153.

worthian, and it is so by intent and not by mere coincidence. Arnold's poems avail themselves of situations that are Wordsworthian, images that are Wordsworthian, phrases that are Wordsworthian. This Wordsworthian matrix is enlisted in what essentially amounts to a denial of the vision of Arnold's predecessor, although, at the very same time, it is relied upon to preserve Wordsworth's ability "to make us feel." . . .

I

Arnold's "Resignation" is his version, or, more properly, his inversion, of Wordsworth's "Tintern Abbey." The parallelism between the two poems is deliberate. It enables Arnold to employ his predecessor's work as a frame of reference, an ironic "touchstone" essential to his own meaning.[3] "Resignation" is almost twice as long as "Tintern Abbey." It abounds in erudite allusions and echoes from sources as varied as Lucretius and Goethe. But the core of the poem is unmistakably Wordsworthian: the setting is the Lake Country of the Romantics; the situation, a return to the earlier associations of the scene by a matured poet and his sister; the import, a creed handed down by the poet to his listener.

In "Tintern Abbey" Wordsworth and Dorothy stand "here upon the banks of this fair river." The poet mourns his lost childhood oneness with Nature but derives joy from the knowledge that his sister still possesses the power that he has lost. The poem ends on a triumphant assertion of his belief in a matured and "sober pleasure" based on the "wild ecstasies" of youth. Memory becomes a source of joy: "Nature never did betray the heart that loved her." The poet, "a worshiper of Nature," can readily become its priest.

In "Resignation" the poet and his sister also stand "on this mild bank above the stream," amidst a lush natural landscape which has

[3] In their otherwise excellent commentary on the poetry of Arnold, C. B. Tinker and H. F. Lowry, though dwelling extensively on the Goethean sources of "Resignation," strangely enough fail to point out that the poem is above all a rebuttal of Wordsworth, who, according to his youthful critic, "should have read more books, among them, no doubt those of the Goethe whom he disparaged without reading him." Only Professor Baum seems to have taken notice of the analogies between "Resignation" and "Tintern Abbey." But he dismisses them cursorily by remarking that the " 'exhortations' " of the poets are after all "quite unlike" each other, thus underestimating the importance of this "unlikeness" for a reading of Arnold's poem (*Ten Studies*, pp. 25–26, fn. 3).

remained unaltered despite the changes they have suffered. "The loose dark stones" have not moved; "this wild brook" runs on, undisturbed. The scene's permanence sharpens the poet's awareness of his own mutability. He, too, hopes to derive a creed based on his observation of Nature. But while Arnold's yearning for sobering "thoughts" suggested by the surroundings is not unlike Wordsworth's, his interpretation of these surroundings is markedly different. Indeed, the ethical creed that he charts out for his sister and the poetic creed he indirectly prescribes for himself are based on a complete re-definition of a Wordsworthian faith in Nature. To Wordsworth, the communion between Nature and man is in itself an abundant compensation for the mutability of life—it brings about a communion between brother and sister, man and man, and confirms the poet in his role of Nature's high priest. To Arnold, on the other hand, the utter impersonality of the scene before him only accentuates the need for an adequate attitude towards a natural world which can no more provide the "tender joy" that Wordsworth was capable of extracting from it than it can act as a stimulus for the heightened sensations sought by his Faustian sister. He must therefore explain to the Romantic Fausta the limitations suggested by landscape, and, simultaneously, delimit his own functions as new kind of poet, a poet deprived of the "rapt security" inherent in the Romantic vision.

To Arnold the landscape is but an emblem of "the general life," an impersonal power which demands the submission of all men. But rather than becoming a mere object subjected to the capriciousness of "chance," man can achieve the dignity of a rule by "fate" if he understands his own position within the "dizzying eddy" of life. This understanding can come only through detachment. It is achieved instinctively by gypsies plodding in their "hereditary way"; it is achieved consciously by those higher beings who can discern through a special insight "what through experience others learn." In outline, Arnold's schematization is not unlike Wordsworth's. He has identified the landscape before him with an order or plan which he, as a detached observer, is able to perceive; he has maintained that this order can be understood instinctively by some and consciously by others; he has established the need for an acceptance of this plan, "the general life." But, of course, it is the valuation which Arnold places on these elements which is entirely opposed to Wordsworth's. Children unconsciously in touch with the divine have become gypsies instinctively attuned to the buffets of life; the redeeming Dorothy has become the unredeemable Fausta; the isolated poet who converts the "still, sad music of humanity" into a joyful faith has become a detached stoic contemplator, content with a "sad lucidity of soul." [4] For what has changed, above all, is the order perceived by the poet and the manner in which the poet's perception has been achieved.

The divine "presence" perceived by Wordsworth resides in the landscape he sees, as well as in himself. It is:

> a sense sublime
> Of something far more deeply interfused,
> Whose dwelling is the light of setting suns,
> And the round ocean and the living air,
> And the blue sky, and in the mind of man;
> A motion and a spirit, that impels
> All living things, all objects of all thought,
> And rolls through all things.

To Arnold, on the other hand, "the something which infects the world" is not an invisible *primum mobile*. It is the aggregate of all that is visible, an impersonal and tyrannical power which offers "not joy, but peace" to him who apprehends its operations:

> Before him he sees life unroll,
> A placid and continuous whole—
> That general life, which does not cease,
> Whose secret is not joy, but peace;
> That life, whose dumb wish is not miss'd

---

[4] Arnold's choice of the gypsies as his prime example is extremely significant. His justification of the gypsies to the sister who dismisses them as being "less" than "man" is nothing less than a direct rebuttal of the position taken by Wordsworth in his 1807 poem, "Gipsies." In this little-known poem, Wordsworth regards the gypsies he has met during an excursion as sub-human, almost devilish creatures who are unaffected by the laws of man and Nature. Shunning their fellowmen during the day, totally oblivious of their natural surroundings, Wordsworth's gypsies raise "bolder" fires at night and thus defy the "mighty Moon" and the "very stars" that "reprove" them for their negligence as much as the poet himself. Arnold's gypsies likewise "crouch round the wild flame." But their purpose is simple: they merely want to stay warm in order to "rub through" life. For, unlike Wordsworth's gypsies, they *are* affected by time and change. Their indifference to Nature therefore is not, as with Wordsworth, a reprehensible act of defiance, but, quite to the contrary, represents an expression of their triumph over a natural world which has, in turn, become wholly indifferent towards them. Arnold's gypsies wait stoically "Till death arrive to supersede, / For them, vicissitude and need."

> If birth proceeds, if things subsist;
> The life of plants, and stones, and rain,
> The life he craves—if not in vain
> Fate gave, what chance shall not control,
> His sad lucidity of soul.

Nature has provided Wordsworth with a "holy love"; it has only confirmed Arnold's saddened intellectual awareness.

"Resignation" and "Tintern Abbey" rely on the modulation of conflicting moods; both poems conclude on the speaker's subjection to a discipline based on Nature. Wordsworth emphasizes the beneficence of this discipline; Arnold emphasizes its grim necessity. In each case, the landscape has acted as a guide. But while for Wordsworth Nature is an active teacher and comforter who readily reveals "a presence that disturbs me with the joy of elevated thoughts," Arnold's "thoughts" are addressed rhetorically to the impassive landscape before him so that it might confirm his own well-rehearsed lesson in the art of "bearing":

> Enough, we live!—and if a life,
> With large results so little rife,
> Though bearable, seem hardly worth
> This pomp of worlds, this pain of birth;
> Yet, Fausta, the mute turf we tread,
> The solemn hills around us spread,
> The stream which falls incessantly,
> The strange-scrawl'd rocks, the lonely sky,
> If I might lend their life a voice,
> Seem to bear rather than rejoice.

The lesson of joy given to Wordsworth is thus subverted. For Arnold's Nature is utterly impervious to the emotional demands of its students. "The meadows and the woods and mountains" speak freely to Wordsworth in the "language of sense." Arnold, however, must scrupulously point out that the language he ascribes to the scene before him is really his own. The turf is "mute," the hills are "solemn," even the rocks are enigmatic and "strange-scrawl'd." The poet thus is forced to superimpose his own order on the scene he sees before him. He can at best attribute an imagined "voice" to the life he sees around him; he can only assume that the landscape would *"seem"* to teach him how to bear.

Wordsworth's vision is transcendent and symbolical: ocean, air, and sky contain the same spirit which dwells "in the mind of man." Arnold's vision is analytical and allegorical: the mind of man can tentatively impose its understanding upon what it apprehends through the senses. Therefore, while Wordsworth's poet is a medium for the divine plan of Nature, Arnold's poet is merely the interpreter of the "dumb" wishes of a neutral universe. Whereas Wordsworth becomes infused and intoxicated by the centrifugal power of Nature, Arnold must stand aside and examine his own relative position in time and space in order to preserve his "lucidity of soul." The scene before him is meaningless in itself. It must be related to Mohammedan pilgrims and Gothic warriors, to Orpheus and to Homer. Intensity is replaced by extensiveness: *"Not deep the poet sees, but wide."* The resolution of Arnold's poem therefore depends entirely on his *a priori* survey of the "general life," a survey brought about by precisely that cultural view which Wordsworth lacked to make "his thought richer and his influence of wider application."

"Resignation" thus represents Arnold's attempt to give a contemporary "application" to Wordsworth's Romantic poem. It is a characteristically Victorian juggling of "heart" and "head": an emotional faith in Nature is qualified by the wider intellectual view afforded by scientific skepticism, historicism, and "Culture." Arnold's qualification also alters Wordsworth's poetic method. The symbolically exalted "green pastoral landscape" becomes an allegorized "green hill-side" arbitrarily invested with qualities corresponding to the human situation. . . .

III

"Resignation" and "Dover Beach" are perhaps the most obvious examples of Arnold's use of a Wordsworthian matrix in his poetry. But they are by no means the only ones. Arnold's "To a Gipsy Child by the Seashore" reverberates with echoes from the "Immortality" ode;[5] his "East London" and "West London" sonnets are the Victorian counterparts of the London sonnets written by Wordsworth in 1802; the conception of the "Marguerite" poems owes much to Wordworth's use of his "Lucy." There are correspondences in situations and phrases. Images, such as the elm-tree in "Thyrsis" (which

[5] Cf. W. Stacy Johnson, pp. 47–51.

recalls the oak of "Michael") or the "sea of life" in "To Marguerite,"
are invested with Wordsworthian properties.

The introduction of these elements into Arnold's own poetry represents more than a mere negation of Wordsworth's vision. There
is a definite effort at conservation on the part of a poet, who, according to Quiller-Couch's witticism, had a notable tendency to regard
himself as "Wordsworth's widow." [6] The younger man, whose boyhood "had been spent in the Lake Country and under Wordsworth's
affectionate eye," [7] tried to knit on his own experience to that of his
predecessor. For not only Arnold, but a host of other eminent Victorians, regarded Wordsworth with a curious ambivalence. Intellectually, they deplored the simplicity of his natural faith; yet, at
the same time, the skeleton of this faith provided them with a vicari-
ous emotional gratification. For Wordsworth was able to do what his
successors could no longer achieve. He could convert grief and pain
into joyous affirmation; he could draw this affirmation from the element which he called "the still, sad music of humanity," and which
Arnold was to re-name "the eternal note of sadness." This is the pattern of some of his greatest poems, "Tintern Abbey," the "Immortality" ode, the opening of *The Prelude*. Even in his "Elegiac
Stanzas," written "in bereavement over the tragic death of the poet's
dearly beloved brother," was he able to draw hope from suffering
and to find soothing emotions by which he could "humanize" his
soul. To the Victorians such a feat was definitely worth observing.

Arnold particularly admired this Wordsworthian power of transforming individual grief into a statement of universal affirmation.
In his "Memorial Verses, April 1850," he pays homage to his dead
predecessor by ranking him above Goethe and Byron. The attitude
Arnold takes toward the Laureate is very similar to that which,
ninety years later, W. H. Auden was to take towards Yeats. The deceased poet stands for a definite period of history, a simpler world-
view which his successor cannot revive. But Wordsworth also stands
for something else:

> Ah! since dark days still bring to light
> Man's prudence and man's fiery might,
> Time may restore us in his course
> Goethe's sage mind and Byron's force;

[6] Quoted by Professor Douglas Bush in "Wordsworth and the Classics," *UTQ*,
II (April, 1933), 359.
[7] Lionel Trilling, p. 19.

> But where will Europe's latter hour
> Again find Wordsworth's healing power?
> Others will teach us how to dare,
> And against fear our breast to steel;
> Others will strengthen us to bear—
> But who, ah! who, will make us feel?

Others can strengthen us to bear by preaching a "prudent" Goethean renunciation; others can teach us to resist despair through sheer vitality. But Wordsworth's "healing power" is as unretrievable as the shining armor of the Sea of Faith. The question of the hour, therefore, is not only *"who* will make us feel?" but also the implicit *"what* will make us feel?" Arnold never doubts that the power to "make us feel" must be kept alive at all costs; but from where is this feeling to be drawn? Nature no longer offers a religion. The Victorian poet can no longer expect to harmonize the "still, sad music of humanity" into a universal chorus of faith. He must therefore do the second best thing. He must cling to the "eternal note of sadness" itself. He can share it with Wordsworth and lament his own inability to replace this sadness with new feelings of joy, "Wordsworth's healing power." Thus, paradoxically enough, the Victorian poet can engender feeling by bemoaning the loss of feeling. He can preserve Wordsworth's emotional core.

Arnold eventually realized that such a diminished conservation of Wordsworth was not a conservation after all. For, by reiterating an elegiac "note of sadness," Arnold had transgressed against his own rules for "the right Art" by omitting the quality of joy, the joy so deeply felt by Wordsworth but denied to Arnold in "Resignation" and "Dover Beach." Arnold renounced poetry and turned to the dissemination of Culture. But even in his new role, he remained faithful to his desire to blend Wordsworth's feeling with the intellectualism of his own age. In 1879, nine years before his death, Arnold offered a selection of Wordsworth's poetry to the Victorian reading public. His revision of entire lines and phrases was regarded by some as a sign of editorial irresponsibility. It suggests, however, the extent to which Arnold had taken upon himself the cultural responsibility of preserving Wordsworth as an emotional fount for his age, a task he had already set for himself, long before, in the creation of his own poems.

The Dover Bitch: A Criticism of Life

by Anthony Hecht

for Andrews Wanning

So there stood Matthew Arnold and this girl
With the cliffs of England crumbling away behind them,
And he said to her, "Try to be true to me,
And I'll do the same for you, for things are bad
All over, etc., etc."
Well now, I knew this girl. It's true she had read
Sophocles in a fairly good translation
And caught that bitter allusion to the sea,
But all the time he was talking she had in mind
The notion of what his whiskers would feel like
On the back of her neck. She told me later on
That after a while she got to looking out
At the lights across the channel, and really felt sad,
Thinking of all the wine and enormous beds
And blandishments in French and the perfumes.
And then she got really angry. To have been brought
All the way down from London, and then be addressed
As a sort of mournful cosmic last resort
Is really tough on a girl, and she was pretty.
Anyway, she watched him pace the room
And finger his watch-chain and seem to sweat a bit,
And then she said one or two unprintable things.
But you mustn't judge her by that. What I mean to say is,
She's really all right. I still see her once in a while
And she always treats me right. We have a drink
And I give her a good time, and perhaps it's a year
Before I see her again, but there she is,
Running to fat, but dependable as they come.
And sometimes I bring her a bottle of *Nuit d'Amour*.

"The Dover Bitch: A Criticism of Life." From *The Hard Hours* by Anthony Hecht (New York: Atheneum Publishers, 1967). Copyright © 1960 by Anthony E. Hecht. Reprinted by permission of Atheneum Publishers. Appeared originally in *Transatlantic Review*.

A Background for "Empedocles on Etna"

by Kenneth Allott

I

In his poem "Stanzas from the Grande Chartreuse," which was first published in 1855 but had probably been on the stocks for several years,[1] Arnold confessed that

> . . . rigorous teachers seized my youth,
> And prun'd its faith and quench'd its fire,
> Show'd me the pale cold star of Truth,
> There bade me gaze, and there aspire.[2]

There has been speculation on the names of the "rigorous teachers" intended to be supplied, but the shortest list would have to make room for Goethe, Senancour, Lucretius, Epictetus and Spinoza, who are among the men with whose writings Arnold struggled most manfully in the 1840s in his pursuit of that "intellectual deliverance" described by him in his inaugural lecture as Professor of Poetry at Oxford in 1857 as "the peculiar demand of those ages which are called modern." [3] Devotion to "the pale cold star of Truth" was never to be denied by Arnold, but here his confession is also a complaint: the "genuine feelings of unrest, loneliness and dissatisfaction" which T. S. Eliot finds in the best poems, and which the younger Arnold was too honest a poet to suppress, indicate that any feeling of joyful emancipation produced by this necessary "intellectual deliverance" was quickly qualified by a sense of loss that

"A Background for 'Empedocles on Etna'" by Kenneth Allott. From *Essays and Studies 1968*, ed. Simeon Potter (London: John Murray, 1968), pp. 80–87, 89–100. Copyright by the English Association 1968. Reprinted by permission of The English Association.

[1] It recalls a honeymoon visit to the monastery in September 1851.

[2] The text is from *Fraser's Magazine* (April 1855). The 1867 readings "purged its faith, and trimm'd its fire" and "high, white star of Truth" in *New Poems* are less candid.

[3] *Complete Prose Works,* ed. R. H. Super, i (1960), p. 19. Cited below as *Prose Works.*

grew sharper with the passing of time. "Forlorn," the epithet chosen by Keats to describe the return to reality in the "Ode to a Nightingale," is Arnold's epithet in "Stanzas from the Grande Chartreuse" as he contemplates "la poussière de toutes les croyances tombées"—

> Wandering between two worlds, one dead
> The other powerless to be born,
> With nowhere yet to rest my head,
> Like these, on earth I wait forlorn . . .

and he begs forgiveness of his "masters of the mind" if his melancholy seems to compromise their "truth." It has to be grasped that Arnold's scepticism was always, except perhaps at the very outset, reluctant. In *Every Man His Own Poet or the Inspired Singer's Recipe Book* (1872) the author (who called himself "a Newdigate Prizeman" and who was in fact W. H. Mallock) begins his recipe "How to write a poem like Mr. Matthew Arnold" with the injunction "Take one soulfull of *involuntary* unbelief" (my italics) and goes on to stress that the tonality of the poetry, for all Arnold's efforts at *Tüchtigkeit,* is one of melancholy and nostalgic regret. The temper of Arnold's mind remained fundamentally religious because, in spite of his youthful revolt against the narrowness and strictness of his upbringing at Rugy and Fox How, and in spite of his knowledge that his father thought him to be both too independent and too indolent, his boyhood, taken as a whole, was a singularly secure and happy one. It is now customary to attribute conflict to an unhappy childhood, but from a psychological viewpoint Arnold's conflicts arose from his inability to feel that an "intellectual deliverance" that cut him off from full communion with the warmth and happiness of the family circle could be anything but culpably unfilial.

Yet the "intellectual deliverance" had begun with Dr. Arnold, who inculcated open-mindedness and a spirit of inquiry on his sons and daughters and his favourite sixth-formers at Rugby in the firm belief that devotion to truth and devotion to Christianity could not be at odds. Matthew saw his father, for all the latter's severity and imaginative limitations (he was shocked by Byron, troubled by Goethe's *Faust*), as an intellectual liberator. Consequently, when he went up to Balliol in 1841 and the beliefs that were never shaken for Dr. Arnold began to grow unreal, he continued to feel, as his training had taught him to feel, that an unavoidable duty was laid on every individual "to get breast to breast with reality." [4] It was a duty not to be postponed. There could be no luxuriating in poetic sensation, no Tennysonian "dawdling" with the world's "painted shell." [5] The problem of man's place in the sum of things became pressing when the original props of belief were knocked away. Mrs. Humphry Ward believed that George Sand's novels opened "a world of artistic beauty and joy" [6] to Matthew and his younger brother Tom at Oxford, but the recently published "Equator Letters" composed by Tom Arnold on his voyage to New Zealand (November 1847–January 1848)[7] show that this is a simplification of the truth. Tom Arnold's interest in George Sand was aroused almost exclusively by her passionate cry against social injustice. Matthew's enthusiasm for the French novelist was more aesthetic, but it is clear that he read her primarily, as he read *Wilhelm Meister* (in Carlyle's translation), for the artistic presentation of a "large, liberal view of human life." [8] There were shifts of emphasis in mental stance between 1843 and 1847, but broadly speaking the "rigorous teachers" were wrestled with by Arnold as an undergraduate, as a young Fellow of Oriel, and later as Lord Lansdowne's private secretary in London, in an attempt to furnish himself with the elements of a creed that would not affront the critical intellect by its supernaturalism but would nevertheless allow him to salvage at least the possibility of reverence from the wreckage of the orthodox beliefs in which he had been reared. He studied Goethe or Lucretius or the *Bhagavad Gita* for enlightenment, but also, obscurely, to obtain spiritual reassurance, and this second purpose grew more explicit as time went on.

So much can be deciphered of the steady reality behind the mask of the light-hearted dandy with which Arnold faced the world at Oxford or in Mayfair. He appeared to be a man who could always be distracted from his books by a day's fishing or an evening's whist. He was ready to talk absurdities and many of his friends thought him frivolous. "I laugh too much and they make one's laughter

---

[4] *The Letters of Matthew Arnold to A. H. Clough*, ed. H. F. Lowry (1932), p. 86. Cited below as "Lowry."

[5] Lowry, p. 63.

[6] *A Writer's Recollections* (1918), p. 12.

[7] *New Zealand Letters of Thomas Arnold the Younger*, ed. J. Bertram (1966), pp. 207–19.

[8] "Emerson," *Discourses in America* (1896 edn.), p. 143.

mean too much," he wrote to J. D. Coleridge in 1844.[9] How successful a mask it was we know because some of his brothers and sisters,
not to mention these friends, were surprised by the earnestness and
melancholy of his first collection of verse, *The Strayed Reveller, and
Other Poems*, in 1849. "The common assumption that he wholly
lacked a capacity for philosophical thinking is mistaken," claims a
recent critic. "It might be said rather that he could not be a dutiful
schoolman, discovering the mind's happiness within the boundaries
set upon thought by any single school or sect." [10] The concealed intellectual effort expended by Arnold in the 1840s was considerable
and the small degree of success achieved in certain directions dis-
heartening. We hear him saying wrily to Clough at the end of 1847
or early in 1848 ". . . you may often hear my sinews cracking under
the effort to unite matter," [11] and to his sister Jane in an undated
letter belonging to the summer of 1849 he explains self-deprecat-
ingly that his poems are fragmentary and "stagger weakly and are at
their wits' end" because "I am fragments." [12] It was not for want of
trying that he was forced to this honest admission.

A few years later Arnold wondered aloud if he had not deformed
his nature and perverted his poetic gift by the earnestness with
which behind his monocle and languid manner he had sought to
construct a philosophy of life in the decade following his father's
death. "I feel immensely—more and more clearly—what I *want*—
what I have (I believe) lost and choked by my treatment of myself
and the studies to which I have addicted myself," he admitted to
Clough in May 1853. "But what ought I to have done in preference
to what I have done? there is the question." [13]

It is, of course, an unanswerable question. To Arnold in the 1840s
it seemed that there was only one course open, and, knowing what
we know now of his temperament and background, it is hard to see
how he could have acted otherwise. He recognized that he must
"begin with an Idea of the world in order not to be prevailed over

[9] *Life and Correspondence of John Duke Coleridge*, ed. E. H. Coleridge (1904),
i, p. 145.
[10] Warren D. Anderson, *Matthew Arnold and the Classical Tradition* (1965), p.
134.
[11] Lowry, p. 65.
[12] *Unpublished Letters of Matthew Arnold*, ed. A. Whitridge (1923), p. 18. The
editor speculatively dates the letter "1853," but the reference to the siege of Rome
by the French establishes the correct date.
[13] Lowry, p. 136.

by the world's multitudinousness," [14] but how was an adequate idea of this sort to be gained? He puzzled himself with metaphysics and was irritated by the arid abstractions of German idealism into some respect for the common sense of Locke, who, however, lacked "the positive and vivifying atmosphere of Spinoza." [15] Spinoza's serenity was vivifying, but his arguments against final causes were dismissed as casuistical. In weaker moments he feared that "We read to avoid the labour of an inward survey and arrangement—and are but heaping up more to be surveyed and arranged in some inevitable future." [16] By September 1849 he had decided that his "one natural craving" was "not for profound thoughts, mighty spiritual workings, etc., etc., but a distinct seeing of my way as far as my own nature is concerned . . ." [17] He could not have settled for so much less than "the truth, the whole truth, and nothing but the truth" if he had not by then convinced himself laboriously that metaphysical questions receive dusty answers:

> Hither and thither spins
> The wind-borne, mirroring soul,
> A thousand glimpses wins,
> And never sees a whole;
> Looks once, and drives elsewhere, and leaves its last employ.[18]

The bearing of this early chapter of Arnold's intellectual history on his poetic development has often been overlooked or insufficiently allowed for. He was a youth of nineteen when his father died suddenly of heart-disease at Rugby in June 1842. Elder sons, says Newman in *Loss and Gain,* "should their father die prematurely, are suddenly ripened into manhood, when they are almost boys." [19] The "first sorrow, which is childhood's grave" [20] completely changed the circumstances of the Arnold family, made Matthew its titular head, and gave to his intellectual explorations a new and more personal urgency. The loss of his father freed him from an antagonism that was never more than a son's need not to be completely overshadowed, but it also gave him the private grief that now it was too

---

[14] Lowry, p. 97.
[15] Lowry, p. 117.
[16] Unpublished note in the Yale MS.
[17] Lowry, p. 110.
[18] "Empedocles on Etna" I. ii. 82–6.
[19] Part I, Chapter 18.
[20] The phrase is from Arnold's Newdigate prize-poem *Cromwell* (1843).

late to justify himself. He "plunged very deeply in the years following his father's death," wrote his brother Tom, "in the vast sea of
Goethe's art and Spinoza's mysticism." [21] Through Goethe read as a
sage rather than as a poet, he came to Spinoza. From both men he
drew the lesson of the inadequacy of Romantic self-assertion and the
necessity of submission to the universal order. Epictetus confirmed
the lesson and also taught him that some questions "are perhaps in-
comprehensible to the human mind" and that it is enough "to know
the nature of good and evil" and "not to trouble ourselves about the
things above us." [22]

Arnold's assent to the eclectic variety of Stoic ethics preached to
Pausanias as practical wisdom in the second scene of "Empedocles
on Etna" was always more intellectual than emotional while he was
still capable of writing poetry. "Close thy *Byron*; open thy *Goethe*,"
Carlyle had trumpeted in *Sartor Resartus,* but Arnold remained in
two minds. He opened his Goethe obediently, but he could not suppress a sneaking admiration for Byron's defiant energy or pretend
that he had no sympathy for the discontented aspiration of Senancour's Obermann. In "Mycerinus," which is probably in conception
one of Arnold's earliest pieces (apart from juvenilia and prize-
poems), there is no submission: the universal order that decrees an
early death for a good man is seen as a "tyrannous necessity." (It is
difficult not to take the poem as an expression of Arnold's rebellious
feelings about his father's death in the prime of life when we read

> . . . on the strenuous just man, Heaven bestows,
> Crown of his struggling life, an unjust close!)[23]

By 1849, when "Resignation" was published at the end of his first
volume of poems as a kind of testament, Arnold had certainly come
to value detachment as a means of "conquering fate," but here the
technique of preaching to another what you still find difficult to
accept yourself, or of reprobating in another the weaknesses identified in yourself—a technique familiar to us from Arnold's scolding
of Clough in letters—is employed on Fausta (Jane Arnold), who is
described as "Time's chafing prisoner." How remote Arnold's "resignation" was from Stoic apathy, which involved a serene acceptance

---

[21] *Manchester Guardian,* 18 May 1888.
[22] Fragment clxxv. Long's translation (1877).
[23] Dr. Arnold told his children stories from Herodotus at Fox How and set
Mycerinus as the theme of the Rugby prize-poem in 1831. Matthew's poem is
based on the account of Mycerinus in the second book of Herodotus.

of the universal order, is underlined when he speaks with profound melancholy of

> The something that infects the world.

What is evident in reading Arnold's first volume of poems, *The Strayed Reveller* (1849), is that his poetic development is less determined by aesthetic considerations than by the tension set up between these and his wish "to get breast to breast with reality." Even such narratives as "Mycerinus" or "The Sick King in Bokhara" and such tableaux as "The Strayed Reveller" or "The New Sirens" are patently something more than narratives or pictures, or, to put it another way, they have been adopted as subjects because they allow Arnold to experiment with different attitudes to life and estimate their adequacy.

"Empedocles on Etna" is seen in a true perspective as Arnold's most comprehensive attempt to "*solve* the Universe" by bringing into unity the fragments of his thought, but paradoxically it is the failure of this intention that is responsible finally for the artistic success of the poem. As a poet Arnold knew very well that a willed unity was only a shot-gun marriage to save appearances and insisted on rendering with integrity the "alternating dispositions," the duality, the "dialogue of the mind with itself," [24] of a divided nature.

II

. . . We do not know why Arnold preferred Empedocles to Lucretius in 1849, but we are safe in assuming that his interest in Empedocles was stimulated by the praise of the Sicilian philosopher in *De Rerum Natura*. Lucretius says of Empedocles that there is nothing in Sicily "more illustrious than this man, nor more sacred and wonderful and dear" and that he announces his discoveries in such a manner that he seems "hardly mortal." [25] Writing to Clough in March 1848, Arnold distinguishes in Carlylean-Emersonian fashion between the "philosophe" who trusts "the logical absolute reason" and the "philosopher" with insight who drives his feet "into the solid ground of our individuality as spiritual, poetic, profound

[24] 1853 Preface.
[25] *De Rerum Natura*, i, 726–33.

persons." [26] As a poet in search of a philosophy he turned first and for preference to the insights of the poet-philosophers, who included for him the authors of the *Book of Job* and the Hindu *Bhagavad Gita* as well as Lucretius and Empedocles. In weighing these two it must have struck him that the Empedocles whom he described in the 1853 Preface as "one of the last of the Greek religious philosophers, one of the family of Orpheus and Musaeus" was closer to his 1848 definition of the "philosopher" than the Epicurean Lucretius whose enthusiasm for science and contempt for religion give him a look of the Voltairean "philosophe." We know now that Arnold's interest in the *Bhagavad Gita* had been aroused by October 1845 and that it increased when he read the poem and what had been written about it. He shows his familiarity with the poem's ideas when early in 1848 he tries to convert Clough to his own enthusiasm.[27] Victor Cousin seems to have directed him to Wilhelm von Humboldt's analysis of the *Bhagavad Gita* in the *Transactions of the Royal Academy of the Sciences,* Berlin (1826).[28] This analysis contains, as does H. H. Milman's review of it and other works on Hindu poetry in the *Quarterly Review* of April 1831, which Arnold certainly read, the assertion of a likeness between the *Bhagavad Gita,* the *De Rerum Natura* and the fragments of Empedocles. Milman, who was Professor of Poetry at Oxford when he wrote this review, says that the Hindu "divine song" in its place in the *Mahabharata* "reads like a noble fragment of Empedocles or Lucretius introduced into the midst of an Homeric epic," and that in its freedom from "redundance of metaphor" it is "Grecian rather than Italian" in taste.[29] Associations between Lucretius, Empedocles and the *Bhagavad Gita* had been formed in Arnold's mind before he began to study the Greek philosopher.

Arnold studied Empedocles in Simon Karsten's edition (Amsterdam, 1838),[30] which provides an introduction ("De Empedoclis Vita et Studiis"), a Latin translation of the fragments printed opposite the Greek text, detailed notes, and a long essay on the philosopher's ideas. Students of Arnold know of this edition, but they have not

[26] Lowry, p. 73.
[27] Lowry, pp. 69 and 71.
[28] "Early Reading-Lists," *Victorian Studies,* ii (1959), p. 261.
[29] *Quarterly Review,* xlv (April 1831), pp. 3–4, 7.
[30] *Philosophorum Graecorum Veterum . . . Operum Reliquiae,* ii (1838). Cited below as "Karsten."

used it. Examination of it shows that the "hints" Arnold claimed
to have found in the philosopher's remains come in many instances
from Karsten's introduction and final essay. For example, the char-
acterization of Empedocles in the 1853 Preface as "one of the last of
the Greek religious philosophers" derives directly from Karsten's
description of Empedocles as "almost the last of those poet-proph-
ets . . . of the line of Orpheus . . . who instruct and govern the
ignorant and simple by sacred ordinances and songs." [31] Again, there
is nothing in the fragments or in the account of Empedocles by Diogenes Laertius to suggest the melancholy disposition and vast discouragement which Arnold fastens on his hero—indeed it is accepted
that Arnold has simply transferred to the philosopher "the feeling
of depression, the feeling of *ennui*" which he found "stamped on the
poem of Lucretius." [32] Yet even for this transfer he found "hints" in
the facts of Empedocles' life—in his exile, in his being one of the
last of the old Greek religious philosophers (which immediately suggested to Arnold a man "wandering between two worlds"); in Karsten's description of the philosopher's lofty solemnity and arrogance
(which made Arnold speak of Empedocles' "proud sad face"); and
in Aristotle's judgement reported by Karsten that the soul of Empedocles was μελαγχολικός. These are some of the "hints" which permitted Arnold to connect the historical Empedocles with Lucretius
and present his own Empedocles as one in whose work "we hear already the doubts, we witness the discouragement, of Hamlet and
Faust." [33]

The melancholy of Arnold's Empedocles is the Romantic melancholy of Byron's *Manfred,* of George Sand's *Lélia,* of Foscolo's
Ultime Lettere di Jacopo Ortis, and, above all, of Senancour's *Obermann.* When Arnold said in 1857 that "the feeling of depression, the
feeling of *ennui*" was "stamped on how many of the representative
works of modern times" [34] it was of these and similar books that he
was thinking. That Empedocles is identified with Senancour through
Lucretius is plain when we notice in "Empedocles on Etna" that
Callicles corrects Pausanias, who supposes simple-mindedly that
Empedocles' trouble is that the times are out of joint, with the
words:

[31] Karsten, p. 33. My own translation.
[32] "On the Modern Element in Literature" (1857), *Prose Works,* i (1960), p. 32.
[33] 1853 Preface.
[34] "On the Modern Element in Literature," *Prose Works,* i (1960), p. 32.

'Tis not the times, 'tis not the sophists vex him;
There is some root of suffering in himself,
Some secret and unfollow'd vein of woe,
Which makes the time look black and sad to him . . .

[I. i. 150–53]

and then discover that Arnold echoes these words in his 1869 essay
on *Obermann*:

But a root of failure, powerlessness, and ennui, there certainly was
in the constitution of Senancour's own nature; so that, unfavourable
as may have been his time, we should err in attributing to any outward circumstances the whole of the discouragement by which he is
pervaded.[35]

From the link Arnold established in his mind between the fragments of Empedocles and the *Bhagavad Gita* we can understand
Clough's gibe in his notice of "Empedocles on Etna" in the *North
American Review* in 1853 at "the dismal cycle" of Arnold's "re-
habilitated Hindoo-Greek theosophy." [36] The pantheist notion of
"A God identical with the world and with the sum of force therein
contained: not exterior to it," [37] which is expressed in Arnold's
poem in the lines

All things the world which fill
Of but one stuff are spun,
That we who rail are still,
With what we rail at, one . . . , [I. ii. 287–90]

derives multiply from a fragment of Empedocles (". . . but [God]
is only sacred and ineffable mind, penetrating the whole world with
rapid thought"),[38] from Arjuna's vision in the *Bhagavad Gita* of the
universe "standing in a vast unity in the body of the God of gods,"
from the Stoic doctrine of the World-Soul and Spinoza's "Deus, sive
Natura," and from Wordsworth's and Goethe's poems, although we
should also note that Arnold's actual words seem to echo Emerson's
"Nature," which was included in *Essays* (1844):

. . . she [Nature] has but one stuff to serve all her dream-like
variety. Compound it how she will . . . it is still but one stuff.[39]

[35] *Essays, Letters, and Reviews by Matthew Arnold*, ed. F. Neiman (1960), p. 161.
[36] *Poems and Prose Remains of A. H. Clough* (1869), i, p. 378.
[37] Yale MS.
[38] Karsten, p. 138. Fragment 360.
[39] *Complete Works of R. W. Emerson* (Bohn's Standard Library edn., 1881), i. p.
229.

Obermann in his pilgrimage to the Dent du Midi reminds Sainte-Beuve of the Lucretian sage raised above the tumult of life: "S'il s'élançait, s'il disparaissait alors, ce serait presque en Dieu, comme Empédocle à l'Etna." [40] He wanders like Byron's Manfred in the Alps, suffering like George Sand's Lélia from "l'excès de douleur produit par l'abus de la pensée." His mind is "over-tasked"—to use the word Arnold applied to both Lucretius and Empedocles. Manfred and Obermann were remembered by Arnold when "in a curious and not altogether comfortable state" he wandered about Thun in 1849 and longed to carry his "aching head to the mountains." [41] He felt himself "over-tasked." "Yes," he writes to Clough in February 1853, *"congestion of the brain* is what we suffer from—I always feel it and say it—and cry for air like my own Empedocles." [42] The network of associated ideas and images drawn from Arnold's reading and personal experience that lies behind "Empedocles on Etna" is far more complicated than I have attempted to show, but even so simplified a diagram of it would justify us in speaking of the poem as a culmination of Arnold's earlier poetic efforts to "unite matter" and "get breast to breast with reality."

"Empedocles on Etna" is not what the Arnold who sought an "intellectual deliverance" wanted to say, but what the truth-telling poet was unable not to say. His philosopher is wretched and cannot live by the philosophy of resignation that he preaches. Arnold states in his plans for the poem in the Yale MS. that the vision of "the stern simplicity" of the real nature of things is "capable of affording rapture and the purest peace," but he did not feel that rapture or experience that peace. He tries hard to make Empedocles a special case by the very variety of the reasons that he adduces to explain his hero's loss of "spring and elasticity of mind," but the truth is that despondency is more real to him than the sentiment that "Life still/ Leaves human effort scope." The ascent of the volcano from the shady, moist "forest region" at its foot to the "charr'd, blacken'd, melancholy waste" of the cone becomes a secular Way of the Cross that ends in self-crucifixion. The ascent re-enacts the journey of the

---

[40] *Les Grands Écrivains Français par Sainte-Beuve,* ed. M. Allem. *XIXᵉ Siècle: Les Romanciers* (1927), i, p. 57. Sainte-Beuve's essay was first published in 1832 and was read by Arnold in the first volume of *Portraits Contemporains* (1845).

[41] Lowry, p. 110. Byron's *Manfred,* as I have shown elsewhere, determined the choice of dramatic form for "Empedocles on Etna" and the evolution of the action—see *Notes and Queries, n.s.,* ix (1962), pp. 300–3.

[42] Lowry, p. 130.

Romantic poet from innocence (Callicles) to experience (Empedocles)—

> We Poets in our youth begin in gladness;
> But thereof come in the end despondency and madness . . .[43]

and also, more broadly, symbolizes what may happen to a man when
he leaves behind as illusions the religious beliefs which have hitherto given his life significance (by being accepted unquestioningly)
and moves into what W. B. Yeats calls "the desolation of reality."
Empedocles "sees things as they are," but the vision is too much for
him. The movement from innocence to experience, from the com-
fort of traditional beliefs to the painful vision of reality, is a movement in time that the poem renders spatially. At one pitch of generalization "Empedocles on Etna" is a poem about the cruelty of
time, and there is more irony than resignation in Arnold's adoption
of a saying attributed to Thales in Diogenes Laertius' *Lives of the
Philosophers*, "Time is the wisest of things, for it finds out everything" as a motto for his 1852 volume. Nothing in Arnold's letters
strikes the reader with more force than his repeated complaints
about the loss of youth, which are the shadow of a pre-lapsarian happiness:

> And yet what days were those, Parmenides!
> When we were young . . .
>
> Then we could still enjoy, then neither thought
> Nor outward things were closed and dead to us;
> But we received the shock of mighty thoughts
> On simple minds with a pure natural joy . . .
>   [II [i] 235–6, 240–3]

There is a passage in what Arnold calls Sainte-Beuve's "very good
article" [44] on Leopardi in the fourth volume of *Portraits Contemporains* which must have seemed to Arnold a wording of his most intimate doubts and fears. Sainte-Beuve writes:

> Il me semble que, lorsqu'on se met en rapport par la croyance,
> par la prière . . . avec la grande âme du monde, on trouve appui
> accord, apaisement. Que si la créature humaine s'en détache au
> contraire et ne trouve pas de raison suffisante pour croire et pour

---

[43] Wordsworth's "Resolution and Independence."
[44] In his notice of Sainte-Beuve for the *Encyclopaedia Britannica* in 1886.

espérer, comme à la rigeur elle en a peut-être le droit, car les preuves de raisonnement laissent á désirer, elle en est à l'instant punie par je ne sais quoi d'aride et de désolé.[45]

Arnold's own version of these reflections appears in a note in the Yale MS. (undated, but almost certainly written between 1849 and 1852):

I cannot conceal from myself that the objection which really wounds and perplexes me from the religious side is that the service of reason is freezing to feeling, chilling to the religious mood.

And feeling and the religious mood are eternally the deepest being of man, the ground of all joy and greatness for him.

"Empedocles on Etna" was rejected as a failure because it left Arnold with a hopeless antinomy: on the one hand, "the pale cold star of Truth" to be followed; on the other hand, the necessity of joy. But joy is impossible if "the service of reason" freezes "feeling and the religious mood"; and the price of joy is beyond the means of the sensitive and honest man if payment has to be made in the currency of illusion. However hard he tried, Arnold could not embrace "truth" and "joy" in a single thought, but was drawn back again and again to the nagging contradiction between them:

> And yet men have such need of joy!
> But joy whose grounds are true . . .[46]

He turned away from the contradiction that had nerved his most complex work by discarding "Empedocles on Etna" in 1853 and defending his rejection of it in a preface which, as a modern critic has said, was "written by Arnold's spectre." [47] It was like the crisis of a long and punishing illness from which the patient recovers to lead a diminished life. The new poems that Arnold wrote after 1852 took less out of him. Gradually there were fewer poems and in the end no poems at all. The nostalgic prefatory quatrain to *New Poems* (1867) shows that Arnold recognized fully what was happening:

> Though the Muse be gone away,
> Though she move not earth today,
> Souls, erewhile who caught her word,
> Ah! still harp on what they heard.

---

[45] The essay is dated 1844. Quoted here from the 1884 edn. of *Portraits Contemporains,* iv, p. 411.

[46] "Obermann Once More," ll. 237–8.

[47] Frank Kermode, *The Romantic Image* (1957), p. 12.

III

After his marriage in June 1851 (when he was still engaged in writing "Empedocles on Etna") and the start of his new duties as a school inspector, Arnold had less time to devote to poetry than in his bachelor days, but the real impediments to poetic composition were not external. The increasing difficulty Arnold found in writing poetry after "Empedocles on Etna" was not a matter of busy tours of inspection, bad hotels and snatched meals (he produced a fair quota of poetic work when conditions were worst in the early years of his appointment), but was due ultimately to his decision to hold back something of himself in the act of creation (which is the true meaning to be attached to the rejection of subjectivity in the 1853 Preface), and this decision is connected with his need to settle down, come to terms with ordinary life, and "mature." It seems, he writes bleakly to his sister Jane a few months before his marriage (25 January 1851), ". . . as if we could only acquire any solidity of shape and power of acting by narrowing and narrowing our sphere," but how reluctantly he faced this prospect is evident when he adds that he is "almost tempted to quarrel with the law of nature" which compels us to leave "the aimless and unsettled, but also open and liberal of our youth" and "take refuge in our morality and character." [48] It was to the same sister in September 1858 that he acknowledged that his tragedy *Merope* (1858) belonged to a less ambitious kind of poetry than "Empedocles on Etna" and stood in need of apology.

> People do not understand what a temptation there is, if you cannot bear anything not *very good,* to transfer your operations to a region where form is everything. Perfection of a certain kind may there be attained, or at least approached, without knocking yourself to pieces, but to attain or approach perfection in the region of thought and feeling, and to unite this with perfection of form, demands not merely an effort and a labour, but an actual tearing of oneself to pieces, which one does not readily consent to (although one is sometimes forced to it) unless one can devote one's whole life to poetry.[49]

[48] *Letters of Matthew Arnold,* ed. G. W. E. Russell (1895), i, p. 14. Cited below as *Letters.*

[49] *Letters,* i, pp. 62–3 (where the letter is misdated "6 August" instead of "6 September").

I find this letter moving, especially Arnold's confession that he is still sometimes forced in spite of himself "to submit . . . to the exhaustion of the best poetical production." In "an existence so hampered as mine is"—he was now a man with a family to support who for financial reasons had taken on the extra task of acting as Marshal when his father-in-law Judge Wightman was on circuit—he pleads that he can no longer bear the labour-pains of poetic creation, which are "an actual tearing of oneself to pieces." Not only is his existence hampered, but the times are against him (as they were against Empedocles). He claims that it is "only in the best poetical epochs (such as the Elizabethan) that you can descend into yourself and produce the best of your thought and feeling naturally, and without an overwhelming and in some degree morbid effort." [50]

It is important to understand what Arnold is saying. He was not Gautier, a poet whom he did not care for, or Mallarmé, whom he would not have understood. When he speaks of transferring his operations to "a region where form is everything" he is not slighting the importance of his dramatic subject in *Merope*—a subject which he had chosen with great care, if rather absurdly, from a number listed in Hyginus, "a Latin mythographer of uncertain date," [51] because it seemed to him to contain an "excellent action," that is to say, one with a powerful appeal "to the great primary human affections: to those elementary feelings which subsist permanently in the race, and which are independent of time." [52] A "region where form is everything" must be translated as "a region where the artist's struggle is exclusively with form and expression because the subject does not involve the perplexities of his own development." This is, of course, the 1853 Preface's denial that a poem should be "a true allegory of the state of one's own mind." [53] The pseudo-classicism of the preface must therefore be seen as a direct evasion of the strains and anxieties of genuine poetic creation.

Merope, which is by common consent a poetic failure, lies at the far end of the line on which "Sohrab and Rustum," which took the

[50] All the quotations in this paragraph are from the same letter of 6 September 1858.

[51] Preface to *Merope*.

[52] 1853 Preface.

[53] Ibid. Arnold is quoting a phrase from David Masson's "Theories of Poetry and a New Poet," *North British Review*, xix (August 1853), p. 338. The phrase caught Arnold on the raw because it was so apt a description of "Empedocles on Etna."

place of "Empedocles on Etna" in Arnold's 1853 volume, and
"Balder Dead" (1855) are important intermediate stations. Both
these poems have some poetic value because Arnold was able to
connect their "excellent actions" with his own experience, because,
in other words, the poems retain in spite of Arnold's infatuation
with a chimerical pure objectivity a subjective element. (A purely
objective poem is by definition a dead poem, since it has not engaged
the poet and therefore cannot be expected to interest his readers.)
Arnold's letter of 6 September 1858 admits implicitly that "Empedocles on Etna" is a poem in which its author had struggled to "approach perfection in the region of thought and feeling" and to
"unite this with perfection of form," and that this struggle had been
"not merely an effort and a labour, but an actual tearing of [him-
self] to pieces." *Merope* was written to "inaugurate my Professorship
with dignity" [54]—Arnold had been elected Professor of Poetry at
Oxford some eight months earlier on 5 May 1857. "Empedocles on
Etna" was written because there was no escape from it, because, as
Arnold told Clough in December 1852, ". . . woe was upon me if
I analysed not my situation." [55] It is a remarkable if unintentional
irony, then, that these two pieces—the one, though flawed, written
at the height of his powers, the other the most frigid of all his com-
positions—should in Arnold's final classification of his poetry in
1885 occupy a special category by themselves as "dramatic poems."

[54] *Letters,* i, p. 60.
[55] Lowry, p. 126.

The Use of Elegy

by A. Dwight Culler

We come now to *Thyrsis,* the elegy on Clough, which was written between 1862 and its publication in 1866. It is usually treated along with *The Scholar-Gipsy,* as a companion to that poem, and of course, there is every reason for doing so. The two poems employ the same locale, they are written in the same stanza and the same pastoral mode, and they were placed one after another in all of Arnold's collections. Still, they were written fifteen years apart, and with Arnold fifteen years—especially when they extend from the early 'fifties to the mid 'sixties—is a long time. Much has happened in that time, and indeed, this "much" is essentially what the poem is about. By separating *Thyrsis* from *The Scholar-Gipsy,* then, and considering it in the context of the elegies, one not only avoids the elementary mistake of saying that Clough "is" the Scholar-Gipsy but he also sees how different the two poems are. For the one is primarily a Romantic dream-vision which creates an ideal figure who lives outside of time, whereas the other is an elegy about a human figure who lived in time and was thereby destroyed.

When Clough died in Florence on November 13, 1861, it was generally agreed that he had not lived up to the brilliant promise of his Rugby years. At Oxford he had "failed" in his examination, and although he had partially redeemed this failure by a fellowship at Oriel, he had perversely resigned his fellowship after a few years, partly out of irritation with the Thirty-Nine Articles and partly out of a restless desire to help in the work of social betterment. He went over to Paris to watch the Revolution of 1848 and to Rome to see Garibaldi fight the French, but he

"The Use of Elegy." From *Imaginative Reason: The Poetry of Matthew Arnold* by A. Dwight Culler (New Haven and London: Yale University Press, 1966), pp. 250–68, 272–86. Copyright 1966 by Yale University. Reprinted by permission of the publisher.

found no sense of commitment, and his new job at University
Hall was not better, but rather worse, than the old one at Oriel.
Nothing opened up in Australia or America, and so he settled
down in the Education Office in a routine task which, unlike his
friend, he did not dignify by literary employment. In 1849 he had
published the delightful, if unregenerate, *Bothie of Tober-na-
Vuolich,* but his next poem, *Amours de Voyage,* rather perplexed
and pained even his most sympathetic admirers. And so, on his
death, it was an open question whether he had failed merely in
the eyes of the world or whether, in some deeper sense, he had
actually been a failure.

Arnold's letters show that his mind hovered around this question and also that he was led back in meditation to those early
days when Clough was the senior and most brilliant member of
that "little interior company" at Oxford in 1845–47.[1] What had
happened to make his life go wrong? Surely at that date anyone would have prophesied greater things of Clough than of the
dandy Arnold, and yet here was Arnold, increasingly acknowledged
as one of the authentic poets of the day, elected Professor of
Poetry at the University of Oxford and delivering at that moment
the lectures on translating Homer which would lay the basis of a
distinguished critical reputation. Comparisons are odious, but one
does not have to be a La Rochefoucauld to say that on the death
of an old college chum they are inevitable. Even in the elegies
which we have already examined there is, without any triumphant
feeling, an unexpressed vein of thought that goes somewhat like
this: "This person, with whom I was once associated, or whom I
admired, is now dead and I am alive. Had I gone on as he did,
I too might be dead, but I turned aside from sickness into health
and so stand here, at Carnac, or before Heine's grave, or meditating
on the strange fate of the two ladies with whom I once had dinner.
And so, paying tribute to what was great in them, I also pass
judgment on their errors and draw from their lives the profound
moral lesson, 'There but for the grace of God go I!' " In the case
of Heine and Obermann, Arnold thought that he could put his
finger on the exact moment when he and they had parted company: for Heine it was in the Hartz mountains, for himself and
Obermann in the Bernese Alps, when he had descended to work

[1] *Letters of Matthew Arnold, 1848–1888,* ed. G. W. E. Russell (New York, London, 1895), *1,* 176–77.

and live, they to languish and die. Similarly, Arnold thought that he could put his finger on the exact moment when he and Clough had parted company, but in this case the scene was not the Swiss Alps but the Cumnor hills, and the date was about a year earlier, in November 1848. Clough had just taken his dramatic departure from Oriel and had published his irrepressible *Bothie of Tober-na-Vuolich,* and so, for the anti-Establishment set, he was the hero of the hour. "—I have been at Oxford the last two days," wrote Arnold, "and hearing Sellar and the rest of that clique who know neither life nor themselves rave about your poem gave me a strong almost bitter feeling with respect to them, the age, the poem, even you. Yes I said to myself something tells me I can, if need be, at last dispense with them all, even with him: better that, than be sucked for an hour even into the Time Stream in which they and he plunge and bellow." Of course, Arnold was being mock-stern, and there was no open rupture; a few years later he and Clough were breakfasting together frequently again, and much of the old intimacy was re-established. Still, something had come between them which could not be ignored, and in February 1853, when Arnold, in answer to his friend's complaint, was writing a long "historical" letter about their relationship, he admitted that "there was one time indeed—shortly after you had published the Bothie—that I felt a strong disposition to intellectual seclusion, and to the barring out all influences that I felt troubled without advancing me." He assured Clough that this estrangement was "merely a contemplated one and it never took place." Indeed, such was the charm of Clough's company and his mode of being that "I could not have forgone these on a mere theory of intellectual diatetics." "I am and always shall be, whatever I do or say, powerfully attracted towards you, and vitally connected with you . . . , for ever linked with you by intellectual bonds—the strongest of all." Still, if "you ask me in what I think or have thought you going wrong," it is in this: that you never would "resolve to be thyself," but were always worrying whether you shouldn't be something different from what you were. "You have I am convinced lost infinite time in this way: it is what I call your morbid conscientiousness—you are the most conscientious man I ever knew: but on some lines morbidly so, and it spoils your action." A few months later he repudiated the idea that he was merely using his friend "as food for speculation": that was a "morbid suspicion" and should be put aside. Still, the discussion of this matter continued through the summer and into the fall, for on October 10, nine days after finishing the Preface of 1853, Arnold wrote: "Forgive my scold the other day—when one is trying to emerge to hard land it is irritating to find your friend not only persisting in 'weltering to the parching wind' himself, but doing his best to pull you back into the Sea also." [2] The allusion to *Lycidas* is significant. By George Sand, Arnold had been called *un Milton jeune et voyageant*. Now that he was reaching the end of his voyage, he was apparently thinking of Clough as his prospective Edward King.

In Arnold's view the moment when Clough had "died" was the moment when he had thrown himself into the Time Stream and made himself subject to change and death. And that was the moment, in 1848, when "Thyrsis of his own will went away." Thus, though the death of Clough in 1861 provided the occasion for the poem, its subject, insofar as it is about Clough, is not his death but his going away. It is about his abandoning the ideal of the Scholar-Gipsy. The Scholar-Gipsy lived in a world outside of Time and so was not subject to death. Thyrsis too could have lived in that world if he had wished, but he would not. "Some life of men unblest / He knew, which made him droop, and fill'd his head." And so, in the earlier poem, he was allowed by the poet to depart, and was only adjured, when once the fields were still and the dogs and men all gone to rest, to return and once "again begin the quest." Meanwhile, in a nook of the high, half-reaped field, the poet would wait for him—would wait till sun-down. Actually, it was just one year that Arnold waited. In the *Stanzas in Memory of the Author of "Obermann,"* dated November 1849, the poet declared that he too "in the world must live," and we recall that in *The Scholar-Gipsy* this shift of locus was acknowledged by the poet's awakening from his dream and finding himself, in mid-poem, no longer with the Gipsy but in the world. But in both poems he drew two distinctions between himself and Clough. One was that whereas Thyrsis "of his own will went away," Arnold was driven by fate. And the other was that Arnold intended so to live in the world as to remain essentially unspotted by it. It is true, when he was writing the *Stanzas*

[2] *The Letters of Matthew Arnold to Arthur Hugh Clough*, ed. H. F. Lowry (Oxford, 1932), pp. 95, 129–30, 136, 144.

in Memory of the Author of "Obermann," he included Clough among those "Children of the Second Birth, / Whom the world could not tame." [3] But the question now was, whether, and in what degree, either he or Clough had been faithful to the ideal since their parting in the high half-reaped field some fifteen years before.

In order to find out, Arnold needed to revisit the fields. In January 1862, in thanking Mrs. Clough for some of her husband's poems which she had sent him, he wrote, "I shall take them with me to Oxford, where I shall go alone after Easter;— and there, among the Cumner hills where we have so often rambled, I shall be able to think him over as I could wish." [4] There can hardly be any doubt that Arnold actually did take something like the walk described in *Thyrsis* and that in so doing he found the structure of his poem. It is the structure of the "place revisited," the device employed in Wordsworth's *Brothers,* in *Tintern Abbey,* and in Arnold's own *Resignation*. Its advantage is that it begets self-consciousness. One becomes conscious of self by being conscious of a place that was formerly associated with the self. In this way too one becomes conscious of time. Place is the medium on which the passing of time is recorded, and so in this place, which is at once recognizably the same and yet bewilderingly different, the poet has an indicator of all that has happened in the intervening years. Simply by traversing the fields he can develop the theme, which is central to the poem, of the contest between permanence and change.

At the beginning of the poem change is triumphant everywhere. "How changed is here each spot man makes or fills." In the spot which man makes, the two Hinkseys, "nothing keeps the same." The examples given, however, show that we are here on the level of mere popular folkways and superstition—things dear to the human heart but whose loss is relatively light and trivial. More serious is the question, "Are ye too changed, ye hills?" for this evokes Wordsworthian and Biblical echoes of the "everlasting hills," from whence cometh our help. If they are changed, then change is triumphant indeed. But as the poet begins his walk he is confident that they are not changed. With only the slightest hesitation ("Runs it not here?") about the track

[3] Ibid., p. 110.
[4] Ibid., p. 160.

by Childsworth Farm, in thought he follows that track to his
very goal, the signal-elm, and from that vantage turns and looks
out over the familiar scene to the well-known Vale, the weirs, the
youthful Thames, and to Oxford, unchanged in its loveliness.
She is lovely at "all times," now in winter as formerly in spring.
Indeed, on this winter eve cold is overcome by spring warmth,
and the poet finds himself, in imagination, safe in his forest
glade. But then, in line 22, with the word *Only*, the same word
which introduced the discordant note in *Dover Beach*, the poet
falters and perceives that he himself is subject to change and that
the signal-elm which he so confidently expected to see—"I miss
it! is it gone?" And with this third question the poet is pre-
pared to enter seriously upon the exploration of his theme.

For if the answer to this question is affirmative, then change
does indeed rule all, not merely the social world of man and the
natural world of the hills, but also the world of spiritual values.
For the tree, though in a sense a part of the natural landscape,
has become a private symbol between Thyrsis and the poet of the
enduring validity of their youthful ideal:

> while it stood, we said,
> Our friend, the Gipsy-Scholar, was not dead;
> While the tree lived, he in these fields lived on.

He was a symbol of that abiding inward life which all men desire,
and thus, with the question about the tree the poet is no longer
exploring the Cumnor hills but is exploring a region of the mind.
When he says, in the next line, "Too rare, too rare, grow now my
visits here," he is not speaking of the natural scene, for he is not
a Wordsworthian poet. He is speaking of the depths of his own
soul, with which he has been too infrequently in communion.
The line echoes another line in the contemporary poem *Palladium*: "We visit it by moments, ah, too rare!" There the reference
is explicitly to the soul, which is compared to the image of Pal-
las Athene, on which the safety of Troy depended. Like the
signal-elm, it was placed on high, far above the city, and we are
told that "while this stood, Troy could not fall."

> So, in its lovely moonlight, lives the soul.
> Mountains surround it, and sweet virgin air;
> Cold plashing, past it, crystal waters roll;
> We visit it by moments, ah, too rare!

The essential question is one of *power*. It is "some loss of habit's power" which first makes the poet falter, and when he renews the attempt, it is with the cry, "Who, if not I, for questing here hath power?" The word has almost Lawrentian overtones of a vital, procreative force, a joyous union with nature and with oneself, which would enable him to recreate the vision of the Scholar-Gipsy once again. Can he do it? As in *Dejection: an Ode,* it is not so much a question of whether the tree is there as of whether he can see it. Essentially, it is a question of poetry. Has he been so long in the world that his poetic powers have been completely dissipated, or do they still survive? If they do, he ought to be able, like his predecessors from old, to "flute his friend, like Orpheus, from the dead." Wordsworth, however, is the only one in Arnold's poetic pantheon whose "healing power" is ever compared to that of Orpheus, and Wordsworth, we know, is dead. And so the poet launches into that lovely stanza,

> O easy access to the hearer's grace
> When Dorian shepherds sang to Proserpine!

which expresses the relative difficulty of writing poetry in a modern, unpoetic age. In ancient times the muses walked the earth, and poets spoke directly to them as to a friend. But now, in a later age, and a northern land, and to an aging poet, what chance that poetry would have this magic power?

Nonetheless, the poet will try:—

> Well! wind-dispersed and vain the words will be,
> Yet, Thyrsis, let me give my grief its hour
> In the old haunt, and find our tree-topp'd hill!
> Who, if not I, for questing here hath power?

What these lines indicate is that Arnold's quest for the tree will be accomplished by giving his grief its hour, that is, by writing an elegy. And so, a hundred lines after the beginning of the poem we get an elegy within an elegy which has as its purpose to determine whether the elegist can sing. If he can, if he proves the vitality of his poetic powers, then, whatever he accomplishes for his friend, he will at least have fluted himself from the dead. As Coleridge said of the damsel with a dulcimer, "Could I revive within me / Her symphony and song," and did so in the act of the poem, so Arnold, referring to the vision of the Scholar-Gipsy,

revives it within him and becomes the poet once again. In this way
he solves a problem which is central to the other great Romantic
poems about the failure of poetic power. The paradox in Wordsworth's *Immortality Ode,* Coleridge's *Dejection: an Ode,* and
Hopkins' sonnet to Robert Bridges is that the poems themselves
belie the event of which they speak. But Arnold has included
within his poem, as its central episode, the act of imagination by
which that poem was restored. "A timely utterance gave that
thought relief," says Wordsworth, but the utterance is outside
the poem. In *Thyrsis* it occupies approximately lines 101–71.

As the poem within the poem is an elegy, its structure necessarily repeats that of the larger poem, and that is why, in lines
101–50, we get a reintroduction of themes already stated in lines
1–40. The theme of the poet's intimate knowledge of the countryside, already stated in the opening stanzas, is now more confidently repeated in lines 105–11, but with this difference, that the
poet now understands that his power derives from this knowledge. Then, just as his confidence had been checked before by
the word *Only,* so now the word *But* reintroduces the theme of
change, which once again floods across the poem. It encompasses
the dingle, the green bank, the girl, and the mowers. "They all
are gone, and thou art gone as well!" And once again it also encompasses the poet.

> Yes! thou art gone! and round me too the night
> In ever-nearing circle weaves her shade.

The effect of this descent of night is to transform the forest
glade into a darkling plain. The soft, spring warmth becomes
chill, the flowers are replaced by brambles, and the luxuriant
Thames valley becomes an "upland dim" in which the fog creeps
from bush to bush. But the more startling effect is upon the
poet's imagination. For as he feels this chill descend, he simultaneously falters in his grasp upon imaginative reality. The language and conceptions of the poem coarsen. The images are too
quickly translated into their moral equivalent, and they are dis-
torted into something altogether out of keeping with the poem.
The descending night with its darkness and its chill becomes
Death, and the poet so far forgets where he is (or rather *when* he
is) as to make his foot "less prompt to meet the *morning* dew."
His way becomes the Way of Life, the hill becomes the Citadel

of Truth, and it is not a low Cumnor hill with an elm atop, but
a mountain towering high in the clouds and bearing upon its
summit the "throne of Truth." In *The Scholar-Gipsy* Goethe
"dejectedly" took his seat upon the "intellectual throne," but
the Scholar-Gipsy never did. Had he been invited to, he certainly
would have done so dejectedly, but he fled such places rather
than sought them. And when we learn that this same mountain
is apparently "the fort / Of the long-batter'd world," we wonder
whether the poet is coming or going. If he is seeking the Scholar-
Gipsy, he is seeking him in the wrong place, and in truth, the
whole conception of this stanza is not idyllic and poetic, but moral
and heroic. It derives not from Romantic poetry but from ancient Stoicism and evangelical Christianity. Probably its actual
source is Hesiod's *Works and Days*: "Full across the way of Virtue the immortal gods have set the sweat of the brow; long and
steep is the path that reaches to her, and rough at the beginning;
but when you reach the highest point, hard though it is, in the
end it becomes easy." [5] For the poet it has not yet become easy,
and his stanza bears the marks of strain and effort. It is one of
the passages most frequently quoted from the poem, as seeming
to contain its moral message, but imaginatively it is the nadir of
the poem. The poet, bewildered and lost, is about to lie down and
give himself to death, when suddenly, by ceasing to try, he is
miraculously saved.

This is the elegiac reversal, and it is accomplished by the
poet's "hushing" his false poetic voice and assuming his true. By
so doing, he is once again placed in his imaginative landscape
and achieves his poetic vision.

> Look, adown the dusk hill-side,
> A troop of Oxford hunters going home,
> As in old days, jovial and talking, ride!
> From hunting with the Berkshire hounds they come.
> Quick! let me fly, and cross
> Into yon farther field!—'Tis done; and see,
> Back'd by the sunset, which doth glorify
> The orange and pale violet evening-sky,
> Bare on its lonely ridge, the Tree! the Tree!

Why does Arnold have his protagonist see the tree in this way?
Part of the answer is that the tree is not to be seen by scaling a

[5] Lines 288–92. Donne's third Satire has also been cited.

mountain-top or battering down a fortress, but in the same way
that the Scholar-Gipsy was seen by boys, blackbirds, mowers,
and poets. You turn around and he is there! Part of it is that
hunters are for Arnold a symbol of joyous vitality, and they stir
up the landscape and make it vibrate a little. Moreover, they are
an element of permanence, riding out of *The Scholar-Gipsy* "as
in old days" and indicating that all is essentially the same. And
finally, they precipitate the poet into that instinctive movement
which is the right one. Where effort had failed, he now "flies"—
that is, he does what the Scholar-Gipsy did, and so, acting like
the Scholar-Gipsy, he becomes the Gipsy and sees his tree again.
Of course, he cannot reach the tree that night, but this too is
proper, for the tree (unlike the throne and the fort) is not something to be reached. As a "signal" elm, it operates from afar, and
the quest itself, not the achievement of the quest, is the essence
of its meaning. So Arnold, in the exactly contemporaneous preface to the *Essays in Criticism,* berates the *Saturday Review* for
falling victim to the "beautiful but deluding idea" that the British
nation has "found the last word of its philosophy." "No," he
says, "we are seekers still!" and he gives to Oxford, "so venera-
ble, so lovely, so unravaged by the fierce intellectual life of our
century," the function of "ever calling us near to the true goal of
all of us, to the ideal, to perfection,—to beauty, in a word, which
is only truth seen from another side." [6] This, too, is the function
of the tree; and so, in recovering his vision of the tree, Arnold
has not reached the end of his road but has merely renewed his
power to continue a seeker still.

But what of Thyrsis? The elegiac reversal of line 157 is not
merely the peripeteia of the elegy within the elegy but is also
the major turn in the elegy as a whole. It is significant, then,
that it involves not the death and rebirth of Thyrsis but the loss
and recovery of the tree, and that the tree, in some sense, is the
central figure of the poem. Arnold conceded to his friend Shairp
that "if one reads the poem as a memorial poem, . . . not enough
is said about Clough in it; I feel this so much that I do not send
the poem to Mrs. Clough." [7] It is not merely, however, that not
enough is said about Clough in it, but rather that so much of

---

[6] *Essays in Criticism: First Series* (1902), pp. x–xi; *The Complete Prose Works
of Matthew Arnold,* ed. R. H. Super (Ann Arbor, 1960–), *3,* 289–90.
[7] *Letters, 1,* 380.

what is said is critical. In the early stanzas Clough is compared to the cuckoo, that "too quick despairer" who petulantly flies away when the first bloom is off the spring, not realizing that summer and autumn "have their music too" and that the cycle of nature will bring a new spring in another year. So, in the cycle of history, if Clough could have waited the passing of storms which a more far-sighted person would have known were transitory, he would have survived into the better times which are already in prospect. But "he could not wait their passing, he is dead." In this way his death becomes slightly ludicrous, the unnecessary destruction of a witless and flighty person who could have been saved by a little forethought. Where the ordinary elegy contains a section in which the poet accuses various powers of negligence in permitting the death of the beloved, Arnold's poem does not employ this convention, for "Thyrsis of his own will went away." His death was really a kind of suicide.

Still, by asserting, with respect to the cuckoo, that rebirth is the law of nature, the poet has opened the way to assert this of Clough too, and the elegy within the elegy is the proposed means of doing this. Unfortunately, when the elegy is accomplished and the poet turns to include his friend in its discovery —"Hear it, O Thyrsis, still our tree is there!"—he finds that his friend cannot hear it and that his death in Florence is a second symbolic desertion of the Cumnor fields.

> Ah, vain! These English fields, this upland dim,
> These brambles pale with mist engarlanded,
> That lone, sky-pointing tree, are not for him;
> To a boon southern country he is fled. . . .

The poet, then, is left alone on the darkling plain. But though he is alone, he will not despair, for the sight of the tree against the western sky is a sign that the Scholar-Gipsy still haunts these hills, "outliving thee." And, if he is "a wanderer still, then why not me?" Together with the Scholar-Gipsy the poet will pursue the "fugitive and gracious light" which is their ideal, and the final vision we have is of the two of them going off together, outliving Clough.

If the poem ended at this point (and in some ways it would be a better poem if it did) we would have to say that *Thyrsis* belongs with those elegies like *Heine's Grave, Haworth Church-*

yard, and *Stanzas in Memory of the Author of "Obermann"* which come to bury their subject not to praise him. Its theme is how Thyrsis abandoned the ideal of the Scholar-Gipsy and so subjected himself to Time and Death, and how the poet, though visiting too rarely this country of the soul, revisits it now and rededicates himself to poetry. However, the poem does not end here, and, whatever may have been the motives, poetic or personal, for Arnold's adding the last three stanzas, these stanzas reinclude Thyrsis within the old ideal. We are now told that although he did go away and lived for a time with "men of care," yet essentially he never abandoned the vision of the Scholar-Gipsy and was a wanderer until he died. Indeed, at the very end of the poem it is his voice which is to come, " 'mid city-noise," and remind the poet, "Our tree yet crowns the hill, / Our Scholar travels yet the loved hill-side."

Poetically, it is awkward to have Thyrsis voice the very words which in the poem he could not hear, and one has the feeling that Arnold, in his desire, perhaps, to do right by his friend, was led to do wrong by his poem. Of course, one recognizes that the "boon southern country" to which Clough fled was not merely Italy but was also a version of that country "far to the south, beyond the blue," where Balder envisioned the rise of the second Asgard. There, wandering in the great Mother's train divine, Thyrsis could easily have achieved any kind of knowledge, and we should have to suppose that he learned about the tree through the "immortal chants of old," which we are told he could hear though he could not hear Arnold's. These chants are particularly the Lityerses songs sung by the Phrygian reapers in worship of the vegetation deity Daphnis. All over the ancient world, under the various names of Maneros songs in Egypt, Linus songs in Phoenicia, and Lityerses songs in Phrygia, these popular chants celebrated the death and rebirth of the harvest gods. More sophisticatedly, they survived in the Greek and Latin classical elegies, and Arnold's stanza alludes especially to the fifth and eighth of Virgil's *Eclogues*. From these *Eclogues* came most of the quotations, including lines alluding to Thyrsis and Daphnis, which form the epigraphs of Clough's "Long-Vacation Pastoral," *The Bothie of Tober-na-Vuolich*. Clough may be supposed, then, to have rejoined in death a better version of the world which he lived in in his life and to have gained an "easy access" to those values from which Arnold, alone in the Cumnor hills, was still debarred.

Such one may suppose to be Arnold's meaning. The only difficulty is that when one compares the "boon southern country" to which Clough has fled with the "upland dim" in which Arnold still wanders, one finds the latter more chaste and more convincing. There is something coarse and flamboyant about the "broad lucent Arno-vale" with its flowery oleanders, when set against the misty English upland with brambles and a "lone sky-pointing tree." The contrast is the same as that which Ruskin drew in *The Stones of Venice* between St. Mark's as a "long low pyramid of colored light," and the gaunt, aspiring height of an English cathedral, or that which Browning drew in *Home-Thoughts from Abroad* between the English buttercup and "this gaudy melon-flower," which symbolized the beauty of Italy. So Arnold is content to be " 'neath the mild canopy of English air" with his tree rather than to enjoy "all the marvel of the golden skies" with a translated Daphnis. And the reader too persists in admiring, more than the subject of the poem, the one who remained behind, faithful to the quiet, austere, and difficult ideal of the Scholar-Gipsy.

If we now pause and consider what we have learned about Arnold's elegies, the first thing we would have to say is that they are the poetic counterpart of his imaginative world. We have perhaps obscured this fact by saying that the elegy is divided into two parts by means of the elegiac reversal. So it is in its actual structure, but the complete world which the elegy presupposes is divided into three parts by means of two elegiac reversals. The first of these is simply the death of the subject, and therefore the first part of the world occurs before the poem opens. To use again the example of *Lycidas*, the first part consists of the happy days when

> we were nursed upon the self-same hill,
> Fed the same flock by fountain, shade, and rill.

This part is terminated by the first elegiac reversal, "But O the heavy change now thou art gone." The second part, then, consists of the body of lamentation and is terminated by the more usual reversal,

> Weep no more, woeful shepherds, weep no more,
> For Lycidas your sorrow is not dead.

The third part is the final phase of recovery and reconciliation. It is obvious that Arnold's poetic myth corresponds exactly with this structure: his forest glade is the happy times together, his burning plain the body of lamentation, and his wide-glimmering sea the period of reconciliation. Moreover, his image of the gorge or strait which connects one part of his world with another corresponds to the structural device of the elegiac reversal, and the River of Life corresponds to the current of thought or feeling which sweeps him through his song. This last device is of great value to Arnold, for it not only gives a strong compulsive movement to his thought, but it also enables him to attribute his views to some power larger than himself. Just as in his essays he will attribute to History or the Zeitgeist the unfavorable judgments which he passes upon his countrymen, so in the elegies he will attribute them to muses, breezes, or fate. In *A Summer Night* it is the midnight breeze which "checks his strain" and reminds him that no one is more worthy of a romantic resting-place than an English gentleman of noble feeling. In *Heine's Grave* it is the Bitter Spirits of Heine's own poetry which mock his efforts to claim the bard as his own and remind him that Heine wanted love and so also wanted charm. And in *Haworth Churchyard* it is again the Muse which interrupts him and angrily denies to the Brontës the reawakening which the poet had promised. In this way Arnold is able to give weight and objectivity to value judgments which are his own.

This correspondence of the elegy to the myth explains the different forms which the elegy takes in Arnold's work. If the subject is an inhabitant of the forest glade, as in the case of Wordsworth, then we get the first elegiac reversal but not the second, for in 1850 Arnold did not believe that the forest glade could ever be recreated again. But if the subject is an inhabitant of the burning plain, then we do not get a first reversal, since his death is not a "heavy change," and the second reversal is a reversal in reverse. This is the form of the elegies on Obermann, Charlotte Brontë, and Heine. Then, when Arnold is a little further along in his own myth, he discovers that persons whom he had thought to be on the burning plain actually were not, and this revisal of opinion constitutes a conventional elegiac reversal in which the subject dies in Arnold's estimation as one thing and is reborn as another. *Thyrsis* is an ambiguous example, *A Southern Night* a much clearer one. It is notable, however, that in the latter case Arnold required two poems in which to make the discovery. In *Stanzas from Carnac,* though he himself was placed by the wide-glimmering sea, he was under the impression that his brother was not. But in *A Southern Night* he found that he was wrong, and so the two poems together constitute a single elegiac form. The one is the "elegiac reversal" of the other. Finally, in the very late elegies, such as *Rugby Chapel,* the second Obermann poem, and *Westminster Abbey*, Arnold hardly bothers with either the forest glade or the burning plain but proceeds directly to the wide-glimmering sea. This means that there is no first elegiac reversal (except perhaps in *Westminster Abbey*) and that the second is a conventional one and comes very early in the poem. In the case of *Obermann Once More* it comes so early that one may consider that poem to be the second part of an elegy of which the *Stanzas in Memory of the Author of "Obermann"* is the first part. The fact that Arnold wrote his elegies in fragments and that these fragments are distributed over his entire poetic career is simply an indication that he spiritually enacted his myth as he went along.

Indeed, taking this larger view of the elegies, we can now see that a great deal of Arnold's poetic production is elegiac in character. *Balder Dead,* as we have already indicated, is essentially an elegy drawn out, by the insertion of inert matter, into epic proportions. *Sohrab and Rustum,* initially entitled *The Death of Sohrab,* is an elegy for lost youth. *The Church of Brou* is an elegy for the Duke of Savoy in which the poet reproduces in words the elegy which the Duchess has carved in stone. The *Sick King in Bokhara* is a double elegy, both for the King, who becomes well, and for the Moolah, who is redeemed through punishment and understanding. *Tristram and Iseult* is another double elegy, Tristram dying as himself to be reborn in the form of his own children, Iseult dying as Ireland to be reborn as Brittany. All the love poems taken together constitute one large elegy in which woman dies as Marguerite and is reborn as Mrs. Arnold. Likewise, the poet dies as passionate lover and is reborn as son or brother. *Empedocles on Etna* is a truncated elegy in which Empedocles dies with only the promise of rebirth when he shall poise his life at last. But more largely, the drama *Empedocles on Etna* "dies" as morbid art through the "elegiac reversal" of the Preface of 1853 in order to be reborn as wholesome

art in *Sohrab and Rustum*. Indeed, in this sense both of Arnold's
first two volumes die in order to be reborn as their successor. Of
The Strayed Reveller, and Other Poems Arnold wrote that he
was impatient at having been "faussé" in it, and to Jane he said,
"My last volume I have got absolutely to dislike." But *Empedocles on Etna* was no better. "I feel now," he wrote to Clough,
"where my poems (this set) are all wrong," and so he withdrew
them from circulation before fifty copies were sold.[8] Not until
his third volume did Arnold produce a work which he did not
immediately dislike on publication, and this attitude toward his
poetry was but symptomatic of his attitude toward life in general.
Speaking of Béranger, he wrote, "I am glad to be tired of an
author: one link in the immense series of cognoscenda et inda-
genda despatched." [9] In this respect, he is strongly to be contrasted with Newman. Newman was a person who was deeply
attached to his own past and who loved to feel it accumulating
behind him. As a result, he kept every scrap of paper that ever
passed through his hands, and writing his *Apologia* was not only
an easy task but was also deeply moving and of great delight.
Arnold, on the other hand, requested that no biography of him
should ever be written, and he undoubtedly destroyed many of
the materials which would have made it possible. The ultimate
reason for this difference is that Newman believed in "two and
two only absolute and luminously self-evident beings, myself and
my Creator," whereas Arnold believed in two and two only luminously self-evident beings, his Best Self and his Ordinary Self.
Newman's task, then, was to strengthen the links between himself and his Creator, Arnold's to repudiate the Ordinary Self and
strengthen the Best Self. Arnold agreed with Goethe, as paraphrased
by Tennyson,

> I held it truth, with him who sings
> To one clear harp in divers tones,

---

[8] *Letters to Clough*, pp. 109, 126; *Unpublished Letters of Matthew Arnold*, ed.
Arnold Whitridge (New Haven, 1923), p. 14; *The Poetical Works of Matthew
Arnold*, ed. C. B. Tinker and H. F. Lowry (Oxford, 1950), p. 502. The letter in
which Arnold criticizes his poems as "fragments" (*Unpublished Letters*, p. 18)
should be dated 1849, not "1853?" as the reference to the French expedition
against Rome makes clear. Thus the allusion is to *The Strayed Reveller, and
Other Poems*.

[9] *Letters to Clough*, p. 93.

> That men may rise on stepping-stones
> Of their dead selves to higher things.[10]

With Arnold the elegies were these stepping-stones. . . .

. . . One would not call *Thyrsis* an act of sibling rivalry, but in it the brilliant pupil of his father is displaced, and Arnold, through the transformation of the imagery, finds his father once again.

This event is finally consummated in *Rugby Chapel*. Arnold's brother notes that in 1842, when their father died, Arnold "could not have written of his father's great qualities with the profound and yearning appreciation which is shown in 'Rugby Chapel,' composed fourteen years later." [11] Actually, though the poem is dated 1857, it was probably not completed much before its publication in 1867, so that in point of fact Arnold waited some fifteen to twenty-five years to compose it. By that time, far from feeling any imperfect sympathy with his father, he had developed a strong sense that in his school work and his religious and social essays he was continuing the work that his father had begun. The beginning of this appreciation may be seen in a letter which Arnold wrote to his mother in 1855. He is thanking her for sending him an early letter of his father's which she had just found, in which the Doctor was making plans for the education and welfare of his then eight-year-old son, and Arnold was touched by the thought of this silent parental love, exercising itself even when he was least aware. "This is just what makes him great," he declared, "that he was not only a good man saving his own soul by righteousness, but that he carried so many others with him in his hand, and saved them, if they would let him, along with himself." This idea—the central conception of the poem—was then reinforced two years later when he read Thomas Hughes' novel, *Tom Brown's School-Days* (1857). For the high point of this work comes on the last day of school when Tom, hitherto a careless fellow and not much an admirer of the Doctor, learns that the Doctor had arranged that he, East, and Arthur should be together in the same study so that Tom would have someone to concern himself about and get into less mischief. It came as a "new light" to Tom to find that, "besides teaching the sixth, and governing and guiding the whole School, editing classics, and writing histories, the great

---

[10] *In Memoriam*, i.
[11] *Manchester Guardian* (May 18, 1888), p. 8.

Head-master had found time in those busy years to watch over
the career, even of him, Tom Brown. . . ." The novel ends, of
course, with Tom on his knees in Rugby Chapel before the
Doctor's tomb and being led by "hero-worship" of him to the
possibility of the worship of One higher than him, "the King and
Lord of heroes." [12]

It is at this point that Arnold's poem begins, and that is one
reason why it was dated November 1857. It was dated from the
time when Arnold's father, through the aid of this somewhat
athletic but moving book, was reborn in the imagination of the
son. As a result, the poem is concerned almost exclusively with
the third phase of the myth. Admittedly, an elegy published
twenty-five years after the event cannot very well say, "O the
heavy change now thou art gone!" It can only say, "Lycidas your
sorrow is not dead." Still, the poem makes this statement rather
early (at line 15 of a 208-line poem), and the form of the statement is curious. It was determined by a review of *Tom Brown's
School-Days* written by the positivist critic Fitzjames Stephen.
"It was Fitzjames Stephen's thesis," wrote Arnold, "maintained
in the Edinburgh Review, of Papa's being a narrow bustling
fanatic, which moved me first to the poem." The function of the
poem was to refute this thesis—"to fix," as Arnold said in strangely
hagiographic language, "the true legend about Papa, as those who
knew him best feel it ought to run." [13] As a result, the elegiac
reversal took the form of rescuing the Doctor, not from death,
but from misconception, and once again, this was done through
the agency of the tomb. In most of the elegies the tomb is placed
at the end of the poem as a symbol of what the subject was. Here
it is placed at the beginning as a symbol of what he was not.
"Gloom" is what characterizes the tomb and what was attributed
to Dr. Arnold by Fitzjames Stephen. "But ah!" says the poet,
"that word, *gloom,* to my mind / Brings thee back, in the light / of
thy radiant vigour," and through this curious method—a kind
of *lucus a non lucendo!*—the elegiac reversal is accomplished.

In the rest of the poem affirmation proceeds unchecked, and it
involves a considerable revision of Arnold's previous poetic equip-
ment. For though we are once again on the burning plain, it
is now uncomfortably recognizable as the wilderness through which

[12] *Letters, 1,* 48; *Tom Brown's School-Days* (2d ed., London, 1857), pp. 407, 425.
[13] *Letters to Clough,* p. 164.

the children of Israel wandered. And the mountain is no longer Etna or an Alp but Mt. Horeb or Mt. Sinai. Moreover, the protagonists are not lonely figures brooding upon some mountain height but a band of pilgrims in the valley struggling to reach the mountain. And on top of the mountain is not a tree or a Palladium or a throne, but an inn, whose gaunt and taciturn host holds his lantern in our faces and asks such questions as we expect to be asked only at the gates of Heaven. "Whom in our party we bring? / Whom we have left in the snow?" And at this point the Romantic hero falls back abashed, and there steps forward a new hero, the Servant or Son of God, who "would not *alone* be saved" but saved others along with himself. It is predicted that under his guidance the company will proceed, "On, to the bound of the waste, / On, to the City of God"—a place which has not hitherto been mentioned in Arnold's poetry, except as the second Asgard.

The last part of the poem may be best understood as a kind of palinode to *Resignation,* the one other poem associated with the death of Arnold's father. It will be recalled that the occasion of that poem was a walk which Arnold took with Jane, probably in 1843, just ten years after the children had taken the same walk on the Wythburn Fells with their father and Captain Hamilton. The difference now was that their father was dead and Jane had suffered a shattering blow in the breaking off of her engagement just three weeks before the wedding. Hence, the theme of resignation. The theme is developed by means of a contrast among three groups of figures representing three different ways of life: first, the daemonic questers who felt that salvation consisted in reaching some Mecca, some Jerusalem, some Rome—some City of God! But the poet sees that these are really thralls to their own passion and that reaching their goal will not really bring them repose. Secondly, there are the gipsies, who ramble aimlessly about the countryside with no idea of a fixed goal until at last death ends their lot. And finally, there is the poet, who sits quietly on the mountain-top and contemplates the whole of life but does not take part in it. He is not unsympathetic to the people —he does not say, "I am alone"—but he does not share their aspirations. And to Fausta's impatience that they are today retracing their steps instead of making furiously for some goal, the poet replies:

> Not milder is the general lot
> Because our spirits have forgot,
> In action's dizzying eddy whirl'd,
> The something that infects the world.

He has rejected Byronism and muddling through, but he does not seem aware that there is any other alternative.

Yet he had overlooked one character in his own poem, and that was his father. In the earlier walk his father had served as leader.

> High on a bank our leader stands,
> Reviews and ranks his motley bands,
> Makes clear our goal to every eye—
> The valley's western boundary.

As they mount up,

> There climbing hangs, a far-seen sign,
> Our wavering, many-colour'd line;

until at last they reach the cool-shaded farms, the "noisy town" of Keswick, and ultimately the "wide-glimmering sea." This role of the Doctor had also been emphasized by Arthur Stanley in his pious *Life,* published in 1845. "Most of all, perhaps, was to be observed his delight in those long mountain walks, when they would start with their provisions for the day, himself the guide and life of the party, always on the look out how best to break the ascent by gentle stages, comforting the little ones in their falls, and helping forward those who were tired, himself always keeping with the laggers, that none might strain their strength by trying to be in front with him—and then, when his assistance was not wanted, the liveliest of all; his step so light, his eye so quick in finding flowers to take home to those who were not of the party." [14] Operating, perhaps, a little too much like Pippa in *Pippa Passes,* this is the same Doctor who reappears in *Rugby Chapel,* but now shepherding, not a band of little children, but the "host of mankind."

> See! in the rocks of the world
> Marches the host of mankind,
> A feeble, wavering line.

[14] Arthur P. Stanley, *Life and Correspondence of Thomas Arnold,* 5th ed. (London, 1845), *1,* 243.

> Where are they tending?—A God
> Marshall'd them, gave them their goal.

Though the way is long and the marchers faint, the Servants or Sons of God give them courage.

> Languor is not in your heart,
> Weakness is not in your word,
> Weariness not on your brow. . . .
> Ye move through the ranks, recall
> The stragglers, refresh the outworn,
> Praise, re-inspire the brave!

So, strengthening the wavering line, they continue their march, "On, to the City of God," which replaces both the noisy town and the wide-glimmering sea of *Resignation*.

"I always think," Dr. Arnold used to say, "of that magnificent sentence of Bacon, 'In this world, God only and the angels may be spectators.' " [15] In *Resignation* Arnold was a spectator, but in *Rugby Chapel* he has adopted his father's and Lord Bacon's opinion. Once again he has distinguished among three ways of life: the majority of men, who "eddy about / Here and there" (like the gipsies); the few, who make for some clear-purposed goal (like the questers); and then, not the poet sitting removed from it all on the mountain-top, but the Servant or Son of God, who saves others along with himself.

The alternatives of the City of God and the sea as the final goal of Arnold's myth correspond to the alternatives of the Best and the Buried Self, and so to the two major characters in the last phase of the myth, the Servants or Sons of God and the Children of the Second Birth. The latter, as their name implies, are simply the Children of the Forest reborn after their experience on the burning plain. They have all the mildness, gentleness, and purity of the first group but without their innocence. Also, as they have been chastened and subdued by suffering, their Joy often approaches Calm. The ideal is first announced in *Stanzas in Memory of the Author of "Obermann,"* where they make up a small, transfigured band who live in the world but are not of it. It is continued in the Marguerite poems, where the poet discovers that the true bent of both their natures is to be gentle, tranquil, true. It is more fully developed in Iseult of Brittany and the poet

[15] Ibid., p. 195.

Balder, and is perhaps most dramatically recognized in the tribute
to William Delafield Arnold and his wife Fanny. Finally, it is
claimed for the poet himself in the poem on Heine: "May a life
/ Other and milder be mine!" In the prose it is exemplified in
the phrase "sweetness and light" and in the mildness and sweet
reasonableness of Arnold's conception of Jesus. In its mingling
of Hellenism and the New Testament it is the very epitome of
the Victorian ideal.

The Servants or Sons of God, on the other hand, are Old
Testament figures and so are distinctly Hebraic. Unlike the Children, they are not simply themselves reborn but are related to
something outside of themselves, namely, God. Arnold hesitates
how to call them:

> Servants of God!—or sons
> Shall I not call you? because
> Not as servants ye knew
> Your Father's innermost mind . . .

The term Servants implies a relationship to the Slave, but with
the suggestion that they differ from the Slave in that the work
they do is God's work, not the world's, and that they do it willingly. So willingly, indeed, that they are more properly called
Sons, and this term relates them again to the Children. Indeed,
they could be considered simply the Children of the Second
Birth at a slightly later stage of their development, when they have
not merely emerged from repression but have actually strengthened
the ego to the point where they are now willing to repress others.
They now feel confident that their True Self is, objectively, the
Best Self; for, as Servants who do their Father's will, their will
is the will of God. The Hellenic Children have discovered what
reason and the will of God are; now they, as the Hebraic Sons,
will make these qualities prevail.

As a result, along with the emergence of this character in Arnold's poetry, there is a great increase in the imagery of warfare
and contention. Examples are *The Last Word, The Lord's Mes-
sengers, Bacchanalia,* and *Palladium.* Where in Arnold's earlier
poems the burning plain was a place where individuals wandered
in their isolation, now it is a place where armies clash in combat.
And they are not "ignorant armies," either, who are unsure which
side they are on. The issues are perfectly clear, and the only

question is whether one fights the good fight or not. The final
stage is perhaps observable in *Culture and Anarchy,* where, asking
how one should deal with rioting, Arnold quotes with approval
his father's view. "As for rioting, the old Roman way of dealing
with *that* is always the right one; flog the rank and file, and fling
the ring-leaders from the Tarpeian Rock!" [16] Though Dr. Arnold
often employed the former method at Rugby, the latter clearly
represents a new use to which mountains may be put in Arnold.
In the early volumes poets brooded upon mountains and occasionally threw themselves into volcanoes. Later, the Servants of
God helped others up the mountains. Now they are throwing
those down who did not behave. Fortunately, this was not Arnold's
final view. The offending passage was removed from the second
edition of *Culture and Anarchy,* and in Arnold's other works the
Servant of God adopts the milder methods of the Children of
the Second Birth.

One may see this in the last of Arnold's major elegies, *Obermann Once More.* We have called this poem the second half of
an elegy of which *Stanzas in Memory of the Author of "Obermann"* is the first half, and in respect to substance that is true.
But in method the poem is a dream-vision and so is better associated with *The Scholar-Gipsy.* As in that work, the poet lies
down in a high Alpine field, presumably with Obermann's book
beside him, and there "muses" upon his author until, as night
falls, the figure of Obermann suddenly stands before him on the
grass. Recognizing his former follower, Obermann begins to speak,
and his speech, which extends to 250 lines, occupies the same
position in this poem as the discourse of Empedocles does in
Empedocles on Etna. Indeed, had it been given on Etna, it would
have provided hope for the dejected Pausanias without involving
him in superstition, and it might have saved Empedocles himself where the myths of Callicles could not help. For what it offers
is not a dry rationalism which denies what it cannot feel or a
poetic fancy which asserts what it does not know, but a moving
vision of human history over the past two thousand years. This
vision, which Arnold will draw out more fully in *Literature and
Dogma,* distinguishes four different historical epochs: the pagan
world in the first century B.C., the new age of faith initiated by
Christianity, the gradual withdrawal of faith during the modern

period, and the new order that is now about to be. Obviously,
this is the Goethean philosophy of history which postulates alternating epochs of skepticism and faith, and Arnold's point is to
emphasize the parallel between the first age and the third and
between the second and the fourth. For just as the emptiness of
paganism could be followed by an age of faith, so the emptiness
of our age can also be followed by faith, and this not because
of any historical determinism but simply through the understanding afforded by human history. For in retelling the Christian
story Arnold emphasizes the subjectivity of religious events. "He
lived while we believed," and his death occurred, not on the
cross but in the hearts of men. So, in the same manner that he first
was born, he can be born again. He was first born when the brooding East so well "mused" upon her problems that "a morning
broke / Across her spirit grey." In this poem Arnold too has so
well "mused" that a morning breaks across his spirit grey. For
him it is the Easter morn of Christ's rising from the dead. Not
in the conventional sense, of course. Arnold has been too well
schooled in the Higher Criticism for that. For him Jerusalem is
merely a "lorn Syrian town" set amid "sun, and arid stone, / And
crumbling wall, and sultry sand," and those who wait outside
Christ's empty tomb await in vain. The only word that comes from
that tomb is that man, "unduped of fancy," must henceforth resign
his "all too human creeds, and scan / Simply the way divine."
He must learn that the values of religion, which were hitherto
thought to be objective and divine, are really subjective and human,
and that only by recognizing this fact can we distinguish the
essence of Christianity from the *Aberglaube,* or superfluous belief,
with which it has been encrusted.

Thus, what started out as an elegy for the author of *Obermann*
has become a vision of the risen Christ. Even the tomb, which is
a central symbol in the poem, is not that by Lake Leman or the
granite terraces of Paris, but is the tomb of Christ. And, though
Christ is not risen in any literal sense, the Obermann who is risen
bears so little resemblance to his predecessor in the other poem,
is so mild and gentle, so deeply inward and spiritually serene,
that he seems rather to embody Jesus than merely to announce
him. The book which he carries in his breast is wisely not named.
Presumably we are to take it as his own. But if we were to open
it and read, it would surely sound like the New Testament or the

Imitatio Christi. For the message of the poem is, Close thy *Obermann* and open thy *Imitatio Christi.*

With this vision Arnold recovers the Joy which he had lost when he left the forest glade and descended to the burning plain. But it is not precisely the same Joy. It is, in the first place, a "joy whose grounds are true" and, in the second, "joy that should all hearts employ." By these two conditions it transcends both the first phase of human existence and the second, and is a synthesis of the two. For on the burning plain, whatever kind of solution the Sage or Strayed Reveller might achieve—not of Joy but at least of Calm—it always involved some removal from his fellow men into an aristocratic seclusion. But Thomas Arnold "would not *alone* / Be saved," and Obermann asks, "Who can be *alone* elate, / While the world lies forlorn?" No, the new Joy must be "joy in widest commonalty spread"—it must be *"one common wave of thought and joy,"* as it was in the first age. But then, it must also be true. The Joy of the Romantic poets, and of childhood, and of the childhood of the world had some element of illusion about it, of a divine illusion, which is unsatisfactory to modern man. "He fables, yet speaks truth," says Empedocles of the myth-making Callicles, and though Callicles had Joy and Empedocles had not, we now need a recovered Joy which will be acceptable to the adult as well as to the youth. The faculty through which we are to find this, according to Arnold, is the "imaginative reason."

We have already observed that imaginative reason is that synthesis of intellect and feeling which is characteristic of the modern spirit. It does not deny the evidence of the senses and understanding, but neither does it deny that of the heart and imagination. It is at once profoundly satisfying and profoundly true. As such, it combines the best elements of science and religion and yet transcends these by remaining poetry. In the late essays "Literature and Science" and "The Study of Poetry" Arnold explores the interrelationships of science, poetry, and religion in such a way as to make religion analogous to the forest glade, science to the burning plain, and poetry to the wide-glimmering sea. Science, for example, tells us things which are acceptable to the senses and understanding but not to the heart and imagination. It makes such statements as Mr. Darwin's that "our ancestor was a hairy quadruped furnished with a tail and pointed ears, probably arboreal in his habits." [17] Objectively, this may have been true, but subjectively it is not. It does not correspond to anything that we know about ourselves or to the powers by which we would build up our life. Religion, on the other hand, says that our ancestors were "two of far nobler shape erect and tall," and this does correspond to what we know about ourselves and to the powers by which we would build up our life. The only trouble is that the statement of religion, which is a beautiful myth about the nature of man, has been taken to be a scientific truth about the origin of man. "Our religion has materialised itself in the fact, in the supposed fact; it has attached its emotion to the fact, and now the fact is failing it." Poetry does not make this mistake. Poetry makes the same statement as religion (the quotation is actually from *Paradise Lost),* but it does not assert that this statement is objectively true. "For poetry the idea is everything; the rest is a world of illusion, of divine illusion. Poetry attaches its emotion to the idea; the idea *is* the fact." [18]

Modern readers, interpreting this passage in terms of their own theories of poetry as an autonomous art, tend to overlook the fact that Arnold distinguishes between "the idea," which *is* the fact, and "the rest," which is a world of illusion. And they also overlook that Arnold is here speaking not of all poetry but only of that which is "worthy of its high destinies," the poetry of the imaginative reason. For some poetry does attach its emotion to the illusion, the divine illusion, and the illusion can fail it. In Arnold's view this is what had happened to the poetry of the English Romantic movement. It was too exclusively a product of the imagination. It was too personal and private, too transitory and unenduring. It "did not know enough" in the sense simply of knowing the great, substantial ideas which had operated in human history. It was very beautiful, but it was essentially a dream. Keats says of Adam that he awoke and found his dream was true, but the Romantic poets awoke and found their dreams were false. One after another they awoke upon the "cold hillside" of a purely phenomenal world. Arnold himself began life upon that cold hillside and was forced to write the greater part of his poetry from that situation. For a long time he wrote it in terms of the senses and understanding. But the late paganism of Epictetus and

---

[17] "Literature and Science," *Discourses in America* (1896), p. 110.
[18] *Essays in Criticism: Second Series* (1900), pp. 1–2.

Lucretius and even Marcus Aurelius was not enough. Religion was morality "touched with emotion," and poetry, if it was not pure imagination, was not pure reason either—it was the imaginative reason. And so, in *Obermann Once More,* Arnold dreamed a dream whose substance was neither the dry rationalism of Empedocles nor the sensuous myth of Callicles but was his own personal myth embodied in human history. And he awoke and found it true. The morning which broke in his dreams actually was breaking when he emerged from his dream. Whereas in *The Scholar-Gipsy* he awoke and found himself back in the phenomenal world, here he awoke and found himself forward in his dream. He had actually dreamed himself off the burning plain into the next phase of human history.

Arnold did this in the same way that Adam did it, by realizing his dream in himself. His elegies repudiate a lower nature and create a higher nature, and insofar as his whole poetry had an elegiac character, this was its larger function. It did not hang nostalgically over the past, lamenting a lost paradise, but tried with honesty and integrity to create a "paradise within thee, happier far." "It might have been thought," wrote Arnold's brother, "that this mood [of mild pessimism in *The Strayed Reveller*] would grow upon him . . . But there was nothing more remarkable in Matthew Arnold's unique personality than his power of recovery and self-correction. Several qualities contributed to this— first, the strength of his intellect . . . ; secondly, that cool, shrewd good sense which never deserted him; thirdly, the affectionateness and kindliness of his nature; . . . [and finally] a clear perception, which was perhaps hereditary, of the necessity and dignity of work." [19] Though in 1849 Arnold felt that he had never yet succeeded on any one great occasion in consciously mastering himself, yet he speaks of the necessity of continually making war on depression and low spirits, and he has the faith that "our spirits retain their conquests: that from the height they succeed in raising themselves to, they can never fall." About this he was not quite right. He did fall, and he had to raise himself again and again, but on each successive occasion the attempt was easier. Auden has said of Arnold that he "thrust his gift in prison till it died," but with this Arnold would not have agreed. It was not his gift that

[19] *Manchester Guardian* (May 18, 1888), p. 8.

he thrust in prison; rather it was an element of darkness which long had troubled that gift. "No one," wrote Arnold in 1865, "has a stronger and more abiding sense than I have of the 'daemonic' element—as Goethe called it—which underlies and encompasses our life; but I think, as Goethe thought, that the right thing is, while conscious of this element, and of all that there is inexplicable round one, to keep pushing on one's posts into the darkness, and to establish no post that is not perfectly in light and firm." [20] In *Obermann Once More* he had reached the light. The dawn breaking over the Valais-depth was now his imaginative present. But having reached it, he must help others to reach it too, for the new Joy must be one that could "all hearts employ." Therefore, in the final moments of his vision he is adjured by Obermann—

> Though more than half thy years be past,
> And spent thy youthful prime—

to use the time and strength that are left him communicating this Joy to others. He has saved himself—now he must save others along with himself, and for this the instrument is prose. It has always been something of a problem why Arnold turned from poetry to prose, and the answer may be given in various ways. But one way of stating it is simply to say that the task of the poetry was done. It told the story of a river which descended from the hills, all but lost itself in the sands of the desert, and finally emptied into the sea. Once it reached the sea its story was done. Milton did not continue *Lycidas* after saying, "Tomorrow to fresh woods and pastures new," nor *Paradise Lost* after saying, "The world was all before them where to choose." Newman did not continue the *Apologia* after he had come into the haven of the Catholic Church. Neither did Arnold continue writing poetry after he had reached the new dawn of *Obermann Once More*.

[20] *Letters to Clough*, pp. 110, 93; *Letters, 1*, 289.

Matthew Arnold's Tragic Vision

by John P. Farrell

Matthew Arnold's provocative 1853 Preface, his lonely pride in *Merope,* and his urgent defense of the classical tradition have inevitably combined to convince readers that his view of tragic experience is identical with the tragic vision that many critics find almost exclusively in Greek and Shakespearean drama. The substance of this vision has been diversely and abundantly described. It remains— and there is reason to think it should remain—beyond exact definition. Its most commonly accepted characteristics are that it sees a local disorder in relation to a cosmic scheme, that it dwells upon a conflict that is noble and significant, that the central figure in the conflict represents humanity in general, and that his struggle is carried out in both pride and humility, in guilt and innocence against powers that shake his world to its foundations. The closest one may hope to get to the essence of this vision is, perhaps, Clifford Leech's simple statement that genuine tragedy "offers us a view of things which aims at comprehensiveness." [1] Arnold's 1853 Preface, based as it is on Aristotle's *Poetics,* reflects these ideas. And it reflects, too, a position in common with modern critics like Joseph Wood Krutch and George Steiner who believe that the emergence of modern skepticism, the Romantic ego, the scientific habit of mind, and the democratic spirit has been fatal to the Greek and Shakespearean tragic vision. Arnold differs from them, one presumes, only in his belief that it could be revived, but his own failure to do so ironically mocks the Olympian prescriptions that he handed down in the Preface.

The purpose of this essay is not to continue the debate on the nature of "true" or "authentic" tragedy or to estimate the state of its

"Matthew Arnold's Tragic Vision" by John P. Farrell. From *PMLA,* 85 (January 1970), 107–15, 116–17. Copyright 1970 by the Modern Language Association. Reprinted by permission of the Modern Language Association of America.

[1] "The Implications of Tragedy," in *Tragedy: Vision and Form,* ed. Robert W. Corrigan (San Francisco, 1965), p. 354.

health. It is, rather, to discuss what the tragic experience meant to Arnold. Such experience has, really, very little to do with the tragic vision implied in the 1853 Preface. Arnold's intimate sense of tragic experience is defined, instead, most fully and explicitly in his essay on Lord Falkland and it appears as the informing vision in several substantial works, *Merope* included. The tragic experience displayed in these works detaches Arnold rather completely from the classical tradition and makes him a representative, for better or worse, of a tradition of tragedy that originated in the nineteenth century and that has been studied, as yet, in only modest dimensions.

It will be remembered that in the Preface Arnold quoted Schiller's comment that "All art is dedicated to joy." [2] Although he applied this remark to the idea of cathartic pleasure that we have long associated, under Aristotle's guidance, with the effect of tragedy, there is reason to think that Arnold was contemplating joy of an entirely different kind. The Preface dwells more on the Hellenic ideal than it does on the nature of tragedy and soon replaces the principle of catharsis with an argument for the power of Greek poetry *in general* to bring composure to the soul. This is a maneuver effected, as William A. Madden observes, by Arnold's "aesthetic temperament":

> In great poetry the terror of life as hell was ameliorated [for Arnold] and converted into delight by the "disinterested" poetic power which, inspired by the Muse, converted the spectacle of life into matter for delight by organizing experience in beautiful language. This was the consummation towards which Arnold's poetry and criticism reached out, the transfiguration of reality by the "Greek spirit." [3]

Arnold's response to Greece, it might be added, is the response of Goethe, a response deriving ultimately from Winckelmann, who had declared that in Greece tragedy had been banished or, where not banished, transfigured into beauty.[4]

To say, then, that Arnold is not possessed of the classical tragic

---

[2] *The Complete Prose Works of Matthew Arnold,* ed. R. H. Super (Ann Arbor, Mich., 1960–   ), I, 2. This edition cited hereafter as *CPW*.

[3] *Matthew Arnold: A Study of the Aesthetic Temperament in Victorian England* (Bloomington, Ind., 1967), p. 185.

[4] See E. M. Butler, *The Tyranny of Greece over Germany* (Cambridge, Eng., 1935), p. 97. Warren Anderson finds little of the Greek tragic vision in Arnold: *Matthew Arnold and the Classical Tradition* (Ann Arbor, 1965), p. 252.

vision seems to me legitimate. The tragic vision that he did have is most concisely formulated in the famous lines which image man as "Wandering between two worlds, one dead, / The other powerless to be born." [5] This predicament is offered in the essay on Falkland as the condition of tragedy. It is a condition produced by revolution. In the tragedy of former ages finite man is made to confront a moral order that is the will of an eternal authority. In the nineteenth century the tragic confrontation is more likely to be not with eternity but with history.

The sense that there is something identifiable as process in history, and that the process exercises enormous control over the destiny of men, became endemic in the nineteenth century. In Nietzsche's view the historical sense had become a sixth sense in his time.[6] The idea of progress is a classic use of the historical sense. But in men who recoiled from the power of history to shatter what had been sacred and to endow what had been unthinkable, there developed what might be called a tragic sense of history. This sense became crucial in the work of men like Yeats, Henry Adams, and Spengler; Raymond Williams has explored its influence on a number of other writers including Brecht, Sartre, Camus, and Pasternak.[7] The tendency to see history as a tragic action is a commonplace in the twentieth century. The nineteenth-century version of this tendency as it exists in Matthew Arnold can be recognized once the general content of the tragic sense of history has been established.

I

Classical tragedy had always universalized its meaning by relating the forces that initiated tragic action to a cosmic, even a supernal order. The moral authority attributed to this order depended upon its superiority to the temporal world. The nineteenth century is marked by its feeling of utter estrangement from any such cosmos. But the nineteenth century evolved something like a cosmic authority out of history, the very record of man's temporal experience. Al-

[5] "Stanzas from the Grand Chartreuse" (ll. 85–86). Arnold's poetry is quoted from *The Poems of Matthew Arnold*, ed. C. B. Tinker and H. F. Lowry (London, 1950).
[6] *The Complete Works of Friedrich Nietzsche*, ed. Oscar Levy (Edinburgh, 1909–13), XII, 176. Hereafter, *CWFN*.
[7] *Modern Tragedy* (London, 1966).

though history as cosmic authority was used, for the most part, in the service of a simple moralism, there is the example of Nietzsche, who rejected historicism as "a disguised Christian theodicy" and discovered in history a tragic myth.[8] Kenneth Burke has pointed out the significance of Nietzsche's position and in doing so has illuminated an essential assumption in the tragic sense of history.

> If tragedy is a sense of man's intimate participation in processes beyond himself, we find that science has replaced the older metaphysical structure with an historical structure which gives the individual man ample grounds to feel such participation. What science has taken from us as a personal relationship to the will of Providence, it has regiven as a personal relationship to the slow, unwieldy movements of human society.[9]

Burke's statement isolates the essence of Arnold's tragic vision: Arnold attempts to generalize the fate of his protagonists by relating their experience to a tragic disorder in the movement of history.

The origins of the tragic sense of history can be detected in the turn which that traditional vehicle of the tragic vision, the drama, took in the eighteenth century. The rejection of the *tragédie classique* in favor of bourgeois drama was accompanied, as Arnold Hauser points out, by a new understanding of the tragic experience.

> Classical tragedy sees man isolated and describes him as an independent, autonomous intellectual entity, in merely external contact with the material world and never influenced by it in his innermost self. The bourgeois drama, on the other hand, thinks of him as a part and function of his environment and depicts him as a being who, instead of controlling concrete reality, as in classical tragedy, is himself controlled and absorbed by it. The milieu ceases to be simply the background and external framework and now takes an active part in the shaping of human destiny.[10]

When one's milieu is thought to be composed not only of contemporary institutions, but of an inexorable Time-Spirit as well, the basis of the tragic sense of history has emerged.

The idealized model of the bourgeois protagonist, at least as a man absorbed by his milieu, is the towering, frustrated, and alien-

---

[8] *CWFN*, IV, 120, and see Nietzsche's remarks on *The Birth of Tragedy* and "Richard Wagner in Bayreuth" in *Ecce Homo*, *CWFN*, XVII, secs. 1 and 4.

[9] "On Tragedy," in Corrigan, p. 285.

[10] *The Social History of Art*, trans. by the author and Stanley Godman (New York: Vintage Books, 1951), III, 89–90.

ated hero of the Romantic imagination whose suffering is caused not by any guilt of his but by a flaw in the world. For many a Romantic hero, the flaw in the world is perceived as a spiritual disease being spread by the historical process. The Romantic movement thus encouraged what George Steiner calls "a strain of melancholy historicism" and this receives its most characteristic expression in Senancour.[11] Arnold's tragic heroes owe a great deal to Senancour's effect on him: though he may find in them, as he found in Senancour, some inadequacy in their temperament, he does not find any guilt in their souls. They are not offenders; they are victims.

The hallmark of the historical process in the nineteenth century is revolution and it is by revolution that Arnold's protagonists are victimized. Revolution has itself seemed inimical to the tragic vision because of the putative optimism from which it springs. However, the vast challenge that revolution makes to orthodoxy cannot occur without a violent reorientation of values. For Arnold, as well as for others, a universe in a state of flux is, potentially, a tragic universe. In Karl Jaspers' succinct statement, "Transition is the zone of tragedy." [12]

Raymond Williams has made a book on *Modern Tragedy* a sequel to *Culture and Society* and *The Long Revolution*, and in it has argued that "important tragedy" has had "its most common historical setting in the period preceding the substantial breakdown and transformation of an important culture." [13] He proposes that once we see revolution as a pervasive animus within a culture, and not just as a single decisive conflict, the action of revolution and the action of tragedy become remarkably similar. "The tragic action, in its deepest sense, is not the confirmation of disorder, but its experience, its comprehension and its resolution. In our time, this action is general, and its common name is revolution." Williams is interested in arguing the authenticity of a certain form of tragedy, and this does not concern us. But his book is much to the point in suggesting that "since the French Revolution, the idea of tragedy can be seen as in different ways a response to a culture in conscious change and movement" (p. 62). Arnold's idea of tragedy is just such a response. The

[11] *The Death of Tragedy* (New York, 1961), p. 119. Erich Auerbach has defined the importance of Senancour in formulating the Romantic view of historical reality. *Mimesis*, trans. Willard Trask (New York: Anchor Books, 1957), p. 412.

[12] *Tragedy is Not Enough,* trans. H. A. T. Reiche et al. (Boston, 1952), p. 49.

[13] P. 54. The same idea is treated briefly in Georg Lukács, *The Historical Novel,* trans. Hannah and Stanley Mitchell (London, 1962), pp. 97–99.

response is determined by a tragic sense of history that involves these attitudes: the attitude that human destiny is profoundly shaped by one's milieu, that this milieu derives its organization from a historical process which is both magnificent and radically flawed, and that the participation of a heroic individual in this process, his confrontation with its revolutionary direction, may possess the dignity of tragic conflict.

II

"Falkland" was first published in *The Nineteenth Century* in March 1877, and two years later was reprinted in *Mixed Essays*. As in three of the other selections in *Mixed Essays*, Arnold approaches his subject through the work of another writer, in this case Clarendon. He takes Clarendon's admiration of Falkland as typical.[14] The aim of his essay, Arnold says, is to explain why Falkland, whose literary and political accomplishments were minimal, impressed Clarendon and has continued to impress later generations. His method is to show that Falkland has, in his character and situation, something which charms the imagination and something which appeals to the intellect. The method is notable since the fusion of imaginative and intellectual qualities is the grand synthesis in whose interest Arnold shaped his critical principles. The essay also makes clear that in Falkland Arnold found much of himself.

After giving an account of Falkland's early years, Arnold dwells on his retirement to a life of contemplation among a small group of friends at Great Tew, his Oxfordshire estate in the Scholar-Gypsy country. He was forced to abandon this life in 1639 by "Charles the First's expedition to suppress the disturbances in Scotland" (*ME,* p. 160). Falkland, a born constitutionalist, could not remain indifferent to so bold a display on the King's part. But he was also offended by the "violent proceedings of the court" during the Long Parliament. "He acted with the popular party. He made a powerful speech against ship-money. . . . He spoke vigorously for the bill to remove the bishops from the House of Lords" (*ME,* p. 160). In a word, Falkland had no liking for the feudal authority of which the King and his court were enamored.

---

[14] *Mixed Essays* (1879) and *Irish Essays and Others* (1882), 2 vols. in one (New York, 1894), p. 155. Hereafter, *ME.*

Having established this point, Arnold is ready to deal with Falkland's subsequent enlistment in the cause of the King. As the Long Parliament continued, the real motivations of the reformers made themselves known. The popular party "had professed at first that the removal of the bishops . . . was all they wanted; that they had no designs against episcopacy and the Church of England. The strife deepened, and new and revolutionary designs emerged. When, therefore, the bill against the bishops was reintroduced, Falkland voted against it" (*ME*, p. 161). To Falkland the vote was a matter of conscience, not a matter of politics. Arnold is setting before us a portrait of the disinterested man, a historical embodiment of those human qualities which all his life he had urged upon his countrymen. The King's party eagerly began to press Falkland into service, but he resisted because "he was for great reforms" and he "disliked Charles's obstinacy and insincerity" (*ME*, p. 162). However, feeling a sense of duty, he overcame his reluctance and accepted a position as Secretary of State. Several months later the Civil War broke out and, in September 1643, Falkland died a hero's death on the field at Newbury. During his tenure of office, he was extremely unhappy. As the war went on, this usually affable man, in Clarendon's description, " 'became on a sudden less communicable, and thence very sad, pale, and exceedingly affected with the spleen' " (*ME*, p. 163).

With this review of Falkland's career completed, Arnold proceeds to develop his thesis: "In the first place, then, he had certainly, except personal beauty, everything to qualify him for a hero to the imagination of mankind in general. He had rank, accomplishment, sweet temper, exquisite courtesy, liberality, magnanimity, superb courage, melancholy, misfortune, early death" (*ME*, p. 165). The ordering of this list is revealing: it begins in the seventeenth century but it ends in the nineteenth century. One is hardly surprised, therefore, that Arnold goes on to compare Falkland to "the Master of Ravenswood, that most interesting by far of all Scott's heroes." Like the Master of Ravenswood, "Falkland has for the imagination the indefinable, the irresistible charm of one who is and must be, in spite of the choicest gifts and graces, unfortunate,—of a man in the grasp of fatality . . . He is surely and visibly touched by the finger of doom. And he knows it himself" (*ME*, pp. 166–167). For the imagination, then, "Falkland cannot but be a figure of ideal, pathetic beauty" (*ME*, p. 167).

Arnold turns next to Falkland's ability to appeal to our "judgment." This involves him in a dispute with the opinion of Dissenters (he quotes from the *Nonconformist*) who see Falkland as weakly inconsistent compared to Hampden, whose death " 'was a martyr's seal to truths assured of ultimate triumph.' " Here Arnold has the real question of his essay established for him. *"Truths assured of ultimate triumph!* Let us pause upon those words. The Puritans were victors in the Civil War, and fashioned things to their own liking. How far was their system . . . an embodiment of 'truth'?" (*ME*, p. 168). Arnold's point, of course, is that humanity won no victory with the triumph of Puritanism. The "right answer" to his question, he says, is to be found in this passage from the historical writings of Bolingbroke:

> Cavaliers and Roundheads had divided the nation, like Yorkists and Lancastrians. To reconcile these disputes by treaty became impracticable, when neither side would trust the other. To terminate them by the sword was to fight, not for preserving the constitution, but for the manner of destroying it. The constitution might have been destroyed under pretence of prerogative. It was destroyed under pretence of liberty. We might have fallen under absolute monarchy. We fell into absolute anarchy.
>
> (*ME*, p. 169)

In other words, the alternatives offered to England for its historical development were equally catastrophic. History had become a tale of ignorant armies clashing by night, leaving a Falkland to wander in some crepuscular no-man's-land. "To escape from . . . anarchy, the nation, as every one knows, swung back into the very hands from which Puritanism had wrested it, to the bad and false system . . . of the Stuarts" (*ME*, p. 169).

Falkland's "judgment" is to be honored because he knew that the truth was not with the Puritans (for Arnold, of course, an indispensable discovery). He joined with the King because "he thought the triumph of the Parliament the greater leap into chaos" (*ME*, p. 173). What Arnold wants to make clear, however, is that Falkland was not saved by having been wise enough to choose the lesser evil.

> The final victory was neither for Stuarts nor Puritans. And it could not be for either of them, for the cause of neither was sound. Falkland had lucidity enough to see it. He gave himself to the cause which seemed to him least unsound, and to which "honesty," he thought, bound him; but he felt that the truth was not there, any

more than with the Puritans,—neither the truth nor the future. *This is what makes his figure and situation so truly tragic.*

(ME, p. 174; my italics)

Falkland's figure and situation are mirrored in *Empedocles on Etna, Balder Dead, Merope,* and in the unfinished drama "Lucretius." These works differ according to Arnold's various intentions, but the experience of Falkland is central to the form of each. Their common concern is with the spiritual erosion that comes of protracted wandering between two worlds. Using "Falkland" as a guide, one may say that the tragic condition for Arnold consisted in the loss of options that led to such wandering. Tragedy is the doom visited upon those noble and attractive men who are left without fulfillment because they are caught in a revolutionary climate in which the engaged forces have become hardened and polarized into equally repugnant camps.

Behind Arnold's meditation on this condition lies a deeply felt personal experience. Indeed, he does not conclude his essay until he has pointed out the relevance of Falkland's "figure and situation" to the Victorian world.

> One might sometimes fancy that the whole English nation, as in Chillingworth's time it was divided into two great hosts of publicans and sinners on the one side, Scribes and Pharisees on the other, so in ours it was going to divide itself into two vast camps of Simpletons here, under the command, suppose, of Mr. Beresford Hope, and of Savages there, under the command of Mr. Henry Richard. . . . What we have to do is to raise and multiply in this country a third host, with the conviction that the ideals both of Simpletons and Savages are profoundly inadequate and profoundly unedifying, and with the resolve to win victory for a better ideal than that of either of them.
>
> *(ME,* p. 175)

To understand fully why Arnold would see a historical order dominated by the contention between Simpletons and Savages as a tragic condition, it is necessary to recall his career as a writer. Arnold had begun his career as a man bitterly alienated from his world, but at some point he realized that the burden of isolation was too great to bear. By the mid-fifties he was convinced that he needed to engage his world rather than repudiate it. As Madden says, "Unlike the early letters, in which he warned Clough that it was better to do and be nothing than engage in philistercy . . . the

later letters and the criticism were firmly set against 'quietism' "
(p. 135). In carrying out this transformation, Arnold looked for an
indication that his age was not implacably hostile to all his values.
He saw, or thought he saw, such an indication in the *Zeitgeist* or
"the modern spirit." More and more he stressed the idea that the
historical process in the nineteenth century was building a mandate
for cultural renewal. In "The Function of Criticism," for example,
he clearly rested the case for his values on the argument that history
was working in their favor.

Arnold's optimism, however, was never very vigorous. If some
signs of the time promised that an era of rebirth was at hand, there
were other, more urgent signs that the revolution actually being pro-
moted by the historical process was dominated by the fruitless and
enervating clash between Simpletons and Savages. This clash appeared to Arnold, therefore, as terrifying for more than its power to
destroy noble souls. It was an action which seemed to demonstrate
that appeals to history were futile. The forces working for a meaningful and elevating revolution were viable, but, in the vast and
obscure operations of the historical process, their fruition was likely
to be indefinitely deferred as the revolutionary energy of the nineteenth century dissipated itself in the kind of struggle described in
"Falkland." This struggle issues in tragic consequences, then, not
only because of its inherently catastrophic nature, but also because
it makes faith in history—that last source of optimism for a man like
Arnold—almost impossible to maintain. This is what Arnold had
learned as he meditated upon the historical process during the decade of the fifties, when all four of the works I shall discuss were
written. Though he emerges in the sixties as a critic who made frequent appeals to history, his appeals are compromised by a persist-
ent tone of despair. Arnold's desperate need to believe in history, as
well as the agony of enduring ceaseless betrayals of his faith, are
poignantly evoked in the last paragraph of "Falkland."

> Let us return to Falkland, to our martyr of sweetness and light,
> of lucidity of mind and largeness of temper. Let us bid him farewell,
> not with compassion for him, and not with excuses, but in con-
> fidence and pride. Slowly, very slowly, his ideal of lucidity of mind
> and largeness of temper conquers; but it conquers. In the end it
> will prevail; only we must have patience. The day will come when this
> nation shall be renewed by it. But, O lime-trees of Tew, and quiet
> Oxfordshire field-banks where the first violets are even now raising

their heads!—how often, ere that day arrive for Englishmen, shall your renewal be seen!

(ME, p. 177)

III

Empedocles on Etna deals mainly with its protagonist's immense struggle to preserve his perception, as Arnold put it, of "the truth of the truth." [15] Empedocles is Arnold's most impressive portrayal of the guiltless hero brought to calamity by some inadequacy inherent in his temperament. But, while the poem's major interest is focused on the nature of Empedocles' failing, Arnold sees the crisis on Etna as precipitated by the revolutionary climate of Empedocles' age. He even has Empedocles suggest that in some prior, ideal age the pursuit of truth was attended by no adversity.

> And yet what days were those, Parmenides!
> When we were young, when we could number friends
> In all the Italian cities like ourselves,
> When with elated hearts we join'd your train,
> Ye Sun-born Virgins! on the road of truth.

(II.235–239)

The historical background that Arnold provides for the drama is derived from the same sense of history that produced "Falkland." The background is, one might say, an elaboration on what Arnold meant when he wrote, "I do not think any fruitful revolution can come in my time," a statement made in the midst of his work on Empedocles.[16]

Pausanius, who naively believes that Empedocles can allay "the swelling evil of the time," makes some pertinent remarks on the ethos of the age. "Broils tear us in twain," he says, "since [the] new swarm / Of sophists has got empire in our schools" (I.i.121–122). Pausanius himself represents precisely the kind of thinking that the sophists have risen to attack. He is a Simpleton of the first order, and is rebuked by Empedocles for his dependence on *Aberglaube* (I.ii.27). Arnold said that *Empedocles on Etna* displays an "impa-

---

[15] C. B. Tinker and H. F. Lowry, *The Poetry of Matthew Arnold: A Commentary* (London, 1940), p. 291.

[16] *Unpublished Letters of Matthew Arnold*, ed. Arnold Whitridge (New Haven, Conn., 1923), p. 14.

tience with the language and assumptions of the popular theology of the day" (*Commentary*, p. 288). Pausanius is the object of that impatience.

The sophists whom Pausanius fears populate the camp of the Savages.[17] Arnold saw gathered in this camp highly heterogeneous groups allied, finally, in their common appeal to rationalism. When Arnold invoked "the modern spirit," he was himself appealing, largely, to the spirit of rationalism. He recalled Pascal's warning to the Jesuits that the world no longer believes what is not evident to it. "In the seventeenth century, when Pascal said this, it had already begun to be true; it is getting more widely true every day." [18] But Arnold profoundly distrusted the rational intellect. This distrust is made clear by his hopeful and arresting claim that "the main element of the modern spirit's life . . . is the imaginative reason" (*CPW*, III, 230).

The Savages were those reformers, in religion, philosophy, and politics whose thought was guided by the *un*imaginative reason and whose sophistries would imprison the human spirit in a network of liberal cant. That Arnold saw the work of this group as in fact savage is evident in his denunciation of such enterprises as Bishop Colenso's Biblical criticism. Colenso seemed an omen: "all reticence is to be abandoned," a surge of liberal speculation will proclaim every doubt and broadcast its conclusions "in the crudest shape, amidst the undisciplined, ignorant, passionate, captious multitude" (*CPW*, III, 54).

A third host could never gain way among a multitude so infamously educated. Yet there was to Arnold an even more disturbing feature in the work of the Savages and that was its undeniable cogency. Empedocles is disabled by the influence of the sophists, as he shows when the problem of "mind" and "thought" brings him to a philosophical impasse:

> they will be our lords, as they are now;
> And keep us prisoners of our consciousness,
> And never let us clasp and feel the All
> But through their forms, and modes, and stifling veils.
>
> (II.351–354)

---

[17] For a view of the sophist-Pausanius duel similar to the one being developed here, see A. Dwight Culler, *Imaginative Reason: The Poetry of Matthew Arnold* (New Haven, 1966), p. 161.

[18] *God and the Bible* (New York, 1903; originally publ. London, 1875), p. 92.

The nullity of Pausanius on the one hand, and the efficacy of the sophists on the other, move Empedocles toward his lugubrious end. By evolving the historical framework of the poem out of the "broils" between the Simpletons and Savages, Arnold suggests how intimately connected this clash of ignorant armies was with his understanding of tragic action. Empedocles quite explicitly warns Pausanius to be "neither saint nor sophist-led" (1.ii.136). And in those climactic moments that depict Empedocles in his last anguish, we hear him rail at both sophistry and superstition.

> The brave, impetuous heart yields everywhere
> To the subtle, contriving head;
> Great qualities are trodden down,
> And littleness united
> Is become invincible   (ii.90–94)

And then:

> —Lie there, ye ensigns
> Of my unloved preëminence
> In an age like this!
> Among a people of children,
> Who throng'd me in their cities,
> Who worshipp'd me in their houses,
> And ask'd, not wisdom,
> But drugs to charm with,
> But spells to mutter—
> All the fool's armoury of magic!
>   (ii.109–118)

Incapable of wandering any longer between the two worlds denounced in these passages, Empedocles has left no place to receive him but the isolated summit of Etna. There he has no alternative but to confront the root of suffering in himself.

In 1855, Arnold remarked to Wyndham Slade: "I am full of a tragedy of the time of the end of the Roman Republic—one of the most colossal times of the world, I think" (*Commentary*, p. 342). This work was never completed, though Arnold showed interest in it for a period extending from at least 1849 to 1866. As the authors of the *Commentary* show (pp. 294–297), the connections of the poem with *Empedocles* are very close. The two figures shared in Arnold's imagination very much the same character.

"On the Modern Element in Literature" presents a Lucretius hardly distinguishable from Empedocles:

With stern effort, with gloomy despair, he seems to rivet his eyes on the elementary reality, the naked framework of the world, because the world in its fulness and movement is too exciting a spectacle for his discomposed brain. He seems to feel the spectacle of it at once terrifying and alluring; and to deliver himself from it he has to keep perpetually repeating his formula of disenchantment and annihilation.

(*CPW*, I, 33)

The sense of history that informs this passage belongs less to Empedocles or Lucretius than to Arnold. When Arnold attributed to Lucretius the need to discover an elemental reality immune to the historical process for the reason that the movement of history seemed by turns alluring and terrifying, and thus exasperating, he was synthesizing the major elements in his own attitude toward history.[19] We note, too, what Arnold himself pointed out: Lucretius lived in a revolutionary time.

Although we do not know a great deal about Arnold's conception of "Lucretius," certain interesting information has survived in the form of manuscript notes for the play. Dwight Culler has examined these and has reported their content. The notes refer mainly to historical background and deal with "the public careers of the various characters—Pompey, Clodius, Milo, Cicero, Scaurus, Caesar, and others."

> From these materials it is possible to gain a fairly good idea of what the drama was about. It was to deal with "the events at the end of 53 [B.C.]"—i.e. with the contest for power between the two political gangsters who represented the parties of Pompey and Caesar—T. Annius Milo and Publius Clodius. . . . Two pages in Arnold's notebook which divide the characters into "Milonians" and "Clodians" suggest that this struggle was to be the main political backdrop to the play. (p. 219)

By 53 B.C., Milo had for several years been the head persecutor and mob agitator for Rome's conservative party. His long and violent rivalry with Clodius, self-proclaimed deliverer of the democratic faction and chief ward organizer for Caesar, had erupted with re-

---

[19] David DeLaura, in an apposite comment, defines "the central intention of *Culture and Anarchy*" as the exposition of an ideal that would terminate "the historical oscillation of Hebraism and Hellenism . . . by somehow combining them in a higher synthesis." See his "Matthew Arnold and John Henry Newman: The 'Oxford Sentiment' and the Religion of the Future," *Texas Studies in Literature and Language*, VI (1965), 599.

newed brutality while both were seeking political office in the year 53. The division of Rome's political forces into Milonians and Clodians indicates that Arnold was contemplating the same kind of hideous struggle between an effete conservatism and a preposterous radicalism that he described in "Falkland." And he could discover in the event that brought their fierce antagonism to a climax a literal instance of ignorant armies clashing by night. At a little crossroads on the Appian Way Milo and Clodius, each in the company of armed guards, met and fought. Clodius, after finding retreat in a nearby tavern, was murdered at Milo's command and mob rioting quickly ensued.

Just how Lucretius would have entered upon this dismal scene we do not know. But we do know the place he held in Arnold's imagination. In what may well have been an important source for Arnold's work on "Lucretius," Mommsen's *History of Rome*, the following estimate is made of *De Rerum Natura*:

> It was composed in that hopeless time when the rule of oligarchy had been overthrown and that of Caesar had not yet been established, in the sultry years during which the outbreak of the civil war was awaited with long and painful suspense. If we seem to perceive in its unequal and restless utterance that the poet daily expected to see the wild tumult of revolution break forth over himself and his work, we must not with reference to his view of men and things forget amidst what men, and in prospect of what things, that view had its origins.[20]

Whether Arnold was influenced by Mommsen or not, some similar view of Lucretius he undoubtedly had in mind. One of the surviving fragments from the drama, which refers to Lucretius, proposes very much the same image of the protagonist as Arnold had used in *Empedocles on Etna*.

> It is a sad sight when the world denies
> A gifted man the power to shew his gift;
> When he is tied and thwarted from his course;
> When his fine genius foams itself away

---

[20] *The History of Rome*, trans. W. P. Dickson (London: Everyman's Library, 1921), IV, 553. Mommsen's work appeared between 1854 and 1856. We do not know exactly when Arnold read it, but it seems inconceivable, given his parentage and his plans for "Lucretius" in 1855, that it was not immediately. Arnold briefly compared Mommsen and Curtius, *CPW*, V, 258.

Upon the reefs and sandbanks of the world,
And he dies fruitless, having found no field.
(*Commentary*, pp. 345–346)[21]

While "Lucretius" lay dormant, Arnold was diligently at work on *Balder Dead*. The cosmic revolution augured by the death of Balder and known in Norse mythology as Ragnarok (the Doom or Twilight of the Gods) intimated in an ancient imagination a tragic knowledge of the conditions that beset Arnold's world. Arnold could hardly fail to respond to the *Prose Edda*, and he was pleased with what he had made of it: " 'Balder' perhaps no one cares much for except myself; but I have always thought . . . that it has not had justice done to it." [22] He had written it, for the most part, in 1854 and published it in the next year as the leading poem in his new volume. It was obviously, in his eyes, a major effort.

Balder Dead is throughout marked by allusions to the doom that has been prophesied for the Gods and Heroes in Valhalla's court. The anguished Hermod recalls the prophecy most poignantly:

> Yet here thou liest, Balder, underground,
> Rusting for ever; and the years roll on,
> The generations pass, the ages grow,
> And bring us nearer to the final day
> When from the south shall march the fiery band
> And cross the bridge of Heaven, with Lok for guide,
> And Fenris at his heel with broken chain;
> While from the east the giant Rymer steers
> His ship, and the great serpent makes to land;
> And all are marshall'd in one flaming square
> Against the Gods, upon the plains of Heaven.
>
> (III.471–481)

These lines envision the coming of the Giants from Jotunheim to overwhelm Asgard. The Giants are odious, of course, representing as they do the forces of evil. In Lok (Loki) Arnold had a uniquely interesting figure for the purpose of his theme. Although Lok was a Giant, he was permitted to inhabit Asgard for a reason never explained in the myth. The Gods loathed him and attempted to keep him in check. But Lok was not cowed. As Hela, his grim daughter and mistress of the underworld, boasts: "Yet he shall one day rise,

---

[21] Culler, p. 220, shows that these lines refer to Lucretius.
[22] G. W. E. Russell, *Matthew Arnold* (London, 1904), p. 42.

and burst his bonds, / And with himself set us his offspring free"
(II.222–223). There is more than a hint here of the movement of
popular democracy against the old order. Whenever Arnold treats
Lok and the Giants in *Balder Dead,* he concentrates on the vicious-
ness of their temper, as in Lok's vile speech upon seeing Hermod
return from his pathetic journey to the underworld to visit Balder
("Like as a farmer, who hath lost his dog / . . . So Hermod comes
to-day unfollow'd home" [III.8–19]). The impression that emerges
from the poem is that the victory of Lok and his tribe will signify
the victory of vulgarity and smallness of temper over a noble tradition.

But it must be pointed out, too, that the Gods are represented as
a good deal less than perfect themselves. Thor, in lamenting at
Balder's funeral, grieves most for the loss of Balder's pacifying
presence:

> For haughty spirits and high wraths are rife
> Among the Gods and Heroes here in Heaven,
> As among those whose joy and work is war;
> And daily strifes arise, and angry words.
>
> (III.79–82)

And Balder himself, speaking to Hermod in the underworld words
that are wholly Arnold's addition to the story, says:

> For I am long since weary of your storm
> Of carnage, and find, Hermod, in your life
> Something too much of war and broils, which make
> Life one perpetual fight, a bath of blood.
> . . . .
> Inactive therefore let me lie, in gloom,
> Unarm'd, inglorious; I attend the course
> Of ages, and my late return to light,
> In times less alien to a spirit mild,
> In new-recover'd seats, the happier day.
>
> (III.503–513)

Balder's description of life in Asgard is reinforced by an earlier reference to the pastime of the Gods and Heroes, which was to hack
each other to pieces during the day, knowing they would be miraculously cured at night (II.10–18).

Balder, then, may be found among that weary company of wan-
derers between two worlds. The peculiar circumstances of his death

dramatize, with mythic power, the ominous configuration of the *Zeitgeist.* Balder is killed by a blind God whose arm is directed by a savage Giant. They act simultaneously. Balder becomes the victim of this ironic cooperation because the Gods, convinced that Balder could not be harmed, decide in their curious way to make a sport of throwing axes and spears at him. But Balder *could* be harmed because Lok, the hidden impostume in the universe, had the malicious cunning to discover the only object to which Balder was vulnerable. The myth spoke to Arnold of perils he knew too well. He had been stricken by the blindness of one order to its fatal weaknesses, and stricken, too, by the impending success of another order destined to rule but formed and fostered in a spiritual wilderness.

The death of Balder is a mythic correlative of the theme of "Falkland." The connection between the two works is evident in the similarity of their conclusions. Speaking from the mists of Hela's realm, Balder invokes some remote future and the promise of "Another Heaven" that no one yet has reached. Anticipating a favorite phrase in Arnold's late prose, Balder declares that "Thither, when o'er this present earth and Heavens / The tempest of the latter days hath swept, / . . . Shall a small remnant of the Gods repair."

> There re-assembling we shall see emerge
> From the bright Ocean at our feet an earth
> More fresh, more verdant than the last, with fruits
> Self-springing, and a seed of man preserved,
> Who then shall live in peace, as now in war.
>
> (III.527–531)

These are the "saving remnant" or the "Children of the Second Birth." They regenerate the world by preserving from the vicissitudes of the *Zeitgeist* their integrity and their humanity. They are the third host. . . .

IV

Although Arnold wrote poems like *Sohrab and Rustum* in which the theme of "Falkland" does not appear, the theme clearly occupied a special place in his imagination. That he should come at last to make explicit in the eighteen seventies the theme of poems he wrote in the eighteen fifties can be explained by the fact that he had by then entered upon the period of his religious prose, whose main concern is the clarification of an ethical ideal secure, on the one hand, from the ineptitudes of orthodoxy and, on the other, from the subtleties of rationalism.[23] If man's moral life could not find this security, a time would come, Arnold feared, "when the mildness and sweet reasonableness of Jesus Christ, as a power to work the annulment of our ordinary self, will be clean disregarded and out of mind. Then, perhaps, will come another reaction, and another, and another; and all sterile" (*CPW*, vi, 127).

A sterile future, indifferent alike to the spirit of Falkland and the spirit of Jesus, is the tragic destiny toward which the historical process seemed to be moving with fearful alacrity. Arnold was prompted to this vision not by maudlin sentimentality but by the whole cast of his mind. It is illuminating to compare his sense of tragedy with that of another writer, Hegel, whose theory of tragedy is also grounded in a view of history. Hegel believed that genuine tragedy arises from the collision of two ethical forces, each of which is in itself justified. Tragedy shows the resolution of this ethical contradiction through the reconciling agency of Eternal Justice, which asserts itself against the "one-sided particularity" from which the contradictory ethical claims have issued.[24] The theory, an application to tragedy of Hegel's philosophy of history, has been criticized as providing, in effect, a rationale for optimism.[25] Out of the synthesis of the colliding forces comes a fuller apprehension of the absolute; the future is nothing but promising.

In Arnold's tragic vision the colliding forces, far from being justified, are both menacing, and man is offered a future not by participating in tragedy (not even in the Nietzschean or Yeatsian sense) but only by utterly and completely escaping it. Arnold sometimes seems to resemble Hegel by his frequent use of dialectical terms to describe reality. Hegel, however, is committed to the dialectic he postulates, and so he can make the tragic experience an ally in man's dialectical progress. But Arnold, in spite of all his apparent relativism, invariably concludes his discussions of dialectical structures

[23] See William Robbins, *The Ethical Idealism of Matthew Arnold* (Toronto, 1959), pp. 30–31.
[24] Hegel, *On Tragedy*, ed. Anne and Henry Paolucci (Garden City, N. Y.: Anchor Books, 1962), pp. 46–51. The passage referred to is from *The Philosophy of Fine Art*.
[25] This criticism is implicit in Nietzsche's attacks on Hegel (e.g., *CWFN*, v, 70–71).

by locating reality in an absolute that is the synthesis of his operating terms. The synthesis, "Culture" or "the imaginative reason" for example, is urged upon us as an ideal; we see that the dialectic has been created in order to be resolved.[26]

Arnold followed the impulses of his whole thought by defining tragedy as a condition in which access to the ideal is blocked by an antithesis that cannot be resolved. Tragedy ends in a sterile future because the essence of tragedy is historical stalemate. We may remain unimpressed by Arnold's attempts to make literary tragedy out of historical stalemate, but his failures, in my judgment, are failures in execution rather than failures in vision. Arnold's tragic vision led him to see the defeat of humanism, one of whose aims is to relate the inspirations of the past to the aspirations of the modern temper. In any historical movement preoccupied with the nullities of the past and the aberrations of the modern temper, this illuminating relationship cannot be made. It is something more than melancholy historicism to see the result as tragic.

[26] See DeLaura, n. 19 above, and Walter J. Hipple, "Matthew Arnold, Dialectician," *University of Toronto Quarterly*, XXXII (1962), 1–26.

Matthew Arnold

by John Holloway

III   The Value Frame

Arnold's preoccupation, as we have seen, is with what states of mind and what attitudes are desirable in human society, and more particularly with what is the desirable temper of mind in which to conduct an enquiry. Apart from a rationalist historical determinism, which plays a minor rôle in his thought, he had no metaphysics which might form apparent premises for the moral principles he wished to assert. But because a certain temper of mind—the characteristic urbanity and amenity of Arnold—is so pervasively recommended to the reader by the whole texture of his writing, he had a quite distinctive means for both making and justifying value-judgements in other fields. He could praise and justify praise, or condemn and justify condemnation, by suggesting that the topic or the belief under discussion would appeal, or fail to appeal, to the frame of mind which appears throughout his work as the fundamental good.

This distinctive method is to preface or envelop the main assertion in clauses which invite the reader to view it with favour or disfavour, and suggest grounds for the attitude he is to adopt. These *value frames,* as they might be called, serve several different purposes in Arnold's work, and are sometimes very elaborate. Although by their nature they do not obtrude on the casual reader's notice, yet their influence on the texture of argument is great. It should per-

"Matthew Arnold." From *The Victorian Sage: Studies in Argument* by John Holloway (Hamden, Conn.: Archon Books, 1962), pp. 215–19, 225–43. Copyright 1953 by Macmillan & Co. Reprinted by permission of Archon Books, The Shoe String Press, and the author.

Author's note: References quote the volume and page of the deluxe edition of Arnold's *Works* (15 vols.), Macmillan, London, 1903. The following abbreviations are used:

CA. *Culture and Anarchy* (1869); DA. *Discourses in America* (1885); EC. i *Essays in Criticism,* First Series (1865); FG. *Friendship's Garland* (1871); and ME. *Mixed Essays* (1879).

haps be said that when they are quoted, one feels at first that the mere trimmings of a sentence have been given and its substantial part omitted: but this impression rapidly fades. Consider an example first: "The aspirations of culture, which is the study of perfection, are not satisfied unless [what men say when they may say what they like, is worth saying]." [1] Here the two elements, first praise, second the grounds for praise, are fairly clear: first, a condition such as the assertion describes would satisfy one whose concern was for *perfection,* and this is as much as to call it *good;* second, it would satisfy the *cultured, aspiring* and *studious,* and these qualities— which *Culture and Anarchy* from beginning to end has endeared to us—are here the grounds of goodness. Compare "the flexibility which sweetness and light give, and which is one of the rewards of culture pursued in good faith, enables a man to see that. . . ." [2] Here one senses that the praise itself lies in "rewards," the grounds of praise in "flexibility," "sweetness," "light," "culture" and "good faith": these are the qualities of mind to which the assertion recommends itself.

Another interesting example of this device is, "Surely, now, it is no inconsiderable boon which culture confers on us if in embarrassed times like the present it enables us to [look at the ins and outs of things in this way] without hatred and without partiality and with a disposition to see the good in everybody all round" [3]—here not only can both praise and grounds of praise be located easily, but two further features appear: the first few words, and the reference to embarrassed times like the present, distinguish the author's tone and hint his personality; and the whole sentence not only puts Arnold's key word "culture" to use, but also enriches its meaning, so that it can be employed more compendiously elsewhere. Sometimes it proves vitally important to control the exact significance of these key-words: thus "essential in Hellenism is [the impulse to the development of the whole man, to connecting and harmonizing all parts of him, perfecting him]" [4] recommends a certain impulse, gives grounds for the recommendation through the word "Hellenism," whose import is already fairly well determined, and thirdly, amplifies this import itself. And this constant amplification of the import,

---

[1] CA. (vi. 15). In the following quotations the assertion itself, by contrast with the value frame for it, is put in square brackets or indicated by them.

[2] vi. 28.

[3] vi. 64.

[4] vi. 154.

or rather, constantly bringing it afresh to the reader's notice, allows Arnold to take liberties. He does so with "Hellenism" on the very next page: "that [. . .],—this it is abhorrent to the nature of Hellenism to concede"—the reader can keep in mind, though, that Hellenism even *abhors* with amenity.

It is easy to see how much these value frames do, not only to recommend assertions and offer grounds for them, but also to elucidate and recommend the temper of mind to which they seem true, and above all to show that their strength lies in their appeal to such a temper. "Do not let us fail to see clearly that [. . .]";[5] "when [our religious organizations . . . land us in no better result than this], it is high time to examine carefully their idea of perfection";[6] "[this] is so evident, that no one in Great Britain with clear and calm political judgement, or with fine perception, or with high cultivation, or with large knowledge of the world, doubts it." [7] On the other hand, there are negative instances that show equally clearly how some false proposition is born of the mental temper which Arnold condemns: "Well, then, what an unsound habit of mind it must be which makes us [talk of . . . as . . .]." [8] In either case it is clear that in cultivating this sense of a right "habit of mind" throughout his argument, Arnold equipped himself with a precise and powerful instrument for giving effect to judgements of value.

Some of these examples influence us less because they describe than because they exemplify the right habit of mind; that is to say, they affect the reader less through their meaning than through their tone. "Surely culture is useful in reminding us that [. . .]" [9] illustrates this tendency. But the significant point, for a comprehensive appreciation of Arnold, is how directly and openly this control of tone develops our sense of the author himself. "Keeping this in view, I have in my own mind often indulged myself with the fancy of [. . .]";[10] "to me few things are more pathetic than to see [. . .]";[11] "the philosophers and the prophets, whom I at any rate am disposed to believe . . . will tell us that [. . .]" [12]—above all, "now does any-

[5] vi. 25.
[6] vi. 27.
[7] ME. (x. 122).
[8] CA. (vi. 16).
[9] vi. 59.
[10] vi. 84.
[11] vi. 22.
[12] DA. (iv. 314).

one, if he simply and naturally reads his consciousness, discover that
[. . .]? For my part, the deeper I go into my own consciousness, and
the more simply I abandon myself to it, the more it seems to tell me
that [. . .]";[13]—Arnold is using forms of words that recommend his
assertion and that develop our sense of himself, all in one. And because the value frame serves this purpose, it is naturally adapted to
serve the complementary purpose: it also, often enough, adds to our
impression of his opponents.

These three functions may be performed together through simple
antithesis. One example quoted above was incomplete: Arnold
wrote, "So when Mr. Carlyle, a man of genius to whom we have all
at one time or another been indebted for refreshment and stimulus,
says [. . .] surely culture is useful in reminding us that [. . .]." Here,
words like "refreshment" and "stimulus," and the blunt "says," give
a tone to Carlyle's assertion, and the whole phrase controls our impression of Carlyle himself; but Arnold's "culture" is *useful* in
reminding (it does not simply say); and Arnold hopes to do something more significant than refresh and stimulate. This is very similar to "Mr. Roebuck is never weary of reiterating . . . 'May not
every man in England say what he likes?'—Mr. Roebuck perpetually
asks; and that, he thinks, is quite sufficient. . . . But the aspirations
of culture . . . are not satisfied unless, [. . .] culture indefatigably
tries . . . to draw ever nearer to a sense of [. . .]." [14] The contrast is
clear; Mr. Roebuck is too satisfied too easily. In the sentence "When
Protestantism . . . *gives the law* to criticism *too magisterially,* criticism *may* and *must remind* it that [its pretensions, in this respect,
are illusive and do it harm]," [15] Arnold's opponents are in the end
described explicitly, by the words here printed in brackets; but they,
and their critic, and the quality of their respective assertions, are already distinguished plainly by the value frame, as the italics make
plain. The complex manner in which "its pretensions . . . do *it*
harm" illustrates what was said above about forms of argument
should not, by the way, be overlooked.

Arnold is able to endow even the simplest negative with significant and contrasting tone: for example, "And, therefore, when Mr.
White asks the same sort of question about America that he has
asked about England, and wants to know whether [. . .] we answer

---

[13] CA. (vi. 181).
[14] vi. 15.
[15] *The Function of Criticism* (iii. 38); my italics.

in the same way as we did before, that [as much is not done]." [16]
Here there is a subtly suggestive difference in the sameness—White's
pestering is monotonous and stupid, Arnold is urbane and patient.
Almost exactly this construction comes again: "And if statesmen, either with their tongue in their cheek or with a fine impulsiveness,
tell people that [. . .], there is the more need to tell them the contrary." [17] Sometimes the denial is fuller: "When Mr. Gladstone in-
vites us to call [. . .] we must surely answer that all this mystical eloquence is not in the least necessary to explain so simple a matter." [18]
And while foisting one tone on his opponents, Arnold can provide
himself with quite another merely by changing the mood of his
verb: "Who, that is not manacled and hoodwinked by his Hebraism,
can believe that [. . .]";[19] "When Mr. Sidgwick says so broadly,
that [. . .] is he not carried away by a turn for broad generalization?
does he not forget [. . .]?" [20]—the question-form itself is all that conveys Arnold's presence, but it is enough.

This quite distinctive device bears both inwards, as it were, and
outwards: it suggests an attitude (and grounds for it too) that the
reader should take up towards the assertion that it introduces; and
through modulations of tone, it can do much to expand and sustain
our notion of the writer's personality, and of that of his adversaries.
In doing so it is one of the more important techniques creating that
bipolarity between himself and them which runs like an axis
through Arnold's work. . . .

V *Articulating the Argument: Arnold and his Opponents*

The desire to have distinctive names for whatever he is discussing
is a feature of much of Arnold's work. In chapter IV of *Culture and
Anarchy,* writing of the "energy driving at practice" and the "intelligence driving at those ideas which are . . . the basis of right practice," he says "to give these forces names . . . we may call them . . .
Hebraism and Hellenism." [21] Elsewhere we find "these favourite
doctrines of theirs I call . . . a peculiarly British form of Atheism

---

[16] CA. (vi, p. xxix).
[17] vi, p. xliii.
[18] ME. (x. 90).
[19] CA. (vi. 193).
[20] vi. 147.
[21] CA. (vi. 121).

. . . a peculiarly British form of Quietism";[22] or "I may call them the ways of Jacobinism." [23] How Arnold introduces the terms "sweetness and light," or "Barbarians, Philistines, Populace," [24] is perhaps too well known to need further remark. The effect of some of these is clear enough—they are what may simply be called *hangdog* names. But Arnold gives a reason for using the last three which indicates how they can contribute to the general texture of his prose. "The same desire for clearness," he writes, ". . . prompts me also to improve my nomenclature . . . a little, with a view to making it thereby more manageable." [25] This is important. To be clear and manageable are not new concepts in Arnold's work. They were the distinctive qualities of his tone, because he made this represent his temper of mind. By providing convenient names for his main topics, he not only influences our attitude through the nuance of those names, but articulates his argument with nodal points that soon become familiar, and easy to trace again. The kind of argument that is his at his most typical, an argument that moves gently forward with a smooth, unruffled urbanity, owes not a little to the familiarity of these coinages, as they so constantly reappear. They do not affect the logic of his discussion, but they transform its quality.

The same principle of style also operates more widely. Sometimes he organizes the whole movement of his thought round a single concept denoted by a single constantly recurring word: an example is the essay *Numbers,* through all the earlier part of which runs the idea of a tiny *élite* which is gradually to leaven the whole of society, and for which Arnold borrows the word "remnant." Much more frequently, a whole essay or a whole book is permeated by certain phrases for ideas which have an abiding place of trust in his mind. "Choose equality," "sweetness and light," "our best self," "spontaneity of consciousness," "a free play of the mind," "a full and harmonious development," "perfection at all points," "the best that is known and thought in the world"—these phrases return constantly, and contribute not only through their meaning, but also by their recurrence. They bring the argument nearer to that easy limpidity which its author wishes to recommend. By being careful to repeat himself verbally, Arnold brings into a bright light the essential simplicity of his thought. He orders his argument with familiar

---

[22] vi. 109–10.
[23] vi. 36.
[24] vi. 20, 79 ff.
[25] vi. 82.

landmarks. By this means he can hope to attune the reader to his message, just as the rich verbal confusion of Carlyle attunes a reader to an outlook which is quite different.

And the key phrases work to Arnold's advantage not only by their recurrence, but also by their origin. The first three in the list above are all borrowed—from Swift, Menander and Plato respectively. That they are borrowed in this way may add to the weight they carry, or it may not. But quoting authorities is so common in Arnold that it adds something quite distinctive to our impression of him as we read. Through it we see his modesty, his circumspection, and, oddly enough, his independence—not of mind, but of prejudice or strong emotion such as might provoke personal, precipitate, passionate comment. His use of authorities is a contrast to that of Carlyle. Carlyle overwhelmingly gives the impression of willingness to form and express opinions; his "quotations" are incidental and subordinate. The reader recognizes them as a game, an expression of the author's exuberance, his intellectual self-confidence and high spirits. Arnold really quotes, he does not invent authorities; and time and again his quotation is introduced at the crucial stage, and his authority constitutes the rock of his argument.

Consider some examples. The discourse *Literature and Science* begins by drawing entirely from Plato, and the fact that Arnold by no means expects his audience to defer to Plato's authority only emphasizes the very aspect of using an authority that we are discussing. Later, however, at a really crucial point in the argument, Arnold reverts to Plato. He has been arguing that men have in their nature four "powers" or tendencies, intellectual, moral, aesthetic and social; and that just as they have a need to relate the points of their knowledge into a system, so they have a need to relate these four powers into a system. How is he to suggest that this need is worthy to be given free play? At this point Arnold withdraws from his argument, and makes a quite fresh start to introduce the authority of Diotima in the *Symposium*. All desire, says Diotima, is at bottom desire for the good; "and therefore this fundamental desire it is, I suppose . . . which acts in us when we feel the impulse for relating our knowledge to our sense for conduct and our sense for beauty. At any rate, with men in general the instinct exists . . . and . . . it will be admitted, is innocent, and human nature is preserved by our following the lead of its innocent instincts." [26] In the address on *Equality*[27]

[26] DA. (iv. 333).
[27] ME. (x. 46).

Arnold goes even further. He begins by asserting that in the Burial Service is to be found the maxim "evil communications corrupt good manners"; but this is quite irrelevant and is never referred to again. Its only significance is to have been quoted from Menander; from whom another maxim (not already quoted anywhere) is "choose equality and flee greed." [28] With that the argument can begin; but as it proceeds, George Sand, Turgot, Voltaire, Burke, M. de Lavelaye, Hamerton, Bossuet, the Book of Proverbs, Pepys and Charles Sumner come one after another, if not to confirm an opinion, at least to provide one which can be discussed and examined. At every turn Arnold seems to avoid taking the initiative, or forcing on the reader something which is merely his own. He even makes his method explicit on one issue: "now the interesting point for us is . . . to know how far other European communities, left in the same situation with us . . . have dealt with these inequalities." [29] All the time he is building up our sense of an author who thinks others' opinions more important than his own.

Perhaps it is also worth mentioning, as examples of some special importance, the first paragraphs of the discourse *Numbers*, deriving as they do from one of Johnson's sayings; and the authority of Burke appealed to at a crucial stage in the essay on "The Function of Criticism";[30] and the works of Biblical exegesis, which constitute one sustained appeal to authority. But the method is so common with Arnold that it cannot be overlooked. Nor can we overlook its significance, if only because Arnold at one point states it: "I am grown so cowed by all the rebuke my original speculations have drawn upon me that I find myself more and more filling the part of a mere listener." [31] Arnold quotes the views of others, rather than express his own, because this modifies our sense of his argument and our view of him. This is not simply to say that he conciliates the reader by refusing to disagree with him, or instruct him directly. Had Carlyle attempted to conciliate in this way he would have had to be at special pains to prevent its being a quite false note, thoroughly discordant with his argument. Once again, our concern is not with a superficial trick of persuasion, but with some modulation of style which is a genuine aid because, through developing our sense of the

---

[28] x. 47.
[29] ME. (x. 52).
[30] See . . . pp. 210–11 [John Holloway, *The Victorian Sage*].
[31] FG. (vi. 391).

writer's personality, it genuinely mediates his point of view. That Arnold sometimes uses this method to excess is undeniable; the problem is to sense its point, where it is used aptly.

Quotation, however, is something which Arnold is fonder of inflicting on his opponents than on his models. *My Countrymen,* for example, opens with a grand review of those who have disagreed with him: the *Saturday Review,* Mr. Bazley (M.P. for Manchester), Mr. Miall, the *Daily Telegraph,* the *Daily News,* Mr. Lowe, John Bright, the *Morning Star,* they are all there, marshalled against Arnold, by himself. *Culture and Anarchy* begins similarly—with Bright, the *Daily Telegraph,* and Frederic Harrison; so does *The Function of Criticism.* In *Equality,* Arnold begins with his opponents—Disraeli, Erskine May, Gladstone, Froude, Lowe, Sir William Molesworth—the moment he has done with Menander. The modest, fair, urbane Arnold shows in what seems like an attempt to do justice to the other side. But Arnold uses his opponents further. He quotes from them, and uses these quotations over and over again; wanting his readers to notice less their meaning (which is often uncertain) than their general tenor and their tone. He thus equips himself with a set of—let us say catch-phrases rather than key phrases— that crystallize the views he is resisting in the same simple and recurrent form as his most favoured expressions crystallize his own views. Both the false and the true are presented with the same urbane simplicity; and while we see Arnold's personality behind his selection and presentation of these phrases, and behind their calm and genial reiteration, we see his opponents in the catch-phrases themselves, a little more clearly and a little more disastrously each time. His own account of these phrases was "profligate expenditure of claptrap." [32]

Certainly, he collected some gems. Frederic Harrison was unfortunate enough to "seek vainly in Mr. A. a system of philosophy with principles coherent, interdependent, subordinate, and derivative." [33] Arnold never really let him forget it subsequently. Harrison it was too who told the working class that "theirs are the brightest powers of sympathy and the readiest powers of action." [34] Under Arnold's reiteration, the readiness takes on a fresh colour, the brightness gets a little rubbed. Arnold also lets us savour Frederic Harrison's ac-

[32] vi. 258.
[33] vi. 299.
[34] CA. (vi. 101).

count of the middle classes, "their earnest good sense which pene-
trates through sophisms, ignores commonplaces, and gives to conventional illusions their true value";[35] and John Bright's "thoughtful-
ness and intelligence of the people of the great towns";[36] and *The
Times'* comment on East End children, "Now their brief spring is
over. There is no one to blame for this; it is the result of Nature's
simplest laws!";[37] and Robert Buchanan's account in the same context of "that divine philoprogenitiveness. . . . He would *swarm* the
earth with beings . . ." [38] and his "line of poetry":

'Tis the old story of the fig-leaf time.

The newspaper account of why a certain Mr. Smith committed suicide, that he "laboured under the apprehension that he would come
to poverty, and that he was eternally lost" [39] does service too; so does
Roebuck's "I look around me and ask what is the state of England?
Is not every man able to say what he likes? I ask you whether the
world over, or in past history, there is anything like it? Nothing. I
pray that our unrivalled happiness may last" [40]—which is a recurrent theme in *The Function of Criticism,* and reappears in *Culture
and Anarchy.*[41] "The Dissidence of Dissent and the Protestantism
of the Protestant religion," which began life as a motto on the
Nonconformist, is resurrected in both *Culture and Anarchy* and the
Discourses in America.[42] *The Times'* instruction to the British Gov-
ernment to speak out "with promptitude and energy" enlivens
Friendship's Garland,[43] where Lowe's fatuous "the destiny of England is in the great heart of England" also rears its empty head.[44]
The desire of the Bishops of Winchester and Gloucester to "do something for the honour of the Eternal Godhead" is saluted every so
often throughout *Literature and Dogma;*[45] and choicest of all perhaps, the "great sexual insurrection of our Anglo-Teutonic race," [46]

[35] CA. (vi. 101).
[36] vi, p. xxiv.
[37] vi. 201.
[38] vi. 202–3.
[39] vi. 157.
[40] iii. 23–5.
[41] vi. 110.
[42] vi. 23, and DA. (iv. 375).
[43] FG. (vi. 322).
[44] vi. 321, 371.
[45] *E.g.* vii. 4, 6–7, 33, 162, 183, 237, 239, 273, 288, 304, 364.
[46] CA. (vi. 190 and 191); FG. (vi. 306 and 307).

product of a disciple of Hepworth Dixon, is one of Arnold's most treasured literary possessions.

Now clearly, to introduce or reiterate so many phrases of this kind does not in itself render the texture of Arnold's argument simpler and more urbane: their straightforward effect is to make it more variegated and less urbane, and it will be necessary to see how he so "places" them in their context that this direct tendency is overruled, and the tone of the quotation is prevented from interfering with the tone of the main text. But what these quotations simplify for us is our conception of Arnold's opponents and their shortcomings. Time and again, always in the same way, they epitomize for us the defect of temper which is what above all Arnold is condemning. In one simple, natural perception, we see what this defect is; and every time they are repeated, the flaw they reveal shows a little more clearly.

The defective temper of mind which Arnold makes plain in what his opponents say, is also plain in what they do. He has no need of rhetoric or eloquence or complex argumentation: the simple facts are silently eloquent by themselves. For this purpose, inventions are as good as realities. *Friendship's Garland* is almost a series of fictitious anecdotes of invented revealing incidents—the Philistine Bottles giving Arnold's hero Arminius a jingoistic number of *Punch* in the train, or sitting in all the Deceased-Wife's-Sisters-Bill glory of his suburban residence; the Honourable Charles Clifford addressing the crowd from the footboard of his hansom; Dr. Russell of *The Times* vainly striving to get astride his warhorse; Cole's Truss Manufactory in Trafalgar Square—"the finest site in Europe";[47] Lord Elcho's hat—"to my mind the mere cock of his lordship's hat is one of the most aristocratic things we have." [48] The technique reappears in *The Function of Criticism*: trying to indicate the fault of temper in a whole series of writings, Arnold again takes a single striking case. "Their fault is . . . one which they have in common with the British College of Health in the New Road . . . with the lion and the statue of the Goddess Hygeia . . . the grand name without the grand thing." [49]

"The grand name without the grand thing"—Arnold is not unaware that, if he selects his opponents astutely, their names alone will

[47] vi. 249.
[48] vi. 262.
[49] *The Function of Criticism* (iii. 36).

be enough to expose their defects; and the method is ingenious, for although it says little explicitly, it makes one unable even to think of Arnold's victim without automatically seeing him in an unfavourable light. Beside the British College of Health we have "Cole's Truss Manufactory," [50] and the *"British Banner"*:[51] Arnold adds "I am not quite sure it was the *British Banner,* but it was some newspaper of the same stamp," which seems to show that he knew how the name, if only he could bring it in, would argue for him. It is not, however, only the sham pomposity of names that he enlists in his argument. "Has anyone reflected," he writes "what a touch of grossness in our race . . . is shown by the natural growth amongst us of such hideous names—Higginbottom, Stiggins, Bugg!" [52] In *Friendship's Garland* Arnold hits at the ludicrous, and also at the ugly, in his opponents, by invented names like "Viscount Lumpington," "the Reverend Esau Hittall," and "Bottles Esquire." [53] Elsewhere, for the same purpose, he selects from the material available. The result is Mr. Bazley, Mr. Blewitt, Mr. Bradlaugh, Mr. Blowitz (perhaps Arnold saw something banausic in the initial *B*), Miss Cobbes and Mr. Murphy. There are other names, too, which might be added to this list; and if any doubt remains whether the method genuinely colours Arnold's argument, a passage in *Culture and Anarchy* shows him somersaulting an opponent's argument of an exactly opposite kind: " 'Well, but,' says Mr. Hepworth Dixon, 'a theory which has been accepted by men like Judge Edmonds, Dr. Hare, Elder Frederick and Professor Bush!' . . . Such are, in brief, the bases of what Newman Weeks, Sarah Horton, Deborah Butler, and the associated brethren, proclaimed in Rolt's Hall as the New Covenant!" Evidently, Arnold hints, "Mr. Hepworth Dixon" is taken in by *not* the grand name without the grand thing. He goes on, "If he was summing up an account of the doctrine of Plato, or of St. Paul . . . Mr. Hepworth Dixon could not be more earnestly reverential." And now Arnold replies with his own selection of names: "But the question is, Have personages like Judge Edmonds, and Newman Weeks, and Elderess Polly and Elderess Antoinette, and the rest of Mr. Hepworth Dixon's heroes and heroines, anything of the weight and significance . . . that

[50] *Loc. cit.*
[51] CA. (vi. 96).
[52] *The Function of Criticism* (iii. 26).
[53] FG. (vi. 286).

Plato and St. Paul have?" [54] Here the first parade of names is enough to reveal the intellectual defects of Arnold's opponent, and the second is enough to conclude the discussion.

Arnold's comment on the ugliness of English names occurs in a passage when he is more serious, and is using a judiciously chosen example in another way, less to epitomize an outlook, than to reveal what it omits. It is of particular interest, not only because Arnold is using quotation, authority, the value frame, and example in a single integrated argument, but also because the contrast between the tone of the text itself and that of the inserted passages is particularly vivid. First, he quotes Sir Charles Adderley, "the old Anglo-Saxon race . . . the best breed in the world," and Mr. Roebuck, "the world over or in past history, is there anything like it? Nothing." Against this comes a simple quotation from Goethe, framed or "placed" by the phrase "clearly this is a better line of reflection"— we see at once how the counter-move is directed against a certain mental temper, and recommends its opposite. Then Arnold returns to his opponents. They would not contradict Goethe, it is simply that they "lose sight" of what he saw: they are carried away by controversy, they "go a little beyond the point and say stoutly—"; so long as they are countered in the same spirit, "so long will the strain swell louder and louder." Instead of this, Arnold proposes another spirit, which he sees in simply giving, without comment, one example, one simple fact. "Let criticism . . . *in the most candid spirit* . . . confront with our dithyramb *this* . . ." (my italics):

> A shocking child murder has just been committed at Nottingham. A girl named Wragg left the workhouse there on Saturday morning with her young illegitimate child. The child was soon afterwards found dead on Mapperly Hills, having been strangled. Wragg is in custody.

"Nothing but that," he goes on, "but in juxtaposition with the absolute eulogies . . . how eloquent, how suggestive are those few lines . . . there is profit for the spirit in such contrasts. . . . Mr. Roebuck will have a poor opinion of an adversary who replies to his defiant songs of triumph only by murmuring under his breath, *Wragg is in custody;* but in no other way will these songs of triumph be induced gradually to moderate themselves, to get rid of what in them is excessive and offensive, and to fall into a softer and truer key." [55]

[54] CA. (vi. 97–9).
[55] *The Function of Criticism* (iii. 25–7).

VI   *Irony*

In that passage the sustained contrast between two tempers of mind, one which Arnold seeks to recommend or maintain, and one which he detects in his opponents, is so clear that the problem of how he maintains this duality is now inescapable; and his chief method, beyond question, is irony. It is widely agreed that by irony an author can seem to the casual or uninformed reader to say one thing, but really say something quite different, clear only to the reader who is initiated or more attentive. But why should such a roundabout method of communication ever be employed? Usually it is hard enough, one would suppose, to convey one's meaning straightforwardly—why, not content with one difficulty, does an author invent another? Sometimes, perhaps, because irony can be like a sophisticated intellectual game, which writer and reader alike may enjoy for its own sake. But there may be a more substantial reason. Irony is a powerful and genuine instrument of persuasion. The meaning of a statement—especially one praising or blaming what is being spoken of, or doing anything of a similar kind—usually determines a characteristic tone in which it is reasonable to write or utter that statement. Outright condemnation of essentials tends to sound indignant, partial condemnation of details to sound mildly disapproving, plain description to sound detached, praise to sound admiring. These are no more than tendencies, but they are tendencies strong enough to be inconvenient to writers who, for example, particularly desire not to sound indignant or benignant; and irony is a means whereby a writer may say something in a tone that normally would be inappropriate to it. How easily that will influence the impression he gives the reader of himself, need not be laboured.

Quintilian says that to write ironically is to praise by blaming, or to blame by praising; of which two the last, of course, is the commoner. This is a method which Arnold uses fairly often. But, more than Quintilian's formula suggests, Arnold adapts the nuance of his blame, and of his praise too, so that it serves the general impression he wishes to give. The blame behind his seeming-innocent praise is relatively constant in kind; the praise itself is such that the uncomprehending complacence with which one fancies his opponents would receive it is enough to condemn them; there is no random hitting, because Arnold's irony is adapted so as to be exactly right for the general tenor of his work. Mr. Gladstone is

> that attractive and ever-victorious rhetorician[56]

who

> concludes in his copious and eloquent way.[57]

Other examples of this lethal innocence are

> the ingenious and inexhaustible Mr. Blowitz, of our great London *Times*[58]
>
> a hundred vigorous and influential writers[59]
>
> the newspapers . . . who have that trenchant authoritative style[60]
>
> this brisk and flourishing movement[61]
>
> our great orator, Mr. Bright . . . never weary of telling us[62]
>
> my nostrums of State Schools for those much too wise to want them, and of an Academy for people who have an inimitable style already[63]
>
> before I called Dixon's style lithe and sinewy[64]
>
> Mr. Lowe's powerful and much admired speech against Reform.[65]

There is no mistaking the trend of these passages. At first glance, they constitute just that genial, deferential praise which we might expect the urbane Arnold genuinely to give to his more forceful colleagues; but when the second meaning comes home, they are seen to diagnose just the smug, busy over-confidence that Arnold has made his inveterate enemy.

In this way Arnold makes his irony show both what he is like, and what his opponents are like. Images can do this as well as descriptions. In *A Courteous Explanation* he finds occasion to write: "(Horace) and his friends have lost their tails, and want to get them

[56] DA. (iv. 280).
[57] ME. (x. 49).
[58] DA. (iv. 311).
[59] FG. (vi. 368–9).
[60] vi. 353.
[61] DA. (iv. 321).
[62] iv. 285.
[63] FG. (vi. 353–4).
[64] vi. 306.
[65] vi. 369.

back." [66] The tail here is a symbol of political liberty. But it is not long before Arnold is utilizing its ironic possibilities:

> I think our "true political Liberty" a beautiful bushy object . . . it struck me there was a danger of our trading too extensively upon our tails, and, in fact, running to tail altogether. . . . Our highest class, besides having of course true political liberty,—that regulation tail that every Briton of us is blessed with,—is altogether so beautiful and splendid (and above all, as Mr. Carlyle says, polite) that for my part I hardly presume to enquire what it has or has not in the way of heads.[67]

Clearly, this beautiful bushy tail is—may one say it?—a two-edged weapon. There is a very similar passage at the end of *Friendship's Garland,* in the letter alleged to have been written by "A Young Lion" from Paris; the hand is the hand of a lithe disciple of Hepworth Dixon, but of course the voice is the voice of Arnold:

> While Sala was speaking, a group had formed before the hotel near us, and our attention was drawn to its central figure. Dr. Russell, of the *Times,* was preparing to mount his war-horse. You know the sort of thing,—he has described it himself over and over again. Bismarck at his horse's head, the Crown Prince holding his stirrup, and the old King of Prussia hoisting Russell into the saddle. When he was there, the distinguished public servant waved his hand in acknowledgement, and rode slowly down the street, accompanied by the *gamins* of Versailles, who even in their present dejection could not forbear a few involuntary cries of "Quel homme!" [68]

—by now the exact nuance of the blame behind the praise is beginning to be apparent, the warhorse has become a hobby-horse, and Arnold, once more, is depicting in his opponents the perennial source of his dislike.

The ambivalency between praise and blame that makes this passage ironical depends very much upon Arnold's giving it to an alleged author doing duty for the real author whom we sense in the background. It is one of his favourite devices to invent figures to speak his opinions for him. In part its contribution is like that suggested above for quotations and authorities; but in part too it sustains that divorce of tone and statement which is the office of irony.

[66] vi. 400.
[67] vi. 400–401.
[68] vi. 345.

Thus, in *My Countrymen,* it is "certain foreigners" who deliver the attack on English life—and a most forceful and outspoken attack it is. But Arnold appears only as their interlocutor in defence of England—an anxious, embarrassed, excessively reasonable defender perhaps (as Arnold was likely to be for any cause) but a defender all the same.

> I used often to think what a short and ready way one of our hard-hitting English newspapers would take with these scorners . . . but being myself a mere seeker after truth, with nothing trenchant or authoritative about me, I could do no more than look shocked and begin to ask questions. "What!" I said, "you hold the England of today cheap . . . ?" . . . Though I could not bear without a shudder this insult to the earnest good sense which, as the *Morning Star* says, may be fairly set down as the general characteristic of England and Englishmen everywhere. . . . I begged my acquaintances to explain a little more fully. . . .
> ". . . and intelligence [they said] . . . your middle class has absolutely none." I was aghast. I thought of this great class, every morning and evening extolled for its clear manly intelligence by a hundred vigorous and influential writers. . . .[69]

But he has just been sent a copy of a speech by Mr. Lowe, telling how the English middle class has been performing unrivalled exploits:

> I took it out of my pocket. "Now," said I to my envious, carping foreigners, "just listen to me . . . Mr. Lowe shall answer you. . . ." What I had urged, or rather what I had borrowed from Mr. Lowe, seemed to me exceedingly forcible, and I looked anxiously for its effect on my hearers. They did not appear so much disconcerted as I had hoped.[70]

In *Friendship's Garland* Arnold uses the same device to escape the awkward tone implied by what he wants to say. Here it is the mythical Prussian, Arminius von Thunder-den-Tronkh, who delivers Arnold's attack direct. And Arnold, speaking in his own person, writes:

> In confidence I will own to you that he makes himself intensely disagreeable. He has the harsh, arrogant Prussian way of turning up his nose at things and laying down the law about them; and

[69] FG. (vi. 363–9).
[70] vi. 369–71.

though, as a lover of intellect, I admire him, and, as a seeker of truth, I value his frankness, yet, as an Englishman, and a member of what the *Daily Telegraph* calls "the Imperial race," I feel so uncomfortable under it, that I want, through your kindness, to call to my aid the great British public, which never loses heart and has always a bold front and a rough word ready for its assailants.[71]

Arminius himself is a likeable figure, with his pink face and blue eyes, his shaggy blond hair, his ancient blue pilot-coat, and pipe belching interminable smoke. But although his personality may be likeable, it is very different from Arnold's, and he can do what would be disastrous for Arnold himself. Arminius and his creator go down to Reigate by rail, and in the carriage is, as Arnold calls him, "one of our representative industrial men (something in the bottle way)." When the manufacturer begins to talk politics, Arnold tries to soothe the conversation with "a few sentences taken from Mr. Gladstone's advice to the Roumanians." But—"The dolt! The dunderhead! His ignorance of the situation, his ignorance of Germany, his ignorance of what makes nations great, his ignorance of what makes life worth living, his ignorance of everything except bottles —those infernal bottles!"—that is Arminius's comment.[72] On another occasion, Arnold "runs" to appease him with a "powerful letter" by Mr. Goldwin Smith, published in the *Daily News,* and "pronouncing in favour of the Prussian alliance . . . 'At last I have got what will please you,'" cries he. But Arminius only gives a sardonic smile, and puts it all down ungraciously to the Prussian needle-gun.[73] "Your precious *Telegraph,*"[74] he says bluntly; and of *The Times,* "that astonishing paper."[75] Arnold contrasts Arminius and himself directly: "'You make me look rather a fool, Arminius,' I began, 'by what you primed me with. . . .' 'I dare say you looked a fool,' says my Prussian boor, 'but what did I tell you?'"[76] Even Arminius himself is made to emphasize just the contrast Arnold wishes us to see. "I have a regard for this Mr. Matthew Arnold, but I have taken his measure. . . . Again and again I have seen him anxiously ruminating over what his adversary has happened to say against his ideas; and when I tell him (if the idea were mine) that

[71] vi. 243–4.
[72] vi. 245.
[73] vi. 246.
[74] vi. 235.
[75] vi. 275.
[76] vi. 274.

his adversary is a *dummkopf,* and that he must stand up to him firm and square, he begins to smile, and tells me that what is probably passing through his adversary's mind is so and so." [77]

This example introduces one of Arnold's most characteristic manœuvres. Having introduced imaginary characters to speak for him, he recommends himself to the reader by interruptions that deny their excesses. Here he adds to Arminius's comment the footnote, "A very ill-natured and exaggerated description of my (I hope) not unamiable candour." In the Dedicatory Letter to *Friendship's Garland* he reports Arminius *verbatim* at length and then appears in his own person to retract: "I doubt whether this is sound, Leo, and, at any rate, the D.T. [*Daily Telegraph*] should have been more respectfully mentioned." [78] Arminius asserts dogmatically that Mr. Lowe is descended from Voltaire's insufferable optimist Pangloss: Arnold says that he believes there is no more than "a kinship in the spirit"—Arminius, he fears, was suffering from a fixed idea.[79] Later, Arminius records an unbelievable interview with Lowe. Arnold observes gravely that since everything he makes Lowe say actually appeared in Lowe's printed speeches, there is reason to fear that the interview was only imaginary.[80] When Arminius tirades against the style of the *Daily Telegraph,* Arnold writes, "though I do certainly think its prose a little full-bodied, yet I cannot bear to hear Arminius apply such a term to it as 'incorrigibly lewd'; and I always remonstrate with him. 'No, Arminius,' I always say, 'I hope not *incorrigibly.*'" [81] And Arnold has a delightful footnote to "Young Lion's" account of Dr. Russell mounting on horseback, in which he confesses sadly to not having found, in Russell's correspondence, quite the confirmatory descriptions that "Leo" spoke of. "Repeatedly I have seemed to be on the trace of what my friend meant, but the particular description he alludes to I have never been lucky enough to light upon." [82] Sometimes the retraction by Arnold is implicit in one word, as when, pretending to report Arminius's own words about his inventor, he writes "the newspapers which you are stupid [*sic*] enough to quote with admiration." [83]

[77] vi. 252–3.
[78] FG. (vi. 237).
[79] vi. 260.
[80] vi. 272 n.
[81] vi. 284.
[82] vi. 347 n.
[83] vi. 235.

The general effect of this device, however, might possibly be misunderstood. Only a child would see Arnold in these disclaimers alone. To a reader acquainted with the methods of irony the first rough impression of his personality, coming perhaps from these by themselves, is immediately corrected by a sense that he is author of the whole tissue of assertion dramatized in character and disclaimer with an edge to it. The undercurrent of meaning establishes that he is fully in earnest, has something he thinks it important to say. But concern for his message has not carried him away, and we see him still able to select exactly the most telling mode in which to express it; we are made to feel that there is no self-importance in a man who can so depreciate himself, even in play. Arnold develops both that first rough impression of himself, and the more complete impression, by explicit means: "for posterity's sake, I keep out of harm's way as much as I can. . . . I sit shivering in my garret, listening nervously to the voices of indignant Philistines asking the way to Grub Street. . . . I write with a bit of coal on the lining of my hat." [84] Here the reference to posterity reminds the reader that it is all a game, though one, perhaps, that serves a serious end. So it is when in *Culture and Anarchy*, he, after some havering, offers himself as an example of the Aristotelian extreme of *defect* in possessing the virtues of his own class. "Perhaps there might be a want of urbanity in singling out this or that personage as the representative of defect . . . but with oneself one may always, without impropriety, deal quite freely; and, indeed, this sort of plain dealing with oneself has in it, as all the moralists tells us, something very wholesome. So I will venture to humbly offer myself as an illustration of defect in those forces and qualities which make our middle class what it is." [85] He has done nothing, he confesses, to help uproot the evils of church-rates, for example. He quite lacks the "perfect self-satisfaction" current among the Philistines. "But these confessions," he concludes, "though salutary, are bitter and unpleasant." Here again the effect is two-fold: first, simply, of Arnold offering himself humbly as an example of defect; and second, less simply, of Arnold being sufficiently at ease and in command of himself (despite the unmistakable note of seriousness) to play a nice, an elaborate game of

---

[84] vi. 395–6.

[85] CA. (vi. 80–81). Cf. vi. 90, "I again take myself as a sort of *corpus vile* to serve for illustration in a matter where serving for illustration may not by everyone be thought agreeable."

self-apology that is also in a way self-praise. But these impressions
converge to make a single effect: that if Arnold ever had, like Dr.
Russell, a warhorse, it had the same history as the Cheshire cat, and
there is nothing left of it but the grin.

This double sense in the reader of Arnold first as simply a man
in the situation he describes, and second as a writer forming that
situation, arises also when he contrasts himself and his opponents.
The *Saturday Review,* he says,[86] maintains that we have "found our
philosophy"; but when obliged to travel almost daily on a branch
line close to the scene of a railway murder, Arnold found his fellow-
travellers so demoralized by fear that to begin with he thought they
disproved this. "Myself a transcendentalist" (the *Saturday Review*
has accused him of it) "I escaped the infection; and day after day,
I used to ply my fellow-travellers with . . . consolations . . . 'suppose the worst to happen,' I said, addressing a portly jeweller from
Cheapside; 'suppose even yourself to be the victim; *il n'y a pas
d'homme necessaire'* . . . All was of no avail. Nothing could moderate . . . their passionate, absorbing, almost bloodthirsty clinging
to life . . . but the *Saturday Review* suggests a touching explanation . . . the ardent longing of a faithful Benthamite . . . to see
his religion in the full and final blaze of its triumph." Here our impression is in part of Arnold living through the experience, and in
part of him as its gleeful inventor; and of his opponents, partly in
their fictitious guise of Arnold's jeweller, partly in their real form,
the *Saturday Review* that can write as it does in a world of branch
lines, railway murders, and fat poltroons. Nor is it impossible for
Arnold to modify his effect by giving us a sense of himself as writer,
even when he is most serious. The passage from *The Times,* quoted
above,[87] about conditions in the East End, is fitted by Arnold into
a personal experience. "This firm philosophy," he writes, "I seek
to call to mind when I am in the East of London . . . and indeed,
to fortify myself against the depressing sights . . . I have trans-
cribed from the *Times* one strain . . . full of the finest economical
doctrine, and always carry it about with me. . . ." [88] Then he continues by quoting Buchanan on the Divine Philoprogenitiveness, observes that this must be a *penchant* he shares with "the poorer class
of Irish" and continues "and these beautiful words, too, I carry

[86] EC. i (iii, pp. ix–x).
[87] See p. 128.
[88] CA. (vi. 201).

about with me in the East of London, and often read them there."
Buchanan's "fine line" of poetry, too, "naturally connects itself,
when one is in the East of London, with God's desire to *swarm* the
earth with beings." There is no mistaking the bitterness, but our
sense of Arnold himself is largely a sense of the control and the grim
humour that give to that bitterness this expression.

These more elaborate examples, then, confirm the view that Arnold uses irony to widen his range of assertion, while still remaining
within the range of tone that his outlook demands. It is one further
method whereby he conveys a certain temper of mind by example
rather than description, and it emphasizes once more that this temper is essentially what his work strives to express. This explains, too,
why he is so prominent himself in his writings, why his personality
is progressively revealed in a favourable light that the hostile reader,
revolting from Arnold's whole attempt to persuade, labels com-
placency. Nothing will rigorously prove this label mistaken; but we
tend less, perhaps, to call Arnold's method complacent, once we
have equipped ourselves with a proper knowledge of its detail, and
its function.

Matthew Arnold's Prose:
Theory and Practice

by Geoffrey Tillotson

III

Newman's sister Harriett noted that those who admired him came to write like him. That was Arnold's double fate—we have recently had a thorough examination of the long master-pupil relationship from Professor DeLaura,[1] on the score both of manner and matter (Professor DeLaura goes into the inspiration Arnold found in Newman's ideas not only on culture but, more strangely, on religion). Arnold himself was proud to acknowledge the two-fold debt, which, he confessed, people had noticed.[2] What mainly concerns us here is his debt for authorial personality since this had its effect on the wording as well as the matter of Arnold's prose.

Arnold tried to be as like Newman as possible without ceasing to be himself. He came to think that he was more like him than Newman could allow.[3] That he could think so showed how little he understood Newman, who was a churchman first and last and wholly, and who had even doubted if Arnold's father was a Christian. Arnold was spared a sharp reply such as Newman made on occasion, when his urbanity was simply so much polish on the blade. Arnold liked wielding the rapier more than Newman did. There was relish

[1] David J. DeLaura, "Matthew Arnold and John Henry Newman: The 'Oxford Sentiment' and the Religion of the Future," The University of Texas, *Studies in Literature and Language,* VI, Supplement 1965.

[2] Letter to Newman, 29 Nov. 1871, in *Unpublished Letters,* ed. Arnold Whitridge, New Haven, 1923, p. 57.

[3] Ibid., p. 59.

in his reference to "the controversial life we all lead," [4] whereas Newman lamented that the age afforded no time for *"quiet thought."* [5]

And yet Arnold found in Newman's occasional sharpness the inch he extended into an ell. The manner of writing sharply he learned mainly from certain small things of Newman, the chief of which was the series of seven letters printed anonymously in *The Times* during February 1841, and soon collected in pamphlet form as *The Tamworth Reading Room.* They show Newman at the peak of his brilliance—when he found occasion to quote from them in the *Essay in Aid of a Grammar of Assent* thirty years later, he ascribed to them "a freshness and force which I cannot now command." [6] Arnold knew these letters well, as we learn from the quotations from them entered into his notebooks. In them Newman came near to cutting a dash—anonymously, except for those who knew his authorship. Here is the opening of the sixth Letter to serve as a sample of the conversational writing that attracted Arnold: "People say to me, that it is but a dream to suppose that Christianity should regain the organic power in human society which once it possessed. I cannot help that; I never said it could." And which Arnold adopted. This comes towards the close of the "Function of Criticism at the Present Time":

> But stop, some one will say; all this talk is of no practical use to us whatever; this criticism of yours is not what we have in our minds when we speak of criticism; when we speak of critics and criticism, we mean critics and criticism of the current English literature of the day; when you offer to tell criticism its function, it is to this criticism that we expect you to address yourself. I am sorry for it, for I am afraid I must disappoint these expectations. [7]

And so on. The likeness to conversational speech is shown in little by Arnold's preference, which he shared with Newman, for beginning his paragraphs—let alone his sentences—with abrupt monosyllables. In this same essay five begin with "But," three with the conjunctive "For," and one each with "Nay," "Or," "Still," and "Again." In the Academies essay two paragraphs begin with the ex-

---

[4] *The Complete Prose Works of Matthew Arnold,* ed. R. H. Super, Ann Arbor, 1960– , III, 272.

[5] *Tracts for the Times.* Oxford and London, 1833–41, No. 41, p. 9.

[6] *Essay in Aid of a Grammar of Assent,* London, ed. 1895, p. 91.

[7] [Arnold quotation] *Works of Matthew Arnold,* ed. Super, III, 283.

clamation "Well," one being a "Well, then," and the other "Well, but." And in the passage about Ruskin I quoted earlier, Arnold's comment, it will be recalled, began with "Now, really, . . ."

Arnold designed his authorial personality to be striking, and his prose to match—a thoughtful critic must have pleased him by describing his style in 1883 as "perhaps, more striking than that of almost any other writer at the present time." [8] In his first prose piece Arnold was striking partly by being superior. He aired his intellectual superiority in such runs of wording as these: "What is *not* interesting, is . . . ," and " 'The poet', it is said, and by an apparently intelligent critic . . ." (in reprinting, Arnold dropped the insulting "apparently"), which is followed by "Now this view I believe to be completely false" (where the "Now" is an aggravation); a little later comes "And why is this? Simply because . . . ," and "No assuredly, it is not, it never can be so"; and again: "A host of voices will indignantly rejoin . . ."; and still again: "For we must never forget . . ." (he uses "we" but the guiltily forgetful reader knows at whom the finger is pointing). These things are more wholly wording than matter—they exhibit the manner of the egoist living in an age of controversy. That manner exists also in the many conversational intensives that Pater would have reckoned "surplusage"—"very," "signal," "very signal," "quite," "really," "profoundly." Along with these intensives go the vivid slang words, chief among which was "adequate," a term he had learned at Oxford.[9] Near to slang are other informalities Newman had given him the taste for—homely expressions like "got talked of" and homely imagery, such as (to draw on the "Literary Influence of Academies"): "that was a dream which will not bear being pulled about too roughly," and "We like to be suffered to lie comfortably in the old straw of our habits, especially of our intellectual habits." I may also note that, like Newman, Arnold prefers that when he strikes out an important phrase it shall be quiet rather than brilliant, as Carlyle's and Ruskin's mainly were —quiet phrases like "the dialogue of the mind with itself" (from the 1853 Preface) and "doing as one likes" (a chapter heading from *Culture and Anarchy*).

Slang, homely and quiet phrases, and homely imagery combine two qualities that Arnold liked to combine—the unassuming and the striking. He liked to blend two opposed æsthetic constituents,

---

[8] Samuel Waddington, *Arthur Hugh Clough*, London, 1883, p. 132.
[9] See G. and K. Tillotson, *Mid-Victorian Studies*, London, 1965, p. 134.

which can be variously described. His sentences are both suave and obstructed, smooth and attitudinising, flowing and striking, urbane and barbarous. They have as much of each kind as can coexist in a state of blendedness. They move easily, but among carefully placed obstacles. Newman described the gentleman as one who "never inflicts pain," and who "carefully avoids whatever may cause a jar or a jolt." Arnold's prose has it both ways by alternating long stretches of the gentleman with a flash here and there of the *enfant terrible*. He gives jars and jolts but so deliberately that we accept them as forming part of an individual version of the gentlemanly. To read him is to watch a performance of one who comes near to inflicting pain either without actually doing so, or with ointment so smartly applied that the sting melts away. Later on I shall qualify this description a little, but it is true in the main. The reader is confident that the writer knows where he is going, whatever bundles of sub-clauses, elaborate adverbs and detachable phrases are thrust into his open arms as he moves ahead. It may have been partly this spikiness of Arnold's that led R. H. Hutton to characterise his prose as "crystal," that of Newman's being "liquid."

Take as a handy instance of all this that note Arnold appended to the first paragraph of the "Function of Criticism at the Present Time" when it was collected in his *Essays in Criticism*:

> I cannot help thinking that a practice, common in England during the last century, and still followed in France, of printing a notice of this kind,—a notice by a competent critic,—to serve as an introduction to an eminent author's works, might be revived among us with advantage. To introduce all succeeding editions of Wordsworth, Mr. Shairp's notice might, it seems to me, excellently serve; it is written from the point of view of an admirer, nay, of a disciple, and that is right; but then the disciple must be also, as in this case he is, a critic, a man of letters, not, as too often happens, some relation or friend with no qualification for his task except affection for his author.[10]

Here there are two sentences with eleven interpolations of one sort and another.

That note also serves to illustrate another characteristic of Arnold's wording. Its flowingness is often secured by the use of the lubricating devices I have already mentioned—"I cannot help think-

---

[10] *Works of Matthew Arnold,* ed. Super, III, 258.

ing," "it is permitted that," and the rest. Spikiness exists in the run of the words in "might, it seems to me, excellently serve," where we not only have the severing of auxiliary from verb but the wide severing across a clause and an adverb—an adverb that is itself spiky because of its smart latinity and ticking polysyllables. In the second paragraph of the same essay we get: "should, for greater good of society, voluntarily doom."

The main means of Arnold's strikingness is this sort of unusual word-order. In the first paragraph of the essay I am drawing my instance from we have the striking word-order of "for now many years," but the expected word-order is often rearranged if not to that degree of strikingness:

> Many objections have been made to a proposition which, in some remarks of mine on translating Homer, I ventured to put forth; a proposition about criticism, and its importance at the present day. I said: "Of the literature of France and Germany, as of the intellect of Europe in general, the main effort, for now many years, has been a critical effort; the endeavour, in all branches of knowledge, theology, philosophy, history, art, science, to see the object as in itself it really is." I added, that owing to the operation in English literature of certain causes, "almost the last thing for which one would come to English literature is just that very thing which now Europe most desires,—criticism;" and that the power and value of English literature was thereby impaired.[11]

Sometimes his inversions become ludicrous—sometimes he does *not* avoid paining us! I have noted elsewhere that

> his article "The Bishop and the Philosopher" (*Essays, Letters and Reviews,* coll. and ed. F. Neiman, 1960, Cambridge, Mass., pp. 45 ff.) has one paragraph beginning "The little-instructed Spinoza's work could not unsettle . . ." and another beginning "Unction Spinoza's work has not. . . ." If he had been more conversant with Dickens's novels he might have been warned by Mrs. Micawber's example: " 'We came,' repeated Mrs. Micawber, 'and saw the Medway. My opinion of the coal trade on that river, is, that it may require talent, but that it certainly requires capital. Talent, Mr. Micawber has; capital, Mr. Micawber has not . . .' " (*David Copperfield,* chapter xvii).[12]

---

[11] Ibid.
[12] *Augustan Studies,* London, 1961, p. 118*n.*

And Arnold can pain us by making a sentence carry too many weights—as in this from one of his ecclesiastical essays:

> But as it is the truth of its Scriptural Protestantism which in Puritanism's eyes especially proves the truth of its Scriptural church-order which has this Protestantism, and the falsehood of the Anglican church-order which has much less of it, to abate the confidence of the Puritans in their Scriptural Protestantism is the first step towards their union, so much to be desired, with the national Church.[13]

A small instance of his deliberate clumsiness comes at the opening of this same essay: "I daresay this is so; only, remembering Spinoza's maxim that the two great banes of humanity are self-conceit and the laziness coming from self-conceit, I think. . . ." Surely it would have been better to write "coming from it" or "that comes of it," better because we stress the ending of a phrase and so here stress the unimportant word, the repeated "self-conceit." Arnold did not make enough use of our pronouns.

This clumsy but deliberate repetition introduces the most notorious item in Arnold's method of wording—his liking for repeating a word or phrase over and over again. For instance, having designed "regularity, uniformity, precision, balance" as a description of the prose achieved by the eighteenth century, he repeats it six times in the course of one (long) paragraph. Such repetition of invented terms is part of his method, but ill-advisedly so. He goes to ungentlemanly lengths in repeating them—his insistence as something of the *entêté* about it. This was a mistake Newman would not have made. Very occasionally Newman did repeat a word mercilessly, as for instance here:

> Again, as to the Ministerial Succession being a form, and adherence to it a form, it can only be called a form because we do not see its effects; did anything *visible* attend it, we should no longer call it a form. Did a miracle always follow a baptism or a return into the Church, who would any longer call it a form? that is, we call it a form, only so long as we refuse to walk by *faith*, which dispenses with things visible. Faith sees things not to be forms, if commanded, which seem like forms; it realizes consequences. Men ignorant in the sciences would predict no result from chemical and the like experiments; they would count them a form and a pretence. What is prayer but a form? that is, who (to speak generally) sees any thing

[13] "Protestantism and the Church of England," *Cornhill Magazine*, XXI (Jan.–June 1870), 200.

come of it? But we believe it, and so are blessed. In what sense is adherence to the Church a form in which prayer is not also? The benefit of the one is not seen, nor of the other; the one will not profit the ungodly and careless, nor will the other; the one is commanded in Scripture, so is the other. Therefore, to say that Church-union is a form, is no disparagement of it; forms are the very food of faith.[14]

It is one thing, however, to repeat a monosyllable, and another to repeat a mouthful. Arnold's repeated things are often whole phrases. It may be that his habit was partly encouraged by his love for Homer. He knew the old epics more closely than any other text, except the Bible—in his lectures on translating them he mentions that for two years they were never out of his hands. Homer sometimes repeats a word of great length, and it happens that a note in Pope's translation provides a comment on Arnold's practice. Pope's seventh note on *Iliad* xix reads:

VERSE 197 [of his translation]. *The stern* Aeacides *replies.*] The *Greek* Verse is

Τὸν δ' ἀπαμειξόμενος π῾οσέφη πόδας ὠκὺς ᾿Αχιλλεύς.

Which is repeated very frequently throughout the Iliad. It is a very just Remark of a *French* Critick, that what makes it so much taken notice of, is the rumbling Sound and Length of the Word ἀπαμειξόμενος: [*replies*]: This is so true, that if in a Poem or Romance of the same Length as the Iliad, we should repeat *The Hero answer'd,* full as often, we should never be sensible of that Repetition. And if we are not shock'd at the like Frequency of those Expressions in the Æneid, *sic ore refert, talia voce refert, talia dicta dabat, vix ea fatus erat,* &c. it is only because the Sound of the *Latin* Words does not fill the Ear like that of the *Greek* ἀπαμειξόμενος.[15]

Pope then proceeds to discuss the modern preference for avoiding the repetition of words, especially of polysyllabic words, and decides that "Either of these Practices is good, but the Excess of either vicious." In Arnold the repetitions are therefore vicious.

There is no offence, however, in what is as common in Arnold as his repeated phrases—his use of long words derived from Greek or Latin, and which if they are repeated, are not noticed as being so. They combine with the other spikinesses to enliven the general flow-

---

[14] *Parochial Sermons,* London, 1834–42, III, 213–14.
[15] *The Iliad of Homer,* London, 1715–20, V, 183.

ingness. To draw on a few pages at the beginning of the same essay on Academies we get "prominently," "pre-eminence," "nascent," "instrument," which are sprinkled here and there among the shorter Saxon words that carry the main burden of the thinking. Once Arnold ended an essay with one of these consciously favoured words. In the course of this same essay on Academies he invented a new sense for the epithet "retarding," the sense of slackening the pace of *intellectual* advance, and so can rely on the last word of his essay to come as a climax:

> He will do well constantly to try himself in respect of these, steadily to widen his culture, severely to check in himself the provincial spirit; and he will do this the better the more he keeps in mind that all mere glorification by ourselves of ourselves or our literature, in the strain of what, at the beginning of these remarks, I quoted from Lord Macaulay, is both vulgar, and, besides being vulgar, retarding.[16]

What was desiderated for the conversational style may be described as "lightness." It may come as a surprise to some that the word "light" was one of those greatly favoured in the mid-nineteenth century. Froude, we recall, called Newman "lightness itself," and Arnold begins one of his greatest poems with

> Light flows our war of mocking words . . .

When his *Essays* came out he hoped that Frederick Locker-Lampson would think its Preface "done with that *light hand* we have both of us such an affection for." [17] They were trying to make the English language more like music composed for that still fairly new instrument, the piano. Gide was to describe French prose as like a piano without pedals. We know how much Arnold admired French prose, but there is something about the English language that prevents its sounding like the amputated instrument of Gide's comparison. Newman and Arnold wanted their prose to be like a piano *with* a sustaining pedal, playing music—shall we say as like the favourite parts of Schubert's as possible, light, airy, flowing, wiry, pale-coloured, preferring to tinkle rather than to pound.

I have said that we make an æsthetic response to the personality shown in writing and that we judge it by the exercise of the intel-

---

[16] [Arnold quotation] *Works of Matthew Arnold*, ed. Super, III, 257.
[17] Augustine Birrell, *Frederick Locker-Lampson*, London, 1920, p. 127.

lect. Our æsthetic response to Arnold's authorial personality is one
of pleasure tempered by intellectual doubt as to whether or not its
pleasantness for the twentieth century was pleasantness for the
nineteenth. For some nineteenth-century readers it was decidedly
that—Arnold had his numerous admirers. Those admirers, however, were already, we guess, in possession of the sweetness and light
he was recommending. To the "elephantine main body" of the
bourgeoisie that Arnold was out to transform, he cannot have meant
very much. He sometimes used the term that Hazlitt had introduced
into the critical vocabulary—"tact." But how little of it he himself
exercised! *Culture and Anarchy* was met with critics who saw its
author as a mere æsthete looking rather out of place in the daily
throng of English business: Henry Sidgwick, for instance, ridiculed
him as a person "shuddering aloof from the rank exhalations of vul-
gar enthusiasm, and holding up the pouncet-box of culture betwixt
the wind and his nobility." [18] They might have stomached his urbanity if it had been like that of Newman—an, as it were, unconscious urbanity. They could not take the urbanity of one who pos-
tured. It seems that he made a big strategical mistake. The writer
who had most effect on English culture was William Morris. For
him urbanity was fluff and nonsense—unlike Arnold, he was once
mistaken for a sea-captain. But if Arnold was bent on being urbane,
he ought to have kept his urbanity more like Newman's, which always seemed to exist by right of second nature.

[18] "The Prophet of Culture," *Macmillian's Magazine,* XVI (Aug. 1867), 280.

Matthew Arnold: Poetry as Religion

by Vincent Buckley

. . . Arnold is the most sensitive—some people would say the most vacillating—of the great Victorian literary men. Yet his basic position is quite simple: it is the notion that poetry is, in some real sense, a religious act. What makes that position so baffling is the variety of his approaches to it. His attempts to specify and enhance the value of poetry show a many-sided concern, and take very different expressions. He wants from poetry teaching and consolation and moral vitality: the teaching and consolation and moral energy which many others in his time, as in ours, expected from religion. But just *what* poetry teaches, and *how* it teaches it, are vexed questions, even for Arnold. And, while we may find his concern with consolation a most subjective one, we can find it baffling that he should so often associate the work of consolation with the work of stimulating and enlarging man's affective faculties, his capacity for sentiment.

Sentiment! There is the weakness of Arnold. It may also have been the weakness of Victorian England; the preoccupation with religion, and the tendency to make religion manageable by reducing it to its "poetry"—to moral sentiment, in short—strike us, perhaps unjustly, as curiously Victorian traits. In a sense, religion overshadowed the Victorians, instead of penetrating them. Even the Oxford Movement was, on the whole, doctrinal without a metaphysic; hence the charges of ritualism could be made, with some plausibility, against many of its members. And the Victorians generally seem to have concentrated too exclusively on religious devotion as the summation, the natural result, of moral sentiment, far too little on the metaphysical and mystical insight which Christianity embodies, and to which it leads.

"Matthew Arnold: Poetry as Religion." From *Poetry and Morality: Studies on the Criticism of Matthew Arnold, T. S. Eliot and F. R. Leavis* by Vincent Buckley (London: Chatto and Windus Ltd., 1959), pp. 25–43. Copyright 1959 by Vincent Buckley. Reprinted by permission of the author and the publisher.

Consequently, when we say that poetry for Arnold is a religious act, and that its virtue consists in its being that, we have to be careful to specify further. There is, for evidence, that notorious passage from his earlier work which he quotes at the beginning of "The Study of Poetry":

> The future of poetry is immense, because in poetry, where it is worthy of its high destinies, our race, as time goes on, will find an ever surer and surer stay. There is not a creed which is not shaken, not an accredited dogma which is not shown to be questionable, not a received tradition which does not threaten to dissolve. Our religion has materialised itself in the fact, in the supposed fact; it has attached its emotion to the fact, and now the fact is failing it. But for poetry the idea is everything; the rest is a world of illusion, of divine illusion. Poetry attaches its emotion to the idea; the idea *is* the fact. The strongest part of our religion today is its unconscious poetry.[1]

The "high destinies" of which poetry is to be worthy are those which result from its being made a substitute, if not for religion, at least for much of the work which religion has traditionally done. For "a religion of preternaturalism is doomed";[2] and if virtuous conduct and moral sentiment are not to perish with it, poetry will have to take its place in a number of ways. The substitution apparently does not seem to Arnold as hard to achieve; for already religion and poetry have much in common; indeed, "the strongest part of our religion today is its unconscious poetry."

This is obviously a contentious notion; and it has been subjected to some sharp analysis. T. S. Eliot, for example, says of Arnold's writings on Christianity:

> They are tediously negative. But they are negative in a peculiar fashion: their aim is to affirm that the emotions of Christianity can and must be preserved without the belief. From this proposition two different types of man can extract two different types of conclusion: (i) that Religion is Morals, (ii) that Religion is Art. The effect of Arnold's religious campaign is to divorce Religion from thought.[3]

[1] *Essays in Criticism,* Second Series (Scholars' Library edition), p. 1. All further quotations will be from this edition.
[2] *Five Uncollected Essays* (Kenneth Allott [Ed.], 1953), p. 20.
[3] Arnold and Pater: in *Selected Essays,* p. 396. Among other very telling criticisms of Arnold's position is that of F. H. Bradley. See in particular the passages quoted by Eliot, *Selected Essays,* pp. 412-14. See also the opinion of a contempo-

The comment is sharp and telling enough; but is it quite accurate? Arnold is not simply concerned to preserve "the emotions of Christianity . . . without the belief." He seems also to have the intention of, as it were, redefining religion, so that it is no longer a *bond* between God and man, a bond of which doctrinal formulations are a necessary illumination and expression, but a state of mind. Religion, that is, has its own best guarantee in the state of mind which it is capable of inducing. In a sense, it *is* that state of mind; and doctrines become redundant in considering or advancing it. It is not precisely an emotion; Arnold is not seeking easy thrills; but his view is nevertheless defective as a conception. It has its root in what we may call a sentiment of the numinous, and it has its active effect in moral sentiment. For Arnold, religion can therefore be defined most nearly in terms of sentiment; and so, as I hope to show later, can poetry. Arnold claims, in other words, to be a refined sort of empiricist, and he shows himself to be a pragmatist of a kind at once subtle and ill-defined.

The various attacks made, by Eliot among others, on Arnold's religious position, and on his apparent confusion of religion with culture, seem to me utterly damaging. And his religious position —in so far as it is articulated as a conscious attitude or belief— must now seem to many of us little short of obtuse. The point of criticising his religious position at all is that his attitude to poetry is so closely associated with it, and gets from it a distinctive colouring. We are not really concerned with him as a religious thinker, but as a thinker about poetry. Yet he does, in some sense, regard poetry as a religious act. That is why I think F. R. Leavis is skirting too perfunctorily about the problem when he writes of the opening passage of "The Study of Poetry":

> The element that "dates" in the worst sense is that represented by the famous opening in which Arnold suggests that religion is going to be replaced by poetry. Few would now care to endorse the unqualified intention of that passage, and Arnold as a theological or philosophical thinker had better be abandoned explicitly at once. Yet the value of the essay does not depend on our accepting without reservation the particular terms in which Arnold stresses the

---

rary critic, F. R. Leavis: "Matthew Arnold as Critic" (*Scrutiny*, Vol. VII, No. 3). Leavis is able to say bluntly that "Arnold as a theological or philosophical thinker had better be abandoned explicitly at once."

importance of poetry in these introductory sentences, and he is not disposed of as a literary critic by pointing out that he was not theologian or philosopher.[4]

This is true; and it needed to be said, if only to refute the scornful view of Arnold propagated by such men as J. M. Robertson. "The Study of Poetry" *is,* as an exercise in literary criticism, largely independent of the pretensions announced in its opening paragraphs. Yet, in the perspective established by my present interest—an interest in Arnold's view of poetry and morality—the stress which Leavis leaves may be misleading. Arnold's claims for poetry are religious claims; and they are intimately connected with his expectations of poetry as a moral force. Consequently they colour not only the degree but the kind of trust which he places in it. The desperation of his moral demands on poetry is a direct result of his defective religious position. And the poets whom he most reveres are in a sense religious poets; they are the poets of an ethical-aesthetic sentiment which is, to Arnold's mind, the core of religion. Or, at least, they are poets who are capable of yielding, in some parts or aspects of their work, the kind of satisfaction which Arnold declares to be moral but which is associated in his mind with religion.

Whatever we may say of his religious position, his view of poetry in this essay is certainly not obtuse. Nor does he, as I have insisted, exactly identify poetry with religion. But his tendency to reduce religion to those elements in it which it shares with some kinds of poetry is a curious way of asserting the value of poetry: curious, if only because it generates an optimism about poetry which the history of this country has made to seem unfounded.

His case, as he announces it in "The Study of Poetry," seems to be something like this: It is in poetry that the essential religious, moral, and aesthetic sentiments coalesce and compose one thing. In the process, nothing is destroyed; on the contrary each of the three components, however alike they have all come to seem, has its true value enhanced. For, on its own, traditional Christianity stands self-condemned through its reliance on historical fact, through its tendency to derive doctrinal formulae from historical facts; ethical systems on their own are lifeless

---

[4] F. R. Leavis, *Ibid.*

and incapable of persuading to an action which is not only virtuous but also cultivated; and "aesthetic" interests, if they are
regarded as self-sufficing, lack a certain broadness, a depth of
humanity, do not conduce to *life*. But, blended as Arnold would
have them blended—in poetry—they provide the contemporary
wisdom of the race.

It is obvious, then, that Arnold believes himself to be freeing
both religion and morals from impurities, and to be preserving
at the same time the central tradition of Western poetry. And
we may sympathise with him. Religion and morals and poetry
cannot afford to be separated from one another. But neither
can any one of them afford to be reduced to either of the others,
or to be made a substitute for either of the others. And that is
precisely what Arnold unintentionally tends to do.

As well as this, we may find it alarming that he should place
so much trust on the *sentiment* of poetry, as of religion and
morals. I hope later to justify my own personal unease. Yet it
must be noticed here that what he wishes to retain of religion,
what he relies on poetry to communicate to the modern world,
is the religious sentiment, resting on a vague numinous awareness of God as other than ourselves, and as (in some very mysterious way) making for righteousness: religion without a definite
object, without a coherent intellectual formulation, without any
spiritual discipline proper to it. Rather, the spiritual discipline
will come from the ennobling effects of poetry; in such a conception, poetry becomes the *ascesis* of Arnold's "religion":

> More and more mankind will discover that we have to turn to
> poetry to interpret life for us, to console us, to sustain us.[5]

Now, this is really fantastic. It does not answer to the facts
of the past seventy years; nor does it, I believe, answer to the
facts of the world to which it was announced, to the England of
seventy years ago. And it has had, during those seventy years,
some unfortunate results; it has influenced Pater and I. A. Richards.
As Eliot points out,[6] it is not a far cry from Arnold's moral beauty
to its apparent opposite, the Paterian cult of experience. It is
not a far cry, either, to Richards' statement: "Poetry is capable
of saving us"—a statement which, in its emotive vagueness, in its

[5] "The Study of Poetry," *op. cit.* p. 2.
[6] *Selected Essays, op. cit.*

blindness to certain relevant facts of modern life, and in its suggestion of a religious feeling and terminology, is little short of irresponsible.

But it is necessary to go beyond an initial notice of Arnold's weakness, to go to other texts besides this controversial paragraph, before we may see what he expects of poetry. In this way, we may see what value he assigns to it. This value is first touched on by the suggestion, made throughout his writings, that poetry is a criticism of life. Perhaps the most moving statement of this position is to be found in his essay on Maurice de Guérin:

> The grand power of poetry is its interpretative power; by which I mean, not a power of drawing out in black and white an explanation of the mystery of the universe, but the power of so dealing with things as to awaken in us a wonderfully full, new, and intimate sense of them, and of our relations with them. When this sense is awakened in us, as to objects without us, we feel ourselves to be in contact with the essential nature of those objects, to be no longer bewildered and oppressed by them, but to have their secret, and to be in harmony with them; and this feeling calms and satisfies us as no other can. Poetry, indeed, interprets in another way besides this; but one of its two ways of interpreting, of exercising its highest power, is by awakening this sense in us. I will not now enquire whether this sense is illusive, whether it can be proved not to be illusive, whether it does absolutely make us possess the real nature of things; all I can say is, that poetry can awaken it in us, and that to awaken it is one of the highest powers of poetry.[7]

Several things about this passage are remarkable: not least its tone, which is very far from that of the brash manifesto or of the arrogant *obiter dictum*. And, despite Arnold's claim to have suggested the nature of only one of the two great kinds of poetry, the poetry of natural evocation, it is fairly clear that here we have the germ of his whole position. Poetry is interpretation, but it is not philosophical explanation or analysis. It is a kind of knowledge, and one which reaches deep into its object; but it is knowledge by sympathy, not by reasoning. It is feeling and thought together. It is a mastering of whatever forces in the world oppress us. It is a power of consoling us, of satisfying us.

[7] *Essays Literary and Critical* (Everyman's Library edition), pp. 51–52.

And it awakens in us a sense and sort of life. These are large claims, and they are claims which are closely linked to one another under the pressure of an unusually focussed mind and sensibility; I hope later to say something about each of them as Arnold develops it.

But he is dealing here with a kind of writing which is not based on moral ideas at all, which has for its genius a power of interpreting the world of "Nature." Guérin was not a moralist, and Arnold does not treat him as a moralist, just as, many years later, he is to make a similar distinction in speaking of Keats. Yet how morally satisfying he finds Guérin's "non-moral" poetry to be! The very movement of his prose, as well as his terminology, testifies that the satisfaction which he expects from this writing is of a moral kind. Arnold finds it morally satisfying because it induces in him—what he seems most to have desired —a kind of stoic calm which has elements of a pantheist exaltation. His position is, plainly, that all fine poetry is moral, whatever its agreed object; it is moral in the manner of its contact with that object, and in its consequent capacity to console the reader. The difference between a moral interpretation and a natural interpretation lies in their objects, not in their moral-poetic value. And all fine poetry is moral not by stating or explaining, but rather by representing its contact with reality.

The first mark of the best poetry, then, is something we may call by the very un-Arnoldian name of realism: that is, fidelity to experience. That is the first thing that ensures its moral content, whether or not it is dealing with a subject (such as the life and rhythm of nature) which seems to be neutral as to moral considerations. It gives the sense, that is, not only of the actuality of things themselves but also of their links with the life of man, and of their existing in some dimension which gives them a more than sensuous importance. It is an important point, though only a preliminary one; and I will not here complain of Arnold's characteristic refusal—in this case admitted—to ask himself what grounds there are for accepting the reality of such a dimension, of his readiness to be satisfied with the sense, the sentiment of contact and to assume the reality of its cause.

His emphasis even on nature poetry is of the most serious kind. We may see its seriousness attested in the very tone of his stern aside; "greatness can never be founded upon frivolity and corruption." [8] Yet he insists that the greatest poetry gets its authority from a different kind of contact with reality—with a reality which is itself moral rather than "natural":

> Poetry is the interpretress of the natural world, and she is the interpretress of the moral world.[9]

The second is generally the more significant; and Guérin, as Arnold has said, is the poet of the first. Yet even as he repeats this fact, he slips insensibly over the borderline into a virtual confusion of the two kinds which he has been at pains to distinguish. We must see in this unconscious striving after the fullest possible significance in the work of a favourite poet his own heavily charged preoccupation with morals:

> To make magically near and real the life of Nature, *and man's life only so far as it is a part of that Nature,* was his faculty. [My emphasis.]

Surely a "moral" activity, if ever there was one.

> To assist at the evolution of the whole life of the world is his craving, and intimately to feel it all.[10]

Surely, in a very real sense of the word, a moral aspiration. And Arnold goes on to speak of Guérin's poetry as expressing "the physiognomy and movement of the outward world." A physiognomy is a remarkably human thing for nature to have, at least when it is felt, as Arnold apparently feels it, to express more than a casual similarity and to denote a real identification of the two orders of being.

In fact, when we are faced with these passages, we can't avoid asking some rather perplexed questions: Is Arnold too exclusively preoccupied with morality, in his wide sense of the word: is this his King Charles' head? Do we not find here certainly a view of morals, but a view of morals in itself puzzlingly naturalistic? Is Arnold engaging in a sort of inversion of anthropomorphism, and an inversion which suffers from the fancifulness of that attitude? The questions are not idle ones, but Arnold's attitude is more complex than we realise at first sight. While stressing the moral orientation of Guérin's response to nature, he makes the comment

---

[8] *Essays Literary and Critical, op. cit.* p. 55.
[9] *Ibid.* p. 68.
[10] *Ibid.* p. 69.

that his management of that response is lacking in moral judgment:

> He is thus hardly a moral agent . . . he hovers over the tumult
> of life, but does not really put his hand to it.[11]

In the context in which it is made, we cannot be sure how
to assess this judgment. We cannot find out whether Arnold
really thinks the lack of a central judging energy (what might
be called explicit moral passion) is a debilitating one for a poet.
The essay on Guérin does not even suggest an answer. I feel
that what draws Arnold to so intimate a sympathy with Guérin
is his feeling of temperamental kinship; and that is possibly why
he does not launch any central criticism of what (judging from
his other critical essays) he would presumably consider Guérin's
deficiency: the lack of any attempt to penetrate beneath his
subject to a reality in itself moral.

It is when he analyses such a surely marginal case as Guérin
that Arnold's view may seem dubious, or his personal preoccupation excessive. The *idée fixe* is always the danger of the openly
moral criterion. But the burden of his approach, when he gets
away from the particular even in this essay, is a quite positive
one. It is the idea that great poetry deals generally with man,
with human destiny:

> [Poetry] interprets by expressing, with inspired conviction, the
> ideas and laws of the inward world of man's moral and spiritual
> nature.[12]

Poetry then is not, at its best, a descriptive art, but an evocative
one. It presents, by evoking it, the interior life of man—an idea
which is made ambiguous by the unexplained association of "ideas"
with "laws." But the presentation of interior states is only one of
the two ways in which it interprets man:

> In other words, poetry is interpretative both by having *natural
> magic* in it, and by having *moral profundity*. In both ways it
> illuminates man; it gives him a satisfying sense of reality; it reconciles
> him with himself and the universe.[13]

In both ways; but if we look at the development of English

[11] *Essays Literary and Critical* (Everyman's Library edition), p. 69.
[12] *Ibid*. p. 77.
[13] *Ibid*. p. 71.

poetry we may decide that the ways are more dissimilar than Arnold suggests, are used with very different imaginative frames of reference. The point is, that he clearly sees them both as having a moral significance and effect. I have already suggested that, for Arnold, even the "natural magic" is natural and magical only when he can see it suffused with moral meaning. And he always treats moral meaning, of course, in terms of its effects on the reader. Moral is as moral does. Most of us can with difficulty keep the moral substance of poetry (if indeed that is an apt way of describing it) distinguished from its moral effects. Arnold cannot keep them distinguished at all; his interest and interpretation are so subjective, his full insight so difficult to express without resorting to the device of explaining each of them by reference to the other. In the passage quoted, however, such words as "satisfying" and "reconcile" have a disturbingly therapeutic air about them; and it may be concluded that they hold good only for Arnold's ambiguous temperament and still more ambiguous spiritual situation. Is it the business of poetry to "reconcile man with himself and the universe"? Arnold's contemporary, the young lady who "accepted the Universe," is an absurd example of the same tendency of thought, though in Arnold the whole tone of his statement helps to redeem it.

And he certainly does not want a narrowly didactic poetry. He considers preaching a debasement of the poet's function. In the passage quoted, he speaks of poetry as *illuminating* man; it does not merely *tell* him his place in the universe, but it makes him *feel* it, gives him the sense and sentiment of it. It brings inward life and outward fact together in an expanding movement. Here again is the vaguely stoic note. It is Arnold's very Victorian emphasis on the "truth of feeling" which makes him distrust didacticism in the sense in which Johnson would have understood and supported it.

There is a philosophy implicit in these suggestions; it is a philosophy of naturalism informed by pantheism and sustained by a Christian sense of duty. It is not that Arnold can be labelled a naturalist, or a pantheist; for his criticism is not hamstrung by his leanings towards an eclectic *Weltanschauung*. It is, however, directed and in a way limited by them. The whole essay on Guérin impresses me as part of Arnold's lifelong meditation on his own vocation, and as a poignant expression of that meditation.

His chief positive point is that poetry is a criticism of life. "Criticism" means a sense for, an interpretation and healing representation. The whole transforming power of poetry is involved in it; and whether its object is the life of man or the life of nature, it is in fact valuable to the extent that it affirms something of the life and nature of man. Good poetry cannot help doing this. And Arnold characterises that life, with a becoming vagueness, as "moral and spiritual."

One of the most noteworthy things about this whole tendency in Arnold is the recurrence of the word "life," and of the suggestion that poetry is a means of vitalising some essential human faculty or inner aspiration. The greatest poetry "appeals to the great primary human affections: to those elementary feelings which subsist permanently in the race. . . ." [14] It treats them as its subject, and it appeals to them as they exist in the reader. Here, in the reminiscence of Wordsworth, we can see an attempt to reconcile man and nature; we can see, too, that strain in Arnold's thinking which makes him conceive in moral terms the sort of preoccupation with nature that Guérin has. In other places, he changes the emphasis by referring to the laws of man's nature. All the time, he is insisting that the ultimate value of poetry lies in its touching some profound truth of man.

It is in this sense that poetry interprets, and it is in this sense that "life" is the subject of the interpretation. But the promise of intellectual richness and vigour which is made here is never fulfilled. Arnold is, in fact, very evasive whenever the question arises of the *truth* of an interpretation. He demands that the truth of poetry be comprehensive and healing, not that it be (so to speak) true. Rather, his attitude is at root a complacent one, since it assumes as truth a characteristically Victorian congeries of ideas and attitudes to man, to moral action, and to nature.

However, it should be clear that "criticism of life" means interpretation, evaluation, feeling for, sympathetic sharing in; it does not mean carping at, or even rational analysis. And the suggestion (more natural to our contemporaries than to Arnold's) that a criticism of life is a criticism of society and its follies is not borne out, either, in his literary essays. What the phrase means can be seen more nearly when we reflect on the number of times, and notably in the essay on Gray, that he speaks of poetry as an

[14] Preface to First Edition of *Poems,* 1853: *Irish Essays,* p. 286.

"interpretation of the world." The immediate function of poetry
is a quasi-religious, not a social one. And the remarks on Burns, in
"The Study of Poetry," show us society as an enabling or disabling
condition of poetry, not as its chief subject.

It is in some such sense, then, that the criticism of literature
is the same as the criticism of life, and not (as Marxist critics
are always in danger of supposing) a criticism of a criticism of
life. We cannot keep too firmly in mind that Arnold's concern
for poetry is a concern for something which existentially preserves and exhibits and enhances the human situation. It is
a concern for a kind of life; and it underlies his habit of advancing his view through a consideration of actual poets and actual
poems. In considering them he does not look for a "truth" which
offers itself for debate, but for one which consoles and helps man
in a more central way. So Wordsworth's "poetry is the reality,
his philosophy . . . is the illusion";[15] and Arnold dissociates himself from the *Wordsworthians,* for, as he says, the works which
these devotees praise are generally those which have a certain
hollowness in them: those in which "the lines carry us really not
a step further than the proposition which they would interpret." [16]

Even in speaking of his "touchstones"—those mighty shadows
of achievement which have met as much misunderstanding as
his phrase about "criticism of life"—Arnold illustrates his central
concern. It is a concern to see the object—in this case, the nature
of poetry—as in itself it really is:

> If we are *thoroughly penetrated by their power,* we shall find that
> we have *acquired a sense* enabling us, whatever poetry may be laid
> before us, to *feel* the degree in which a high poetical quality is
> present or wanting there.[17]

The attitude which my italics emphasise is at the very antipodes
from that mechanical application of standards of which Arnold is
so often suspected. His interest, as I have said, is in whatever is
living and profound and accessible in poetry; it is this that has
moral interest, and a beneficent effect on man's capacity for living.

As he himself insists, his concern for life is a concern for morals;
and we shall therefore be interested in what he thinks and feels

[15] *Essays in Criticism,* Second Series, *op. cit.* p. 88.
[16] *Ibid.* p. 89.
[17] *Ibid.* p. 12. My emphasis.

about life. And here the promise of a dynamic or visionary force in his interpretation of life, of a forceful and metaphysical insight in his interpretation of poetry, is not fulfilled. When he says that poetry is "the noble and profound application of ideas to life," the ideas are generally moral ones, and the "life" that part of human experience which offers itself for illumination through moral ideas. We shall have, later, to ask what is the nature or status of these moral ideas on which he is content to rely; here, it is necessary only (and with a certain unease) to take note of their pervasiveness in his writings:

> If it is said that to call these ideas *moral* ideas is to introduce a strong and injurious limitation, I answer that it is to do nothing of the kind, because moral ideas are really so main a part of human life. The question, *how to live*, is itself a moral idea; and it is the question which most interests every man, and with which, in some way or other, he is perpetually occupied. A large sense is of course to be given to the term *moral*. Whatever bears upon the question, "how to live," comes under it.[18]

This may well be so, but it takes us no further towards any truth about poetry. It is not appropriate here to criticise the remarkable looseness of his language, in which, for example, the question "how to live" is said to be a moral *idea*. But the objection which Arnold is trying to anticipate is precisely the objection which Eliot brings: That Arnold, in his attempt to affirm two values at once, confuses life with morals. And he is striking at a real weakness in Arnold's position. Unless the meaning of "moral" is enormously broad, the injunction does not do justice to poetry; unless it is narrow enough to be recognisable as what it is intended to be, then there is no sense in using it at all. And, after all, do men, should men, go to poetry to find out "how to live"? All that Arnold can say in reply is that "conduct is three-fourths of life," and that Wordsworth is intensely moral because he grapples with the real issues of life:

> We say, for brevity's sake, that he deals with *life*, because he deals with that in which life really consists.[19]

And, again, he is open to objection. We may object that, while

---

[18] *Essays in Criticism*, Second Series, *op. cit.* p. 84.
[19] *Ibid.* p. 87. It is a further objection to Arnold's position that we can reasonably ask in what sense conduct is "three-fourths of life."

he turns an adequately critical eye upon received religion, he does not turn an adequately critical eye upon received morality; for in both cases, what he could take as "received" was what Victorian England took as received. But part of his dilemma is the need to preserve morals, and moral sentiment, while getting rid of what is bothersome to him in Christianity—its doctrinal content. Consequently, the sharply critical analysis of contemporary religion is possible to him only while he is passive, and even silent, in his criticism of "the best" contemporary moral thought and feeling. It would be a mistake to assume that *Culture and Anarchy* provides that criticism; it is not that criticism, but a substitute for it. Hence, we may see one reason for the pervasiveness of his concern with morals: that he needs it to replace religion. And if his view is lacking in dynamism, it is also curiously narrow. His choice of the word "moral" to indicate his concern, and his insistence on it, reflect a lack in him. So, as Eliot insists, does the choice of the phrase "criticism of life":

> If we mean life as a whole—not that Arnold ever saw life as a whole—from top to bottom, can anything that we can say of it ultimately, of that awful mystery, be called criticism? We bring back very little from our rare descents, and that is not criticism.[20]

Eliot, of course, has apparently misunderstood the sense in which Arnold uses the word "criticism," yet in so far as his objection is to the choice of that particular word to express what Arnold does mean, he seems to me to have made a telling point. Whatever poetry is or does, why characterise it by a word like "criticism"? Its use betrays a lack in Arnold, a certain shallowness which his subtlety of mind and his seriousness of diction serve, unfortunately, to disguise. It is the same lack which we detect in his recurrent use or suggestion of the word "moral." There is surely a way in which we experience poetry, a way which the word "moral" would seem quite incapable of fixing or defining. And it does not matter, in terms of my present discussion, how broadly Arnold claims to use the term. It is its very *choice* that is in question.

[20] T. S. Eliot: "The Use of Poetry and the Use of Criticism," p. 111.

It is interesting, by the way, to contrast Arnold's social interests to Newman's. When Newman looks about him at the contemporary world, he is immediately and overwhelmingly aware of a metaphysical conflict taking place between Good and Evil. When Arnold looks about him, he sees only a certain deprivation and a certain possibility; he sees anarchy and culture; and while the one is accidental to human life, the other has no more than a human origin and centre.

Other commentators have been disturbed by the pervasiveness of Arnold's moral preoccupation, and in a couple of cases the grounds of their unease are interesting. James Bentley Orrick, for example, charges him with misunderstanding and even flagrantly misinterpreting Goethe; and he attributes the misinterpretation to Arnold's desire to "moralise" the views of a man who was one of his literary heroes.[21] Another critic, Edwin Berry Burgum, sees Arnold as so immersed in his moralising that he simply repeats, in a cruder form, the semi-platonic didacticism of Philip Sidney:

> Arnold's conception of the Christian gentleman was only Sidney's ideal of the courtier, with the stress shifted from manners to morality.[22]

Now, I agree that there is a good deal of truth in both of these criticisms. But we must keep the issue in perspective. Arnold's view of virtue, of moral *behaviour,* is very little different from that of his father, or of any other virtuous, thoughtful, and cultivated Victorian gentleman. And if his sense of the moral reality of poetry ended there, he would have very little interest for us as an important literary thinker. But it does not end there. In fact, he does not ask of poetry that it *teach* such truths of behaviour, or stress the necessity of them. His expectation of it, though no doubt limited by the conventional nature of his moral ideas, is of a completely different, a more subtle kind. Certainly, he expects poetry to induce in the reader a capacity for action; and he conceives that action in terms of virtue; but he expects poetry to induce such a capacity by playing not upon the intellect or the will but upon the whole affective personality of the reader. Poetry variously calms and consoles, braces, edifies, ennobles, vitalises, gives joy. It is in its capacity to do such things that its moral reality consists. And it is in its being this sort of moral reality that its quasi-religious character lies.

Arnold's stress upon the power of poetry to "stay and console" is obviously connected with his recurrent feeling that life (in a

---

[21] J. B. Orrick: "Matthew Arnold and Goethe" (Publications of the English Goethe Society, New Series, Vol. I, edited by J. G. Robertson: Alexander Mooring, 1928). Orrick comments that "Goethe, however, as we have seen, goes to Greek art for a very different reason, for an escape from the 'moral interpretation' which Arnolds sees in him and in the Greeks alike": p. 49. Orrick's view seems to be that Goethe and the Greeks are naturalists, while Arnold is a moraliser.

[22] Edwin Berry Burgum: "The Humanism of Matthew Arnold" (*Symposium,* Vol. II, No. I, Jan. 1931), p. 97.

different sense from that in which conduct is three-fourths of life)
is capable of being an oppressive mystery, and that poetry is the
chief way of mastering it. We have already found him praising
poetry for its capacity to waken in us a sense of natural things
which allows us to be "no longer bewildered and oppressed" by
those things. And he exalts tragedy for a similar reason:

> For only by breasting in full the storm and cloud of life, breasting
> it and passing through it and above it, can the dramatist who feels
> the weight of mortal things liberate himself from the pressure, and
> rise, as we all seek to rise, to content and joy.[23]

In another place, he explicitly associates the notion of mastering
a hostile world with the interpretative power of poetry; he speaks
of our need "to master the world and give an adequate interpretation of it." [24] Here the term "master" plainly means not
only to get imaginative control of, but also to overcome the
world's capacity to disturb and oppress. And we must ask in what
sense Arnold conceives poetry to be the confronting of a mystery.
It seems to me that he does not want it to express an insight into
causes, but a sympathetic insight into natural or moral *states*.[25]
And he wants, in the poet and the reader alike, a balanced fusion of
thought and feeling sufficient to help transcend the vexations of
existence and its philosophical problems. It is here, in his sense of
philosophical *problems*, that he differs from Eliot, with whom
this strain in him has otherwise much in common. Yet he conceives the fusion largely in terms of *sentiment*. He wants poetry to
induce, as it reflects, *life*, vitality, under the aspect of serenity, disinterestedness, a largely stoic calm. It is in this sense that poetry
is to be a "magister vitae." But in practice, in his actual critical
judgments and in the reasons which he gives for making them,
this comes to look very much like ennobling sentiment, a sentiment
which is "bracing and edifying." If he is a Romantic, it is a self-
qualifying, self-moderating Romantic, who desires "classical" serenity in place of romantic excitement. Such serenity is a means of
gaining ground upon the chaos of life:

> No one has a stronger and more abiding sense than I have of
> the "daemonic" element—as Goethe called it—which underlies and

[23] *Irish Essays: And Others*, p. 221.
[24] *On the Study of Celtic Literature* (Everyman's Library edition), p. 110.
[25] v. E. K. Brown: *Matthew Arnold: A Study in Conflict* (Chicago, 1948), pp.
40–41, for a similar opinion.

encompasses our life; but I think, as Goethe thought, that the right thing is, while conscious of this element, and of all that there is inexplicable around one, to keep pushing on one's posts into the darkness, and to establish no post that is not perfectly in light and firm. One gains nothing on the darkness by being, like Shelley, as incoherent as the darkness itself.[26]

The concluding sentence is admirable; but the whole passage leaves quite unresolved the issue of the "daemonic" element and of what attitude the poet should take towards it. Here is Arnold preferring to reach some personal *answer* to the mystery of experience rather than to keep an intense sense of it and, in whatever way is suitable, to close with it. This is the social Arnold, the Arnold who fits so well into Victorian progressivism, the Arnold of the Enlightenment; for, in fact, his facile metaphor gives us nothing at all that is valuable, either for poetry or for life. But, despite this strain in him, he does not really expect poetry to be a means of enlightenment in the historical sense. The reproach which he made to Clough so early in his literary life represents a constant position:

> . . . all the exacerbation produced by your apostrophes to duty . . . to *solve* the Universe as you try to do is as irritating as Tennyson's dawdling with its painted shell is fatiguing to me to witness: and yet I own that to re-construct the Universe is not a satisfactory attempt either—I keep saying Shakespeare, Shakespeare, you are as obscure as life is. . . .[27]

Life is obscure, but part of its obscurity is its aspect of a hostile mystery which has to be overcome or resisted. The point made here is, that it is not to be most efficiently resisted through the systematising intellect, but through ennobling sentiment. The best answer to the hostile mystery is not understanding of its causes, but healing and consolation.

It is from a sense of a world to be "mastered" that the roots of Arnold's interest in the consoling power of poetry grow. The words *heal, stay, console,* are scattered throughout his criticism. Poetry has, it is true, the ultimate aim of steadying men for virtuous action; but its immediate effect is to stay and console.

[26] Letter to his mother, March 3, 1865: *Letters:* [ed.] G. W. E. Russell, Vol. I, p. 249.
[27] *Ibid.*, p. 63: Letter to A. H. Clough, 1847.

This is, in a way, a negative criterion. It is rescued from sterility in Arnold's criticism by always being associated with, or at least implying, something much more positive: the work of bracing and edifying. In the essay on George Sand, for example, he speaks of Nature as a source of "healing and delight for all";[28] and what is interesting in the remark is the open association of healing with delight. Again, he uses of Homer the words "tonic and fortifying."

Stated in this way, it all seems to have a very medicinal flavour, and to be, on that account, rather ludicrous. But Arnold intends it to appear medicinal; poetry is spiritual medicine. And it loses its ludicrous side when we notice that he is constantly driving towards the notion that poetry serves man by animating him:

> The cause of its greatness is simple, and may be told quite simply. Wordsworth's poetry is great because of the extraordinary power with which Wordsworth feels the joy offered to us in nature, the joy offered to us in the simple primary affections and duties; and because of the extraordinary power with which, in case after case, he shows us this joy, and renders it so as to make us share it.[29]

[28] *Mixed Essays* (1880 edition), p. 332.
[29] *Essays in Criticism*, Second Series, *op. cit.* p. 91.
This is Arnold towards the end of his literary life. But a very similar testimony is offered in *Letters to A. H. Clough*, Nov. 30, 1853, p. 146.

Matthew Arnold:
Conservative Revolutionary

by A. O. J. Cockshut

Arnold was the most versatile of all the Victorian sages; several aspects of his varied achievement are not relevant here. I do not consider him at all as a literary critic, and I make use of his poetry and sociological writings only when they seem to throw light on his religious views. No one, I feel, has ever summed up Arnold completely. It should be clear at the start that this chapter does not attempt to do so. His religious works, with which we are mainly concerned, may not be his best. If so, this is unfortunate, but it cannot alter the fact that they are far the most important for our present purposes.

Arnold wrote in the chapter on "Sweetness and Light" in *Culture and Anarchy*: "The great men of culture are those who have had a passion for diffusing, for making prevail, for carrying from one end of society to the other, the best knowledge, the best ideas of their time; who have laboured to divest knowledge of all that was harsh, uncouth, difficult, abstract, professional, exclusive; to humanise it, to make it sufficient outside the clique of the cultivated and learned, yet still remaining the *best* knowledge and thought of the time, and a true source therefore of sweetness and light." By this standard he was content to be judged; and so this chapter is concerned not only with what Arnold thought about Christianity and ethics, but also, and even more, with what he desired to teach the people about them. Arnold was not a subtle thinker, but he was a brilliant rhetorician; he is the most persuasive of all the great Victorians. And *Culture and Anarchy* alone could be turned into a complete text-book of all the arts of public controversy. For this reason I concern myself mainly here with the "popular editions" of his four overtly religious works and of *Culture and Anarchy*. The four are *Literature and Dogma, God and the Bible, St. Paul and Protestantism,* and *Last Essays on Church and Religion*.

Arnold's method in all his controversial works is essentially the same. He takes a striking new name for a well-known moral or social fact, such as Hellenism and Hebraism, or Barbarian, Philistine and Populace. He defines his term, but then gradually allows the definition to grow outwards until it seems to cover a whole tract of human experience. Thus Hellenism means primarily the love of knowledge, and Hebraism fidelity to moral principle; but their total meaning is known only to those who have read the whole of *Culture and Anarchy*. This accumulative type of definition, and the curious but effective circular style of arguing that goes with it make it very difficult to summarise Arnold's thought adequately. But his religious position seems to be mainly based on the following assumptions:

1. There is a general tendency in the universe that makes for righteousness.
2. Jesus was always over the heads of his reporters.
3. Miracles do not happen.
4. Conduct is three-fourths of life, and charity and sexual purity are the key principles of conduct.

Very little argument is given in support of any of these propositions; and the first and the third, in particular, stand with no support at all. They are simply axioms.

A fifth assumption is vaguer, and more difficult to assess, but is just as important to his argument. It can be summed up roughly as the irreversible power and progress of the spirit of the age. "But now," he says grandly at the conclusion of *Culture and Anarchy,* "we go the way the human race is going, while they [our liberal practitioners] abolish the Irish Church by the power of the Nonconformists' antipathy to establishments, or they enable a man to marry his deceased wife's sister."

More specifically in the chapter on "Our Masses and the Bible" in *Literature and Dogma,* he quotes Cardinal Newman: "The Fathers recognised a certain truth lying hid under the tenor of the sacred text as a whole, and showing itself more or less in this verse or that, as it might be. The Fathers *might have traditionary information* of the general drift of the inspired text which we have not." And Arnold comments: "Born into the world twenty years later, and touched with the breath of the 'Zeit-Geist,' how would this exquisite and delicate genius have been himself the first to feel the unsoundness of all this."

"Twenty years later." In round numbers this is the period of time between the birth of Newman in 1801, and the birth of Arnold in 1822. The Spirit of the Age, in fact, is on Arnold's side. This is very telling, especially as it enables Arnold to preserve a kind of modesty in contradicting a man whose genius he really (and not as a mere compliment) loved and reverenced. The reader may easily be cajoled into thinking that this is a case of the familiar contrast between foresight and hindsight—as if Arnold were saying, "So-and-so quite reasonably supposed during the war that there would be widespread unemployment when it ended. We now know, of course, in the sixties. . . ." But it is not really like that at all. In matters of permanent truth (and Arnold was explicitly trying to establish the permanent truth about religion) the Spirit of the age is a most uncertain ally. If Arnold had this great advantage over Newman because he was born in 1822, and Newman in 1801, what advantage might not a man born in 1840 have over both? Thomas Hardy was born in 1840, and he thought there was a general tendency in the universe making against righteousness. He might regard Arnold with the same reverent pity that Arnold bestowed on Newman. How was it that this extremely obvious point escaped the attention of Arnold's acute and well-trained mind? It escaped his attention because he assumed that any broad tendency that had shown itself over a considerable period could only continue to develop and increase. Thus Arnold always writes as if he knows the future. People believed in miracles two hundred years ago. Some disbelieve and some doubt them now. Therefore still more will doubt and disbelieve in the next generation. Arnold felt safe in leaving the vindication of his argument to the unborn. In the short run, his feel of the way the world was going served him well; he was more sensitive perhaps than any of his contemporaries to the currents of the nineteenth century. But no one can really predict the future accurately and in detail. And the study of the past does not support the view that tendencies once begun can never be reversed. If it did, we should be living under Nazi rule to-day.

II

The first problem about Arnold's religious teaching is; if Arnold disbelieved in miracles and thought dogmatic theology useless, why did he wish to attach his moral system to Christianity at all? His two central moral tenets were charity and purity; and his constant claim for them was that they were verifiable. If you follow Arnold's moral doctrine, you will know by experience that it is right. Jesus, therefore, according to Arnold, did not reveal anything, he discovered certain inherent, verifiable truths about human nature and about life itself. And these can be summarised by saying that charity and purity work, and lead to happiness.

All this is rather conventional; and many Victorian agnostics would have said something of the same sort. So it is essential to grasp the very great difference between Arnold and the ordinary agnostic whether in Arnold's time or ours, who will so often say that he accepts Christian morality, but not Christian dogma. At first sight Arnold, with his rejection of dogma and miracle, his rather irresponsible editing of the gospels to make them agree with himself, seems to belong to a familiar type. He did not; the difference is crucial, yet it is not easy to explain.

Very roughly the difference can be summarised by saying that Arnold's system really was religious, though not, in any acceptable, historical sense, Christian. Arnold himself defined religion as "morality touched with emotion." This has usually been dismissed as entirely inadequate to describe religion as it has actually been in the world. It has also been dismissed, less justly, as a dim and tedious precept for living. *Morality* and *emotion* are heavy words; they convey little excitement. Arnold's phrase is apt to remind us of the extra fillip given to school discipline by "the honour of the house" or by singing "Forty years on." But when one returns to the definition after reading through Arnold's religious works, one finds that the emotion he meant was very deep indeed.

Arnold was not just another high-minded agnostic, using selected parts of the Christian moral tradition for his own purposes. Despite his rejection of miracles, he believed with all his being in the death and resurrection of the self, the need for each soul to be baptised into Christ's death. He believed, in his own way, in the truth of the text, which stands as an epigraph to *The Brothers Karamazov*, "Except a corn of wheat fall into the ground and die, it abideth alone: but if it die, it bringeth forth much fruit." I mention Dostoevsky, not because even his literary greatness could add authority to such a text, but because it may help to convey something of Arnold's loneliness in the Victorian scene. In a Protestant country like England the Bible is a common possession of all. People quote it without believing it, or even, as they quote Shakespeare, without knowing that they do so. But alone among Dostoevsky's agnostic contemporaries in England, Arnold seems to feel the psychological impact of the Christian idea of death and resurrection in its full poignancy. Arnold is a lonely figure, for he is separated from Newman and Pusey by his conviction that miracles do not happen, and from Huxley and Herbert Spencer by his deeply-felt awareness of the meaning certain key miracles could have for man's soul. In fact, if we make due allowance for the differences of national temperament, for Arnold's urbanity of expression and Dostoevsky's feverish intensity, Arnold is very near to Shatov, the Slavophil hero in *The Devils*. Arnold, like him, believed in Christ, but could hardly believe in God.

It is in his attitude to the Crucifixion that Arnold's religious ideas stand out most clearly in their lonely grandeur. For the Christian, the Crucifixion, though profoundly important, does not make sense alone. The Resurrection completes its meaning. For a man like Mill, and for most of those who in the nineteenth century saw themselves as followers of Christian moral teaching without being believers, the Crucifixion is a tragedy. It is the most terrible example that history records, but similar in kind to a thousand others, of what happens to goodness when authority or the passions of a mob wish to suppress it.

Arnold takes a third and perfectly distinct view. The Crucifixion for him is the final, most exacting test of the moral doctrine that we must die into life, that we must not shrink from the ultimate self-sacrifice; and (this is very difficult to accept or perhaps even to understand, but it is nevertheless essential to Arnold's whole system of religious thought) he believed that the final sacrifice leads to resurrection, renewal, fulfilment and happiness. How can it, if miracles do not happen, if Christians have always been deluded in believing that Christ rose again and lives? For Arnold this Bodily Resurrection is a kind of levity, not sufficiently serious to match the greatness of the moral need. Nevertheless he says solemnly that in the right use of the doctrine lies salvation.

For Arnold, the Resurrection is contained in the Crucifixion—or rather is contained in the joyous Christian acceptance of it. The Resurrection is contained in the moral achievement of saying "Father, forgive them, for they know not what they do." However we may choose to characterise this doctrine, as noble or obscure or unrealistic, it is essential to understand that, for Arnold, it was no poetic metaphor but one of the most fundamental truths of the universe.

But, whatever we may think of it, Arnold's version of the resurrection must seem very far from the simple common-sense approach which he is always extolling, and professing to offer us. He is always appealing with confidence, as before a jury of plain, sensible Englishmen, to common knowledge and experience. For instance: "That there is an eternal not ourselves that makes for righteousness, and is called God, is admitted; and indeed so much as this, experience proves. For the constitution and history of things shows us that happiness at which we all aim is dependent on righteousness." Admitted? By whom? Not by Professor Huxley, for instance. Nor would Newman have found this at all an adequate account of the meaning of the word God. More blatantly, while discussing Hebraism and Hellenism in *Culture and Anarchy*: "Science has now made visible to everybody the great and pregnant elements of difference which lie in race, and in how singular a manner they make the genius of an Indo-European people vary from those of a Semitic people." What science? By means of what experiments? On such points Arnold is silent.

The extraordinary contrast between the manner of the moderate, experienced man of the world, and the semi-mystical moral vision is fundamental to Arnold, and accounts for a good deal of his fascination. And it may in part explain both the pervasiveness of his influence, and the fact that he has no *followers*. A great deal of what serious agnostics of the twentieth century say about the relation between morality and religion shows traces of Arnold's influence. He is so persuasive, so beautifully urbane and balanced in his presentation of what is really a very extreme position. But, partly for the same reason, he has no followers and founded no sect. For a person who followed Arnold uncritically would have to try to be like himself, mystical at the centre and an urbane, subtly

argumentative man-of-the-world at the same time. This is a very
rare type. It may be exaggerating a little to characterise it as the
heart of George Fox and the manners of Lord Chesterfield, but
even an exaggeration may show how impossible it was for Arnold
to found a sect.

Here Tolstoy (Tolstoy the prophet, I mean—the author of *What
is Art?*, not the author of *War and Peace*) is a perfect and in-
structive contrast. Tolstoy attempts to set up religion and morality
on a basis of pure reason, ignoring tradition, human nature, and
common sense. He arrives at conclusions which are quite simple
and intelligible, unlike Arnold's, but which have generally been
felt to be inhuman and fanatical. Tolstoy, accordingly, has influenced a small band of devoted disciples, but his influence has,
in these few cases, almost excluded all other influences. Outside
this small circle, and despite his immense fame as an artist, Tolstoy's
views on sex, on art, on money are quoted only to be condemned.
Tolstoy with his demoniacal consistency was a born heresiarch.
Arnold was an influence; and echoes of his supple and accommodat-
ing doctrine can be found to this day in the voices of men who
have never consciously learnt from him.

                                    III

    But though it will now be clear why certain Christian phrases like
"baptised into Christ's death" meant so much to Arnold, it still
may not be obvious why he clung so tenaciously to what he called
Christianity and to the Bible, when by any accepted definition he
was not a Christian at all, and when he believed a great deal of
the Bible to be childish fairy-tale. Why was he so anxious to believe,
in the teeth of all the evidence that *his* Christianity was actually
the religion preached by Christ? Why did he say, for instance, in
the introduction to *God and the Bible*, "Jesus had died and risen,
but in his own sense not theirs." What this obviously means is
"in my sense," and it leaves Arnold in the rather absurd position of
saying that Jesus and he are the only two people who have really
mastered the difficulties of theology. Now Tolstoy does this too, but
his doing so only underlines the extreme unlikeliness of Arnold's
doing it. For it is an attitude proper to a fanatic, proper to Tolstoy,
foreign to Arnold. Indeed one of Arnold's finest debating tricks

is an ironic modesty, which disarms criticism, and over and over
again makes his opponents appear to be impudent novices. Here
is an example, from *Culture and Anarchy* of Arnold's habitual
tone when speaking of himself; dozens of parallel instances could
be found. "Knowing myself to be indeed sadly to seek, as one of
my many critics says, in a 'philosophy with coherent, interdependent, subordinate and derivative principles,' I continually have re-
course to a plain man's expedient of trying to make what few
simple notions I have, clearer and more intelligible to myself by
means of example and illustration. And having been brought up at
Oxford in the bad old times, when we were stuffed with Greek
and Aristotle, and thought nothing of preparing ourselves by the
study of modern languages—as after Mr. Lowe's great speech at
Edinburgh we shall do—to fight the battle of life with the waiters
in foreign hotels, my head is still full of a number of phrases we
learnt at Oxford from Aristotle, about virtue being in a mean, and
about excess and defect and so on." It seems almost incredible that
the same man could walk into the blatant egoistic trap contained
in the words, "Jesus had died and risen, but in his sense, not
theirs."

Clearly a strong impulse must have been required to cancel out,
on this one topic, the deeply ingrained irony, the elusive moderation, the practised debating skill. It would seem that though, in
strict intellectual terms, Arnold was a revolutionary, his feelings
were much more conservative than his thoughts. There is a type of
revolutionary, perhaps it is a type particularly common in England,
that retains names as sacred while it alters facts. The history of our
constitution would no doubt provide examples. Arnold wanted to
have it both ways. He wanted to inaugurate a new religious doctrine, and to feel at the same time that he was treading the
ancient paths. Hence the new nineteenth century doctrine has to
be ascribed to the first century. It is significant that while Arnold
speaks with melancholy indulgence of those who retain what he
considers the impractical illusions of the old dogmatic theology,
he attacks with real animosity iconoclasts more uncompromising
than himself. Much of the introduction to *God and the Bible* is
devoted to a fierce attack on W. K. Clifford. Here too, the ironical
method and the calm assumption of superiority over all opponent
break down.

W. K. Clifford (1845–79) the brilliant and short-lived ·

tician, was one of the few Victorians who was not an agnostic, but a dogmatic atheist. Of Clifford's attack on Christianity, Arnold writes: "One reads it all, half sighing, half smiling, as the declamation of a clever and confident youth, with the hopeless inexperience, irredeemable by any cleverness, of his age. Only when one is young and headstrong can one thus prefer bravado to experience, can one stand by the Sea of Time, and instead of listening to the solemn and rhythmical beat of its waves choose to fill the air with one's own whooping to start the echo." (It is amusing to notice that while it was Cardinal Newman's great misfortune that he was born twenty-one years before Arnold, it is Clifford's that he was born twenty-three years after him.)

And Arnold goes on, in even more striking terms, to say "Compared with Professor Clifford, Messrs. Moody and Sankey are masters of the philosophy of history." That is, for Arnold, almost as strong a statement as he could make. Revivalist preachers, stressing especially the doctrine of salvation by faith, Moody and Sankey were apt examples of all that Arnold disliked in popular Protestantism. And over and above his intellectual and religious grounds for disliking them, Arnold had a temperamental aversion from crude mass emotions. For mass emotions can only stifle that shy, half-strangled, still, small voice of deep feeling that we find for instance in the "Stanzas from the Grande Chartreuse":

> Oh, hide me in your gloom profound
> Ye solemn seats of holy pain!
> Take me, cowled forms, and fence me round,
> Till I possess my soul again!
> Till free my thoughts before me roll,
> Not chafed by hourly false control.

People who feel in this way are generally, and Arnold certainly was, more resistant to mass emotions than men of placid temperament. And   e men who stir up mass emotion, are infinitely better, in   s, than the brilliant atheist.

          ly speaking, Arnold, who rejected a personal God,
          acle, was nearer to Clifford than he was to Moody
          as soon as we compare Arnold to the true icon-
          e man who regards the past as a burden and a
          nore in religion than a superstitious muddle
          f science, then we see the strength of Arnold's

If we follow the hint offered by his treatment of Clifford and examine Arnold's conservatism, we shall find abundant evidence to confirm it. The poem "Rugby Chapel," written some fifteen years after his father's death, is proof not only of the abiding influence of his father's personality, but also of Arnold's need to feel that he was carrying on the same work as the man who shaped the lives of Stanley and Clough and so many more. Perhaps no one but Matthew himself felt this continuity between the work of the simple-minded, serious father to whom religion was everything, and the son the apostle of culture and Hellenism. But the son could not endure to suppose that the continuity did not exist.

It is startling to notice, too, how high a place in his scheme Arnold awards to the Old Testament as against the New. All his Hellenism, his self-imposed moderation, his progressive outlook were powerless to spoil for him the permanent appeal of the Old Testament conception of righteousness. One would have to go to a Covenanter or to Nietzsche to find a comparable exaltation of the Old Testament. Sweetness and light!

But, of course, he had practical as well as temperamental reasons for clinging to the Christian name and to the Anglican system. Arnold was very practical; and he knew that a revolution of thought, though not of feeling, was best presented to Englishmen in conservative terms. He knew the immense hold the Bible had on the English people.

Moreover, he knew that no band of agnostic apostles, preaching moral imperatives and sweetness and light, could have what the Anglican clergy already possessed, a platform. When Mrs. Humphry Ward's Robert Elsmere was driven by his doubts about miracles to resign his living, a great part of his misery and perplexity was due to the feeling that he would never again, however devotedly he pursued secular social work, have the range of influence that he had had as rector of a parish.

" 'Shall we try London for a little?' he answered in a queer strained voice, leaning against the window and looking out that he might not see her [his wife]. 'I should find work among the poor—so would you—and I could go on with my book. . . .' She acquiesced silently. How mean and shrunken a future it seemed to them both, beside the wide and honourable range of his clergyman's life as he and she had developed it." Arnold felt this and he felt also a deep reverence for the words of the Prayer Book and

Authorised Version. The loneliness of the agnostic, his loss of corporate emotion, even when he seemed intellectually triumphant, appalled Arnold. In his bitter essay on "Our Liberal Practitioners" in *Culture and Anarchy*, he wrote, "It does not help me to think a thing more clearly that thousands of other people are thinking the same; but it helps me to worship with more emotion that thousands of other people are worshipping with me. The consecration of common consent, antiquity, public establishment, long-used rites, national edifices, is everything for religious worship." It is not surprising that, thinking on these lines, Arnold occasionally turned his thoughts to an older, more universal system of public worship than the Anglican. In a passage which Mr. Eliot's bitter attack has made famous, he wonders whether there will arise among Catholics "Some rare spirit" who will realise that liturgy and worship are more universal than dogma. Here again, as in the passages where he explains what Jesus really meant, the rare spirit is an easily-penetrated disguise for Arnold himself. If taken literally the remark is silly, and Mr. Eliot's exasperation justified. For Catholics dogma must always be more important than liturgy; and one can sympathise with Mr. Eliot's often-expressed disgust when Arnold attempts to turn what Mr. Eliot believes to be a divinely founded Church into a national cultural society. But if Arnold's words are taken, not at their face value, as a suggestion about future policy for the Catholic Church, but as a statement about psychology, surely they have considerable weight; ordinary people are much more easily influenced by ceremonies than by ideas. This is the truth recognised by Pascal when he advised the unbeliever to hear Mass; and it is a truth which the Catholic Church herself, ever realistic, recognises in practice, despite her unchangeable adherence to dogma. Galling though it must be for a Catholic or an Anglican to have their Churches patronised and recommended by a man who does not accept one single Christian doctrine in its plain sense, Arnold was here being realistic too, and, if his premises are accepted, perfectly logical as well.

If Arnold's feeling for the grandeur of Catholic worship sets him apart from his father, he thoroughly agreed with him about the Establishment of the Church. For both father and son, Church and State were not finally distinguishable. Each was an aspect of the soul of the nation; each tended to make good what was lacking in the spirit of the individual. "One may say," Matthew wrote in

the preface to *Culture and Anarchy*, "that to be reared a member
of a national Church is in itself a lesson of religious moderation,
and a help towards culture and harmonious perfection." And this
conviction was no doubt reinforced by his feelings as a literary
critic. In his literary essays, Arnold wrote much about the grand
style. The Church of England possesses a sense of style. The
Nonconformists, in his opinion at least, did not. How spiteful he
always is about Nonconformist "bun-fights," about the narrowness
of their interests and the pettiness of their lives. How he sneers at
their supposed desire to marry their deceased wife's sister, and to
have their own burial grounds. The famous urbanity wears thin
here; and he never seems to have considered the possibility that
the lives of non-conformists were narrow because of their financial
and social condition, and were actually made less narrow by the
chapel. If these sneers are unworthy of Arnold at his best, he felt
much more seriously that it is pushful and egoistical to insist on
praying impromptu when the wisdom of past generations is available to guide. For Arnold, the non-conformists were wantonly
neglecting the best that had been thought and said in the world.
Once again Arnold the literary critic, and Arnold the eccentric
amateur theologian were at one in preferring the traditional
Anglican ways.

Indeed, Arnold possessed a combination of qualities that is not
very common. He was intensely conservative, he was intensely
practical, and he was sceptical about doctrines and historical
events (though not about values). Both the first two qualities drove
him to seek for the continuity of religion in an institution; while
his scepticism made it necessary for him to give a new, personal
meaning to all the beliefs and customs of his chosen institution;
the Anglican Church. Moreover, the combination of conservatism
and scepticism made him feel that the search for continuity was
peculiarly urgent, and the consequences of failure terrible. That
is why he turned with such ferocity, as we have seen, on men
like W. K. Clifford, who threatened to discredit all traditional
modes of feeling in the name of science.

We shall never understand Arnold if we liken him to the
Protestant modernists—let us say to Dean Inge. Inge was for
clearing away the accretions of custom and habit that centuries had
scattered over the fundamental truths about God and the human
soul. Arnold did not believe the Christian doctrine of God at all,

and he loved the liturgical traditions, the accumulated moral wisdom of Christendom, which seemed to the Protestant modernists childish and out of date. Arnold was nearer in spirit to the Catholic modernists, who, in the years following his death, would accept the whole Christian system, but attempt to give it a new and private meaning. Like them, Arnold, who disbelieved in miracles, could accept the poetic value of any miraculous doctrine, provided that it was interpreted symbolically, and that it was morally edifying.

Dean Inge was trying to get back to the hard core of historical truth. For Arnold, the only essential core was in the mind of man—certain moral truths which Jesus had discovered. Arnold was far more radical than Inge in his criticism of doctrinal truths, far more conservative in his treatment of feelings and institutions. He accepted the whole Christian system as if it were a work of art, of saving art; and, just as the poet cannot lie because he "never affirmeth," for Arnold, as for the Catholic modernists, a doctrine which contains a spiritual truth could never be false. In the end, whatever we think of him, Arnold is formidably original. He undertook the immense task of transforming the religious consciousness of mankind.

Chronology of Important Dates

1822	Born December 24, oldest son of Thomas Arnold and Mary Penrose Arnold.
1828	His father becomes headmaster of Rugby School.
1836	Enters Winchester College.
1837	Enters fifth form at Rugby.
1841	August: His father appointed Professor of Modern History at Oxford. October: Goes into residence at Balliol College, Oxford.
1842	June 12: His father dies of heart attack.
1843	Wins Newdigate Prize for *Cromwell*.
1844	Wins B.A. (second class).
1847	Becomes secretary to the Marquis of Lansdowne.
1849	February: Publishes *The Strayed Reveller, and Other Poems*.
1851	April: Appointed inspector of schools. June: Marries Frances Lucy Wightman.
1852	October: Publishes *Empedocles on Etna, and Other Poems*.
1853	November: Publishes *Poems,* including Preface.
1857	May: Elected Professor of Poetry at Oxford (until 1867). November: Inaugural lecture, "On the Modern Element in Literature."
1858	Publishes *Merope*.
1861	Publishes *On Translating Homer*.
1862	Publishes *On Translating Homer: Last Words*.
1865	Publishes *Essays in Criticism*.

1867   Publishes *On the Study of Celtic Literature; New Poems.*

1869   Publishes *Culture and Anarchy.*

1870   Publishes *St. Paul and Protestantism.*

1871   Publishes *Friendship's Garland.*

1873   Publishes *Literature and Dogma.*

1875   Publishes *God and the Bible.*

1877   Publishes *Last Essays on Church and Religion.*

1879   Publishes *Mixed Essays.*

1882   Publishes *Irish Essays.*

1883   October: Begins American tour lasting until March 1884.

1885   Publishes *Discourses in America.*

1886   Retires from school inspectorship.

1888   Dies April 15. November: *Essays in Criticism,* Second Series, published posthumously.

Notes on the Editor and Contributors

DAVID J. DeLAURA, editor of this volume, teaches at the University of Texas at Austin. He has written *Hebrew and Hellene in Victorian England: Newman, Arnold, and Pater* and is editor of John Henry Newman's *Apologia pro Vita Sua* and of *Victorian Prose: A Guide to Research.*

T. S. ELIOT, this century's preeminent poet-critic, referred to Arnold in many contexts and carried on his tradition in his own work as editor.

J. HILLIS MILLER teaches at Yale. His publications include *Charles Dickens: The World of His Novels, The Disappearance of God: Five Nineteenth-Century Writers,* and *Poets of Reality: Six Twentieth-Century Writers.*

U. C. KNOEPFLMACHER, of the University of California, Berkeley, is the author of *Religious Humanism and the Victorian Novel, George Eliot's Early Novels: The Limits of Realism,* and *Laughter and Despair: Readings in Ten Novels of the Victorian Era.*

ANTHONY HECHT, a member of the faculty at the University of Rochester, won the Pulitzer Prize in poetry for *The Hard Hours.*

KENNETH ALLOTT, A. C. Bradley Professor of Modern English Literature at Liverpool, is editor of *The Poems of Matthew Arnold.*

A. DWIGHT CULLER, who teaches at Yale, has written *The Imperial Intellect: A Study of Newman's Educational Ideal* and *Imaginative Reason: The Poetry of Matthew Arnold.*

JOHN P. FARRELL teaches at the University of Kansas and has written on Arnold and Dickens.

JOHN HOLLOWAY, of Queens' College, Cambridge, is the author of numerous volumes of criticism and poetry, as well as of an autobiography, *A London Childhood.*

GEOFFREY TILLOTSON, late of Birkbeck College, University of London, wrote many studies of Augustan and Victorian literature. He was joint author of *Mid-Victorian Studies* with his wife, Kathleen Tillotson.

VINCENT BUCKLEY, who teaches at the University of Melbourne, has published poetry and is the author of *Poetry and Morality* and *Poetry and the Sacred.*

A. O. J. COCKSHUT, who teaches at Oxford, has published books on Dickens, Scott, and Trollope, as well as *Anglican Attitudes* and *The Unbelievers.*

Selected Bibliography

Editions and Bibliography

The Complete Prose Works of Matthew Arnold. Edited by R. H. Super. Ann Arbor: University of Michigan Press, 1960–   .

DAVIS, ARTHUR KYLE, JR. *Matthew Arnold's Letters: A Descriptive Checklist.* Charlottesville: University Press of Virginia, 1968.

Letters of Matthew Arnold, 1848–1888. Edited by G. W. E. Russell. 2 vols. New York: The Macmillan Company, 1895.

The Letters of Matthew Arnold to Arthur Hugh Clough. Edited by Howard Foster Lowry. London and New York: Oxford University Press, 1932.

The Note-Books of Matthew Arnold. Edited by H. F. Lowry, K. Young, and W. H. Dunn. London: Oxford University Press, 1952.

The Poems of Matthew Arnold. Edited by Kenneth Allott. London: Longmans, 1965.

The Poetical Works of Matthew Arnold. Edited by C. B. Tinker and H. F. Lowry. London: Oxford University Press, 1950.

The Victorian Poets: A Guide to Research. Edited by Frederic E. Faverty. Cambridge: Harvard University Press, 1968.

Books

ALEXANDER, EDWARD. *Matthew Arnold and John Stuart Mill.* New York: Columbia University Press, 1968.

ANDERSON, WARREN D. *Matthew Arnold and the Classical Tradition.* Ann Arbor: University of Michigan Press, 1965.

BAUM, PAUL F. *Ten Studies in the Poetry of Matthew Arnold.* Durham, N. C.: Duke University Press, 1958.

BONNEROT, LOUIS. *Matthew Arnold, poète: essai de biographie psychologique.* Paris: Didier, 1947.

BROWN, E. K. *Matthew Arnold: A Study in Conflict.* Chicago: University of Chicago Press, 1948.

BUSH, DOUGLAS. *Matthew Arnold: A Survey of His Poetry and Prose.* New York: The Macmillan Company, 1971.

CULLER, A. DWIGHT. *Imaginative Reason: The Poetry of Matthew Arnold.* New Haven and London: Yale University Press, 1966.

DeLAURA, DAVID J. *Hebrew and Hellene in Victorian England: Newman, Arnold, and Pater.* Austin: University of Texas Press, 1969.

GOTTFRIED, LEON. *Matthew Arnold and the Romantics.* Lincoln: University of Nebraska Press, 1963.

JOHNSON, W. STACY. *The Voices of Matthew Arnold: An Essay in Criticism.* New Haven: Yale University Press, 1961.

MADDEN, WILLIAM A. *Matthew Arnold: A Study of the Aesthetic Temperament.* Bloomington and London: Indiana University Press, 1967.

NEIMAN, FRASER. *Matthew Arnold.* New York: Twayne Publishers, 1968.

RALEIGH, JOHN HENRY. *Matthew Arnold and American Culture.* Berkeley and Los Angeles: University of California Press, 1957.

ROBBINS, WILLIAM. *The Ethical Idealism of Matthew Arnold: A Study of the Nature and Sources of His Moral and Religious Ideas.* London: William Heinemann Ltd., 1959.

ROPER, ALAN. *Arnold's Poetic Landscapes.* Baltimore: The Johns Hopkins Press, 1969.

STANGE, G. ROBERT. *Matthew Arnold: The Poet as Humanist.* Princeton: Princeton University Press, 1967.

TINKER, C. B., and H. F. LOWRY. *The Poetry of Matthew Arnold: A Commentary.* London: Oxford University Press, 1940.

Shorter Studies (not included in the present volume)

ALLOTT, KENNETH. "Matthew Arnold's Reading-Lists in Three Early Diaries." *Victorian Studies,* 2 (1959), pp. 254–66.

CURGENVEN, J. P. "*The Scholar Gipsy:* A Study of the Growth, Meaning and Integration of a Poem." *Litera* (Turkey), 2 (1955), 3 (1956).

———. "Thyrsis." *Litera* (Turkey), 4 (1957), 5 (1958), 6 (1959).

DeLAURA, DAVID J. "Arnold and Carlyle." *PMLA,* 79 (1964), pp. 104–29.

DONOVAN, ROBERT A. "The Method of Arnold's *Essays in Criticism.*" *PMLA,* 71 (1956), pp. 922–31.

DUDLEY, FRED A. "Matthew Arnold and Science." *PMLA,* 57 (1942), pp. 275–94.

EGGENSCHWILER, DAVID L. "Arnold's Passive Questers." *Victorian Poetry,* 5 (1967), pp. 1–11.

FORSYTH, R. A. " 'The Buried Life'—The Contrasting Views of Arnold and Clough in the Context of Dr. Arnold's Historiography." *ELH,* 35 (1968), pp. 218–53.

HIPPLE, WALTER J. "Matthew Arnold, Dialectician." *University of Toronto Quarterly,* 32 (1962), pp. 1–26.

HOUGHTON, WALTER E. "Arnold's 'Empedocles on Etna.'" *Victorian Studies*, 1 (1958), pp. 311–36.

JOHNSON, E. D. H. *The Alien Vision of Victorian Poetry*, 1st ed., 1952. Hamden, Conn.: Archon Books, 1963, pp. 147–213.

KERMODE, FRANK. *Romantic Image*, 1st ed., 1957. New York: Vintage Books, 1964, pp. 12–19.

KNIGHT, G. WILSON. "*The Scholar Gipsy:* An Interpretation." *Review of English Studies*, n.s. 6 (1955), pp. 53–62.

KREIGER, MURRAY. "'Dover Beach' and the Tragic Sense of Eternal Recurrence." *University of Kansas City Review*, 23 (1956), pp. 73–79. Reprinted in *The Play and Place of Criticism*, Baltimore: The Johns Hopkins Press, 1967, pp. 69–77.

——. "The Critical Legacy of Matthew Arnold: Or, The Strange Brotherhood of T. S. Eliot, I. A. Richards, and Northrop Frye." *Southern Review*, n.s. 5 (1969), pp. 457–74.

LEAVIS, F. R. "Matthew Arnold." *Scrutiny*, 7 (1938). Reprinted in *The Importance of Scrutiny*, edited by Eric Bentley, New York: George W. Stewart, 1958, pp. 319–32.

MADDEN, WILLIAM A. "The Divided Tradition of English Criticism." *PMLA*, 73 (1958), pp. 69–80.

PEARSON, GABRIEL. "The Importance of Arnold's *Merope*." In *The Major Victorian Poets*, edited by Isobel Armstrong, Lincoln: University of Nebraska Press, 1969, pp. 225–52.

RAY, LINDA LEE. "Callicles on Etna: The Other Mask." *Victorian Poetry*, 7 (1969), pp. 309–20.

SPENDER, STEPHEN. *The Struggle of the Modern*, Berkeley and Los Angeles: University of California Press, 1963, pp. 246–55.

STEVENSON, LIONEL. "Matthew Arnold's Poetry: A Modern Appraisal." *Tennessee Studies in Literature*, 4 (1959), pp. 31–41.

WARREN, ALBA H., JR. *English Poetic Theory, 1825–1865*, 1st ed., 1950. New York: Octagon Books, 1966, pp. 152–70.

WELLEK, RENÉ. *History of Modern Criticism, 1750–1950: The Later Nineteenth Century*, Vol. IV. New Haven and London: Yale University Press, 1965, pp. 155–80.

WILLEY, BASIL. *Nineteenth Century Studies* London: Chatto & Windus Ltd., 1949, pp. 251–83.

WILLIAMS, RAYMOND. *Culture and Society, 1780–1950*, 1st ed., 1958. New York: Harper & Row, Publishers, 1966, pp. 110–29.